# CRIES
# PANTHER
## *On Mockingbird Hill*

For Beth,
Thank you for
hearing the cries listening,
of others and respond,
Best regards
Sue

# SUE SKILTON ORRELL

Cries of the Panther
On Mockingbird Hill
All Rights Reserved.
Copyright © 2020 Sue Skilton Orrell
v3.0 r1.0

The opinions expressed in this manuscript are solely the opinions of the author and do not represent the opinions or thoughts of the publisher. The author has represented and warranted full ownership and/or legal right to publish all the materials in this book.

This book may not be reproduced, transmitted, or stored in whole or in part by any means, including graphic, electronic, or mechanical without the express written consent of the publisher except in the case of brief quotations embodied in critical articles and reviews.

Marsutonell Press

ISBN: 978-0-578-22968-3

Library of Congress Control Number: 2020902731

Cover Photo © 2020 www.gettyimages.com. All rights reserved - used with permission.

PRINTED IN THE UNITED STATES OF AMERICA

Sex abuse survivor breaks more than sixty years of silence after a cousin publishes a false claim that she accused her father of the crime.

*"Even if I hadn't lived in the area and time, this book is a delightful read. Ms. Orrell keeps your attention and makes you eager for more."*
Georgia Hatcher (high school friend with broad knowledge of Volusia County and many people in the DeLand area)

*"I received the draft and have read it. All I can say is WOW! Beautifully written. I know you spent a massive amount of time on it. I can't imagine you having to relive some of the events as you wrote. Thanks so much for allowing me to read the draft."*
Robert S. Orrell (Bob) (cousin and respected author of genealogy)

*"Sue honestly, I really don't have anything to add. You've done an incredible job."*
Jodi Holler Underhill (resident of DeLand Florida; her father knew my father)

# TABLE OF CONTENTS

*James <u>Bruce</u> Orrell, Jr., 1924*

# *DEDICATION*

## *TO*

## *JAMES <u>BRUCE</u> ORRELL, JR.*

### *(1902-1976)*

**HUSBAND**
*of*
*Alice Skilton Orrell*
*(1905-2001)*

**FATHER**
*of*
*Robert Skilton Orrell*
*(stillborn – January 1, 1927)*

*Margaret Ann Orrell*
*(1930-2012)*

*Mary Alice Orrell*
*(b. 1933)*

*Martha <u>Sue</u> Orrell*
*(b. 1941)*

*Richard Bruce Orrell*
*(b.1944)*

# EXTENDED DEDICATION

To Margaret, my oldest sister—you suspected and cared enough to try to warn me; if only the warning had come in time.

To Music—your constancy gave me hope.

To the Very Reverend Joe Reynolds, retired Dean, Christ Church Cathedral (Episcopal), Houston, TX—You taught me the psychological and spiritual truth of forgiveness and the value of carrying my own pride.

To my very special friend, John L. Mohney, D.O.—Your gifts of homegrown roses, time together, and relaxing trips inspired me.

To all the children I loved and taught—Your natural ways of plugging the holes, mending the tears, and reweaving the shreds of my heart left devastated by the loss of my birth children enabled me to find the strength to get out of bed each morning, get to school, and to be open to the gift of wholeness your presence in my life offered.

And finally to my dear brother, Richard B. Orrell—You are my youngest sibling, a cherished friend, and wise patriarch of our extended family. Your unconditional love for me never wavered, even when my decision to publish this memoir put you in a place of discomfort as you simultaneously empathized with me and sympathized with our sister, Mary.

Thanks be to ALL.

# INTRODUCTION

*An empty bag cannot stand upright.*

Benjamin Franklin
(1706-1790)

I must have been a little over three years old when the nursery worker in Sunday School unintentionally let me feel that I was not as smart or creative as I felt. She had provided materials for all of us to draw something. Her motivating lesson lead-in was, "Who can make a flower?"

With excitement, I set to work on drawing the most beautiful flower I could imagine—individual petals attached to a dark center, a long stem, green grass below, and blue sky above. After a few minutes, the teacher asked, "Who has made a flower?" My hand flew up.

"Class, Martha Sue says she has made a flower. See her picture of a flower? I think it is a sunflower, but she could never make a flower, could she? Only God can do that."

I feel certain that the teacher had no harsh intent, but her discount of my best efforts filled me with shame and disappointment. I wanted to explain myself to the teacher, but lacked the confidence to even try to clarify my claim.

When the family was in the car on the way home after church, Mother asked what I had done in Sunday School. When I started to tell her about the flower incident, I started crying.

Mother said, "You musn't cry about such a little thing. You are so much more mature than all the others in that class." She continued to lecture me about setting an example for the others so that they would know how to behave. I was simply bewildered and overwhelmed by the loss of joy mixed with the shriveled sense of my own abilities. I was not looking forward to returning to Sunday School the next week.

Childhood left early and adolescence came late. Both were initially denied their times, stunted and shunted out of their roles. Close to three decades after the flower drawing incident, each ultimately claimed their rightful place in my life. While neither childhood nor adolescence can literally be relived at later dates, both can be felt through psychological and emotional states of free play and incremental growth toward maturity. Both can guide and be guided.

When childhood and adolescence retreated and faced probable extinction, my false sense of being mature for my age wrapped itself around me like chainmail clanging to be recognized for what it was—a constant reminder that my assumed reality stiffened every growth path within me. The "branding" of me as mature for my age stifled vitality and squelched the joy that should have been part of those formative years. Attempts at free movement chaffed every inch of my body while constricting my heart and lungs—the invisible equivalent of a tight Victorian corset.

With good fortune, it was not a closed matter of too little too late. As my young body inevitably grew, adjustments had to be made to the emotional chainmail. Occasionally, I glimpsed aspiration trying to break through the admonition to act mature. Those glimpses included such things as nicer housing and furniture in some of the homes I visited. They also included seeing peers, both friends and relatives, have fun without so much constraint as I felt. Of course, I couldn't articulate what I was noticing, but the realization was settling into my self-image and creating a sense of both rebellion and acquiescence.

Through extensive reading and therapeutic treatment, I was able to reclaim the wounded child within and to experience the late blooming of a healthy adolescence well beyond an arbitrary chronological age. Long before the targeted reading and therapy, my sheer stubbornness, which Mother had been forced to contend and compete with was a source of strength and stamina. Maybe it had something to do with our red hair.

Without knowing what to call my silent dialogue with myself (no, I never heard voices), I often focused on what I now know were affirmations. Those affirmations became guides and empowered my resolve to find and express who I was and to grow into as much of my potential as I was able to do. For example, when I noticed that Mother seemed to get her way more than Daddy did, I told myself that I would not be bossy when I grew up. Too young to understand the decision-making complexities that go on between couples and within households, it simply seemed to me that Mother insisted on doing what she wanted to do and that Daddy seldom had or took the same opportunity.

At about age five, when we lived in the Hialeah area of Miami, Mother tried to insist on driving to church even though the streets were flooded. Daddy said, "Alice, we don't know which streets are still flooded, and the car may stall in the water. We should just stay home today."

Mother said, "But what will they do for music? Margaret and Mary and I are needed in the choir. There may not be anyone to sing or play the piano if we don't go."

With strong disagreement between them, Mother set out driving with a promise to turn around and return home if the roads had more than a few inches of water on them. I begged to stay home with Daddy and Richard. As a compromise, Mother agreed to that, hoping to ease Daddy's concerns. "I will not be bossy" became one of the early mantras that settled into my mind.

The rough road of healing and restoration of childhood and adolescence was as bumpy as the washboard surface of the unpaved Spring Garden Ranch Road that led to Mockingbird Hill, but carried far graver consequences if a part of my emotional vehicle became stuck, needed repair, or became so worn that repair was impossible.

My façade of maturity had been so thoroughly ground into my psyche that acting any differently never crossed my mind. Mature girls did not cry or act silly. Big girls did not play with dolls. Big girls were able to squelch emotional expression in hopes of a payoff that would grant some of the privileges of older sisters. Big girls didn't need naps. Big girls got to go to town more often and sometimes even were given a special treat before returning home. And above all, big girls never let the panther's cries on Mockingbird Hill prompt their own tears. But not all girls who utter the chant of maturity have even a basic understanding of the term's true meaning. For me, it meant emotional pretense and skillful mastery of self-deceit. If not confronted and treated, such self-deceit will almost always lead to self-defeat.

The early observations that I made regarding my parents' interactions with each other made me sense that something was wrong in my home environment. That realization coincided with what I believe was my first emotional bump in the road. It was a jab to the heart that set me up to be susceptible to feelings of deprivation, envy, shame, and detachment as my parents dealt with their own consequences of the decisions they had made. The experience that generated this insight taught me that voluntary detachment hurt much less than suddenly severed attachment. That conclusion gave me a small amount of control and at the same time taught me a means of coping with all that made me want to cry, even though I knew that real tears would mark me as the baby who had no right or means to equal my two older sisters' status of relative maturity.

With only intuition to alert me to the lack of ease and comfort in my home environment, I set out to make sense of what I observed, what I felt, and what I feared. Although I make no claim to believe in predestination, as I traced the threads of my life's tapestry, I couldn't help but see an unwritten script that I had no acceptable option but to follow. Choices were few, and consequences dire.

# PROLOGUE

*Resolve to be thyself, and know that [s]he*
*who finds [her]self, loses [her] misery.*
Matthew Arnold
(1822-1888)

Y2K had fizzled. Cell phones were shrinking and multiplying. It was less than a decade until I would retire; and the paint on the house my husband and I had just bought was dry. It seemed that life was good—a respite from the distant past with joy in the present and hope for the future. An incoming call on the land line jangled my mind and set it spinning.

Uncharacteristically, I was home alone when the call came in. For a second, I was thrilled to hear my brother, Richard's, warm baritone voice. But I soon heard ire mixed with warmth; a swirl of sadness and incredulity signaled that something was terribly wrong—so wrong that he could not control his vocal response to it. "Did you buy one of Curtis Winfrey's books—the one he claims is a book of genealogy?"

I recalled that one of our cousins was in the process of writing his branch of the family's genealogy. "No. I knew he was working on a book, but I lost track of him years ago and didn't even know he had finished."

"Margaret received the one she ordered today. You know, she rarely asks for help, but she just called and asked me to go over to her apartment right away. I've never seen her so upset. She was nearly in hysterics. When I got there, she handed me the book and pointed to the passage she wanted me to read. Let me read you what Curtis wrote." After citing the page number, he went on:

*'James Bruce Orrell Jr. stands accused of child sexual abuse by his daughter, Martha Sue Orrell.'*

What do you have to say about this, Suzie? Can you make sense of it?"

Stunned, almost in shock at my silence being broken in this way, I stumbled through a labyrinth of language and concluded, "All I can say is that I have never made, nor would I ever make, such an accusation because it wouldn't be true. Curtis Winfrey added two and two together and came up with about seven."

"What should I tell Margaret?"

"Tell her what I said. Send me the book, and I will turn it over to my husband. This is not the sort of thing he usually handles in his law practice, but he will either know what to do or pass it on to someone who specializes in such matters."

After we said our good-byes, I hung up the phone and went to the piano in hopes that the keys would still my shaking hands and calm my racing pulse.

Because I am the only one who knows my truth and because I am now willing to share it with others, focusing on writing and eventual publication of my own book had to become my concerted commitment. The justification I needed to come out of the closet of cultural and familial secrecy broke the bars that had imprisoned me for over five decades.

As I used the process of writing to work through the process of healing, I claimed the fundamental truth that my story deserves to be heard. No other justification is needed. My father's name deserves to be cleared, and, in turn, my name also deserves to be cleared of the false accusation published by Curtis Winfrey.

Prior to the phone call, I was not certain whether Richard knew about my history of sexual assault and abuse, but it seemed likely because Mother knew. When she visited me following my loss of a still-born son, she found a way to let me know that my then-husband had told her. At that time, I was almost thirty-eight years old and had carried the weight of silence since I was thirteen. It would take another year after Rich's phone call before an incident that occurred as we held vigil for Mother's final breath forced my hand and gave me the courage to pull him aside to tell him that as soon as I had time and energy (meaning as soon as I retired), I was determined to find a therapist who could help me work through the long history and attempt to make sense of how I survived and managed to achieve much of what I set out to do.

Near the time of my high school graduation, the brother-in-law who was the perpetrator declared himself an evangelist. When I first attempted to write about my history and my feelings about it, I titled the poem, "The Reverend Rapist." I decided that the title was too raw and not poetic enough, so shortened the poem and retitled it to "Storm in the Night."

About the same time, Curtis Winfrey was in the process of gathering data for his proposed book of genealogy. His grandmother was my Aunt Bessie, one of Daddy's sisters. Curtis was a little older than I. Although I had seen him at a few family gatherings, I had not known him well. Through the correspondence regarding the family history, we discovered that we both dabbled in poetry. We shared several letters that included some of our poetry.

Initially, I was happy to find a cousin who also wrote poetry and who was interested in family history. Then, as our personal histories took us farther apart, and as his data-gathering wound down, I lost track of him.

# STORM IN THE NIGHT (1973-74)

(second draft—shared with Curtis Winfrey)
Sue Orrell

Like a brooding thunder-storm cloud,
He hovers over the huddled heap
Of fear-gripped girl
That lies by their bed
On a pallet
In the middle of the night.
His eyes slobber messages
Of silent verbal venom,
With x-ray vision cripple covers
That tighten and shout for a gale
To blow away the storm
Of horrible memory—
And terror of tomorrow,
Until the paralyzed heap
Recovers strength to
Turn, cough, bury face
And rouse one who sleeps—
Finally hears him ease in
Beside his wife and their daughter.
The trembling girl remembers:
A hurricane ALSO has a calm core
Before its second and fiercest
Rape of the coast—
And tries to sleep
And tries to sleep.

If Curtis Winfrey had attempted to verify his interpretation of the poem, he could have avoided making the mistake of misinterpretation. His understanding that I was sexually attacked and abused was accurate, but he had absolutely no basis for connecting the dots to my father. The poem printed here is an exact duplication of the version that Curtis saw. Within the context of the poem, the first rape had occurred the previous summer, and the second rape was to occur just a month or two after the pallet incident mentioned in the poem. At that time, I was in the eye of my immediate storm.

Perhaps Curtis Winfrey's unprofessional and insensitive statement was a favor more than an attack on my integrity or on my father's honor. Without the mandate created by the published falsehood, I probably would have remained silent for the rest of my life. The internal struggle would not have been resolved, and psychic scars that are now nearly invisible would have continued to cripple my sense of self and worth.

Curtis died not long after his spurious book was published, but not before he and his publisher (Gateway Press, Baltimore, MD) responded to my husband's demand letter for apologies and removal of the erroneous statement from any future printed copies. But the books that had already been sold still bear the ugly lie that cannot be erased from the minds of the nearly 100 people who purchased a copy.

Perhaps the best way to understand my journey is to begin with the family tales of my maternal and paternal grandparents who established residence in West Volusia County, Florida in the early 1900's. Much of the uniqueness of this sojourn relies on the setting, birth orders, and cultural climate of the time.

*Grandmother Orrell holding Sue*

# CHAPTER I

# GRANDPARENTS MOVE TO VOLUSIA COUNTY

*If you tell the truth, you don't have to remember anything.*
Mark Twain
(1835-1910)

Visits to my home town in the last fifty years were not frequent, but each time I drove down Woodland Boulevard, I felt the steering wheel tug for a turn onto East Rich Avenue. Driving past 408 and making a U-turn a house or two away, I would position myself so that I could stop and take a picture that included the third-story window where Mother had practiced her elocution lessons. She always appreciated getting a print of the picture and noticed if the color of the exterior paint had been changed. When she saw the *Yard of the Month* sign or the bronze plaque that announced the house's listing on the *Historic Homes* registry, she would clasp the picture to her chest, close her eyes, and say something like, "Oh, how I miss the years I spent there so long ago."

After thinking of my mother's childhood home as one of the many Victorian homes in DeLand, Florida, only recently I learned that the correct architectural identification is Southern Vernacular. Others in the family had referred to it as Craftsman style. I wonder if Gramma and Grampa Skilton were aware of its design lineage when they built it in 1915.

In the fall of 2015, a long-term dream came true when I was able to visit the home and see the interior of the first floor and the extensive gardens. Looking back, I wonder why I had not paid closer attention to that street and that house during my growing-up years. Perhaps it was how remote it was from my childhood home. More likely, I didn't dare identify with it because I sensed that seeing it caused Mother a type and depth of pain that I could not put words to and couldn't share—almost as disturbing as when she visited her parents' and two of her siblings' graves in Oakdale Cemetery.

More than a few times, I knocked on the door, but never found the owners home. Then, as I took what I expected to be my final drive down the street before having to head home to Houston, I saw an older couple sitting out on the porch in the late afternoon. My rental car's back wheels rested on the sidewalk after I parked behind the owners' car, which was shaded by the *porta cache*. The gentleman walked over to the six or seven steps leading up to the porch and waved to me with a cordial smile as I opened the car door. I asked, "Will the car be okay here for a few minutes? I'd just like to ask you a couple of questions."

"Sure. Come on up and join us. Would you prefer red or white?"

"White, please, on such a warm, sunny day."

Assuming that I was simply the next tourist who had read about historic homes in DeLand, he thought that I might like to see the house that he and his wife had owned and loved for many years. When I introduced myself and told them that my grandparents had built the house, their faces lit up and conversation leaped from cordial to animated. One of the things they pointed out was that the plans for the house had come from a Sears house kit. I hadn't known that Sears marketed house kits. They were popular at the time, but Grampa Skilton used only the plans, not the materials. According to the owners who told me the history, he went up to Georgia and bought cypress rather than using the more common local lumber cut from pine trees.

We had been talking and sipping our wine for at least an hour when the lady said, "Well, don't you want to see the interior? We love to show the house, but limit tours to the first floor. You'll be able to see much of your grandfather's handiwork."

"That's a dream I thought would never come true. Would it be possible to see the back yard too? I've heard that there is a carriage house, but I can't see it from the street."

With warmth of prideful hospitality, they ushered me into the house where I could see first-hand so many things Mother had described in her frequent tales of the home of her childhood. There was a piano where hers would have been and a small reed pump organ in another area. The gentleman pointed out the wood trim that he said Grampa Skilton had chosen to leave natural rather than to stain. The lady showed the expanded modern kitchen and spacious raised deck looking out onto the back gardens that extended to the next block. Pointing to the carriage house, the man said, "We'd like to do something with the carriage house, but found out the foundation is made of a type of brick that will not support any additional weight. We use it for storage, including some of the woodwork trim that was removed when the house was air conditioned before we bought it."

He went on to caution me not to trip over cement boundary blocks that had been placed in the ground where an alley might have been laid out. The citrus trees had suffered from a fungus, but he was hopeful that they had recovered and would bear fruit the next season.

Mother had described the Victorian furniture and the layout of the downstairs. She especially enjoyed telling about how Aunt Miriam, her sister about seven years older, had a habit of sleepwalking. When one of the older sisters had a beau over for an evening of courting, they would sometimes sit on the swing on the front porch. One of the rules was that the porch light had to be left on until the gentleman who was calling left.

More than once, either Aunt Helen or Aunt Jessamine would be out on the porch swing with their date, and Aunt Miriam would come sleepwalking down the stairs with a chamber pot in her hands. Mother always said that she looked like a zombie hunting a place to empty the pot. The dilemma was what to do to make certain that Aunt Miriam did not try to come out onto the porch and either spill the chamber pot in the living room or on the front porch if she managed to get the door open. When I viewed the stairs, I could envision Aunt Miriam coming down in her nightgown with the chamber pot in her hands.

As I looked at each detail of the downstairs in the Skilton home, it was as though I was Mother standing there in the glow of déjà vu that I knew she would feel. My own joy at seeing my grandfather's handiwork and seeing the home that haunted Mother's memories made me wish I could stay longer. But I reluctantly headed for the rental car still blocking the sidewalk.

Aunt Helen used to say, "You know, you come from sturdy stock. You must get to know your Skilton history."

Sturdy *stock*, sturdy house—related—bound to and bound by strong values and long history. The heritage that had been passed down through the published genealogy, the few pieces of china with the picture of the ancestral Skilton home in Connecticut on them, updates from the Skilton Foundation along with pictures from the annual reunions in Connecticut, all came to life and connected viscerally while viewing the ground floor of the Skilton house at 408 East Rich Avenue in DeLand, Florida.

The original Skilton home in Southington, Connecticut had been built between 1640 and 1660. I had seen it in 2005, but was not able to go inside because it was a private residence and the owners were not home. That classic saltbox house is the one that is pictured on the Skilton china. But Mother's parents and all of their children were born in Watertown, Connecticut, not far from Southington.

Foreshadowing my undergraduate academic career at Stetson University, Gramma Skilton played the organ at First Methodist Church, DeLand, and Grampa Skilton directed the choir. Over forty years after their untimely deaths, I would fulfill my senior internship as a Church Music major at Stetson as Organist/Choirmaster at the same church. Even though the internship was an academic requirement similar to student teaching for an education major, I was paid, and kept that position for a full year.

One elderly gentleman had the nerve to offer to personally increase my salary if I would play less music by Johann Sebastian Bach. I wrote up a brief overview of the importance of Bach's music to organ repertoire and made an estimate of the percentage of standard organ repertoire his music represented. My rationale for selecting service music must have satisfied Mr. Smith because I never heard from him again. I often wondered, though, if perhaps the dean or the organ professor had a chat with him after I told them about the incident.

Mother's entire family had been involved in the music program of that church. One of her brothers-in-law, Uncle Alden (Boor), liked to tell the story about visiting the church when he was a student at Stetson. He noticed a beautiful young woman sitting in the choir, leaned over to his friend and whispered, "You see that soprano on the front row? The one who just sang the solo? I'm going to marry her."

Without hesitation, as soon as the service was over, he introduced himself to her, met my grandparents, and asked for the privilege of courting their daughter, Helen. He and Aunt Helen celebrated over 60 wedding anniversaries before her death. Not long before Parkinson's disease was diagnosed, she told me that as she aged, the most terrible thing was to try to sing and have either no notes or untrue sour notes come out of her mouth. With tears brimming on her lower eyelids, she said, "You know, Uncle Alden fell in love with my voice before he even knew my name. Now, I can't stand to hear my own voice when I try to sing."

Following his retirement from the University of Chicago, where he had taught chemistry, Uncle Alden and she had settled in New Smyrna Beach, about 18 miles from DeLand. They were active in their local church, but came over to be supportive when the choir I directed sang a special Christmas or Easter program. Aunt Helen was quite emotional and would tear up when she invariably said something like, "I just wish your Gramma and Grampa Skilton could be here to see and hear you in the same church where she played the organ and he directed the choir. Now, you are doing both. I don't know how you manage to direct the choir mostly with your head while you play the organ. They would be so proud of you."

Both of my parents' families had moved to Florida in the early 20th century prior to the great boom of the 1920's. Mother's family came from Connecticut, and Daddy's from South Carolina. His family settled in Seville in the northern part of Volusia County. Mother's family spent a little while across the St. John's River from DeLand in Cassia, which is in Lake County. They soon bought the property in DeLand, though, and built the home that Mother never stopped missing.

The Skilton home in DeLand set the standard by which Mother would inevitably judge all other houses. It wasn't the largest or the most elaborate house in DeLand, and it wasn't right on the Boulevard, but it was more than adequate for a family with seven children, and was beautiful. No matter how diligent she was in her attempt to compensate for living without that much space and beauty in her adult life, the twinge of pain that sometimes bordered on bitterness would occasionally find its way into Mother's verbiage, attitude, and mostly-hidden internal baggage. Her pain was gnarled into rough-hewn cloth woven from the death of an older sister in the flu epidemic of 1918. Her only brother, George, died young not long after she and Daddy were married. Both of her parents died within four months of each other. The subsequent loss of the house itself was, in effect, one more death to be endured and mourned.

After her father's death, the house was sold and the contents divided among her older siblings. She was fourteen years old when her mother died and had just turned fifteen four months later when her father died. Her oldest sister was appointed her legal guardian, but she opted to live with her closest girlfriend's family. As long as she lived, she still referred to the girlfriend's mother as Mother Telford.

The burden of loss was strapped onto Mother's psyche and soul. Had she been old enough to be given some of the furniture or household goods, such possessions might have offered some degree of comfort. But her strict religious views regarding self-sacrifice forbade her to acknowledge the losses for what they were and allow herself to feel okay despite longing for a beautiful home with comfort and gentility of lifestyle in strong but subtle display. Hers was a constant battle to glorify the reality of poverty that dogged her marital life, from weathering the Great Depression to ultimately living on a pittance of retirement income as a widow for twenty five years.

In time, I would understand that she made a choice to squelch her feelings rather than to acknowledge the loss and deal with the pain. She went beyond teaching worthwhile values by, in effect, disowning the reality of appreciating nice things. She even wrote a song, "These Are the Things that Money Can't Buy." The sentiment of the song is true, but she made more of it than simply claiming a value and passing it on to her children. By necessity, she turned her multiple losses into a chant of beatitude—a type of whistling in the dark that had a hollow ring to me, as I observed her internal conflict long before I could articulate even to myself what it was that disturbed her and, in turn, disturbed me.

For instance, I recall her telling me what the word *trousseau* meant. Since my sisters were eight and eleven years older than I and had married young, the word had been used in my presence, but I didn't know its meaning. Like she said of her parents, Mother loved words and was always happy to discuss definitions.

Rather than simply telling me that it meant that brides were expected to have enough clothes to last for several years, she told me the story of how Mother Telford and her own older sisters, most of whom were already married, had helped her gather together her own trousseau when she and Daddy married. She went on to tell me that she had to wait at least three years before she could afford to buy a new outfit after her wedding. That was a bitter experience for her. In addition to money being tight in those years following their marriage in 1926, Mother didn't know how to ask for her needs to be met. I asked her why she didn't let Daddy know that she needed a new outfit, and she said, "Why, if I had ever told him that, I would never have gotten over it."

As I see it from my vantage point, she never got over it anyway and only made a difficult situation worse by refusing to speak her mind. For her, though, having to express needs or wants equaled begging, which she refused to do. In her mind, if she was loved, then the one who loved her would anticipate her needs and wants and meet them without any prompting from her. This, perhaps, was a common outlook for her generation, but her viewpoint was exaggerated by her birth order and childhood experiences that reinforced the distortion of the view.

Mother kept a bag of *feely* things for any children in the house to play a game of tactile identification. Among the dozen or so objects that could be felt by a blindfolded participant was a swatch of maroon velvet fabric she had kept from a dress that was part of her trousseau. She told me about what care her sisters and Mother Telford had taken with making sure she had ample outfits for any occasion. They even crocheted insets for her negligee and slips. The piece of velvet fabric may have been a carefully saved scrap from when the fabric was cut to be sewn or perhaps she had cut it from the dress itself when she discarded it.

Likewise, Daddy maintained a connection with his boyhood home in Seville and would take a Sunday afternoon drive up there every few months to make sure my brother, Richard, and I were familiar with his family roots. We would visit two or three homes where he and Mother would chat with elderly people who still remembered his parents. He also would stop and visit some of his boyhood friends who had stayed in the town of their upbringing. With an air of affection and no intent of disrespect, he would let us know we needed to hurry with our Sunday lunch by saying, "We haven't been up to Seville lately. How 'bout we take a little run up there and see how *Old Man* (family name) is doing. I bet he hasn't had many visitors lately."

Daddy habitually identified the older generation by Old Man or Old Lady so-and-so. I think he developed the habit partially to distinguish between father and son when so many boys went by Junior. Daddy was a junior himself, but he always was known as Bruce, his middle name.

His family was about the same size as Mother's, but he didn't talk about the family history as much as Mother. One of his sisters, Aunt Bessie, seemed to be more interested in the genealogy and occasionally visited relatives in the Carolinas or Tennessee and reported on her visits. I listened to her tales of visiting various cemeteries, towns, and people. It made me wonder why Daddy didn't do the same. Now I think it was simply a matter of different interests combined with a tighter budget.

Like Mother's, his family was close-knit. But their birth orders were opposite. Mother was the baby of her family and had been born when her parents were forty-four years old. Daddy was the oldest son with fraternal twin sisters being the oldest siblings and another sister being two years older than he. His younger siblings included one sister and three brothers. So, Mother's family included seven children, and Daddy's included eight.

Now I wish I had bothered to get acquainted with those older folks in Seville and had listened to their stories. At the time, though, my attention was directed to whatever tree was in the yard and how fast I could climb to the top branch. Rightly or wrongly, I didn't read Daddy's feelings as the same as Mother's. Since Daddy was the oldest son in his family and Mother was the youngest child, their outlooks were more opposite than similar. As the oldest son, Daddy had grown up expecting to take on a disproportionate amount of responsibility for his mostly younger siblings, and Mother grew up receiving adoring attention from five older sisters and one brother whether she expected it or not. In many ways, Daddy never learned to be a child, and Mother never grew up. Yet, they were both warm, loving parents who were responsible community members, whose integrity could never be questioned, and who unfailingly let all of us know we were loved and cherished.

Daddy's family attended church in Seville but probably was less involved in their church than Mother's. His father, though, was an entertainer in DeLand on weekends. As a one-man band, Granddaddy Orrell was frequently the featured performer in the bandshell. He also travelled to other towns to perform and was best known for playing the autoharp and singing ballads. It seems likely that he sang quite a few Scottish and Irish songs because I grew up knowing several that I had learned when Mother played the piano and she and Daddy sang together. Mother knew some of the light classics, but Daddy knew just as many folk songs. His father died in 1937, so his mother, Grandmother Orrell, was the only grandparent I knew. His grandmother came from Scotland, which accounts for his knowing Scottish folk songs.

Although I don't consciously remember hearing Grandmother Orrell sing to me as she rocked me, Mother often reminded me of Grandmother's special song for me. Borrowing the tune used for the verses in the Gospel hymn, "Bringing in the Sheaves", she made up these words:

> Gramma's little wildcat, Gramma's little wildcat,
> Gramma's little wildcat, Precious little girl.

Gramma's little wildcat, Gramma's little wildcat,
Gramma's little wildcat, Precious Martha Sue.

Mother did me a permanent favor by passing on these words to
me because they gave me a glimpse into how Grandmother perceived
my personality. The words also illustrated my stubborn independence
and determination to act upon my own preferences at a very young
age. Resisting sleep has been a lifelong pattern, making me an extreme
night owl, just like many others in my immediate family. More importantly, as I grew in years and understanding, recalling those words
made me feel that Grandmother had allowed that part of my personality
to be recognized and accepted, even if she did do her best to lull me
into naps.

It was my good fortune that my life started in and centered around
DeLand, Florida. I am thankful that my maternal grandparents found
their way to that Central Florida town, home of Stetson University, and
that my formative years were spent there. Likewise, I am grateful that
Daddy's family also settled near DeLand.

Not long before I completed the Bachelor of Music degree at
Stetson, I was walking across campus and met my voice teacher on
the sidewalk. He was new to the university and was trying to get acquainted with his students. He asked me where I was from. "Right
here—DeLand."

"No, I mean originally."

"That's what I mean—I was born here—DeLand Memorial
Hospital—I graduated from DeLand High School."

With a studied, quizzical look on his face, he said, "Then, where
are your parents from?"

"Daddy's from South Carolina, and Mother's from Connecticut."

Like a student who has just understood a concept or figured out an
answer, his face lit up as he snapped his fingers and said, "That's it! I
may never get your vowels straightened out."

We chuckled and went on our opposite ways—he to his office in
DeLand Hall, and I to the Hat Rack for lunch.

*Mother on bike, Sue in basket, Mary standing (Grace Avenue)*

*Daddy, Margaret, Mary, and Sue (Grace Avenue,
DeLand, FL—Mary & Sue holding dolls)*

## CHAPTER 2
# BIRTH OF THE POST SCRIPTS

*The Angel that presided o'er my birth*
*Said, "Little creature, formed of joy and mirth,*
*Go love without the help of any thing on earth."*
William Blake
(1757-1827)

Just 45 days before Pearl Harbor was bombed, my parents hurried out the door of their tiny house to make the three-mile drive from the north side of town to the centrally-located DeLand Memorial Hospital. They were in the same 1935 Plymouth that would provide transportation for my family for at least fourteen additional years beyond my birth. Ole Betsey had many adventures in her long life.

Daddy, so far as I know, never bought a new car. Rather, he would buy a used car from one of his customers when the car was about five years old. He knew the cars he bought were of good value because he was the mechanic who had taken care of them since they were new. He had just sold whatever car he had previously owned and had bought Ole Betsey from the in-laws of the service station owner where he worked.

Less than three years after my birth, the same car would make the same trip when my brother was born. And less than a year after his birth, Ole Betsey would rally to the call to take the entire family and everything we owned to Bremerton, Washington. Eventually, it became the piece of junk that my oldest brother-in-law used for practicing his automotive tinkering skills.

In the early morning hours of October 23, 1941, Ole Betsey faithfully obeyed Daddy's demands expressed through the accelerator. If Mother was relatively relaxed in early labor, Daddy coaxed a few more miles per hour from the sturdy six-year old car. If she was riding the crest of a contraction, he tenderly let up on the speed demand, hoping a lower bounce over the concrete seams of the highway would help ease the pain. The streets in DeLand were a mix of seamed concrete and brick. Some of the streets away from the center of town were narrow and had a metal lip along the outer edge of the road. The lip served as a warning to let the driver know if the car was about to run off the road. Staying in the narrow lane without hitting the metal lip was a challenge when I eventually tested and honed my driving skills in Ole Betsey.

I can only imagine how uncomfortable that ride to the hospital must have been for Mother as the car jostled over the uneven pavement. Daddy undoubtedly felt a great deal of frustration as he was torn between driving as fast as practical while at the same time being concerned for Mother's safety and comfort. Having musical talent and training must have averted some of Mother's physical distress as she listened to the sound of the tires rolling over the seams in the concrete. She may have even expressed the rhythm aloud as Ole Betsey did its best to put those three miles behind them: ka-thump, thump, ka-thump, breathe. Perhaps this was, in effect, a Lamaze technique years before the use of that approach to pain management was popular.

Doing the best he could, my father pulled into the hospital driveway about 10-15 minutes after leaving the house. By the time they completed the paperwork for admission and were assigned a room, I was tired of waiting. Perhaps the same rhythm that attracted Mother's attention also fed my musical sense as a precursor to my own interests and future career. I tolerated the constant rhythm of the road, but I drew the line once we arrived at the hospital. The rhythmic jostling over the seamed concrete was just what I needed to help me make my entrance.

My entry into the world occurred on the exact date that Dr. Hahn had calculated. I was on the way! Knowing from experience that Mother birthed babies quickly, she and Daddy left soon after she wakened him and let him know that labor had begun. According to the diary she kept during her pregnancy with me, she also called Aunt Mae, who had been her sister-in-law prior to her brother's untimely death. By then Aunt Mae had married Uncle Henry (Todt), who was apparently in the military at that time. It appears that Aunt Mae came to the house and stayed with my older sisters, Margaret and Mary, while Daddy took Mother to the hospital.

They made it to the hospital with no mishaps, and I remained patient for a couple of hours, but as they wheeled Mother down the hall toward the delivery room, I decided the hall would be just fine as a place for delivery. She told me many times about how easy my birth was for her, even if it was in the hall with no privacy.

Though her body seemed to be perfect for giving birth, Mother was not able to sustain all of her pregnancies. In addition to a couple of early miscarriages, she had delivered a premature stillborn son less than eight months after their marriage. By the time Margaret was born, they had been married for four and a half years. The loss of their first child added to her wealth of stored grief that had begun when she was only thirteen years old when her sister, Elsie, died during the flu epidemic. Her mother's death occurred in late 1921, followed four months later by her father's death. It was seventeen years later when her only brother, George, died.

Mother told me that she and Daddy were better prepared financially for my birth than they were for either of my sisters' births. They had weathered the Great Depression and managed to help others on both sides of the family. Mother had been teaching, so they felt they could readily take on the additional financial responsibilities that another child would require. Following the Depression, they had been left with some debt that distressed my financially conservative father. As part of his father-daughter talks, Daddy told me that he had charged groceries at a local store during the Depression and was deeply embarrassed when it took him much longer than anticipated to pay off the debt. He was usually on the quiet side, but enjoyed telling stories about the old days. When he told me about charging groceries, he would always end the story with, "Don't *never* let yourself get into debt. Once you do, it feels like a lifetime sentence."

Other than carrying a house mortgage, he maintained that financial stance as long as he lived. Once they had paid off the Depression grocery bill and the burden lifted, they could begin to enjoy a little discretionary income. After Mary entered school, they began to consider the possibility of having another child. Of course, they were hoping for a boy, but they prepared Margaret and Mary for becoming older sisters to either a sister or a brother.

The timing of my conception was perfect, even though it was long before reliable birth control was readily available. The rule (or perhaps law) was that women had to discontinue teaching as soon as they began showing. Mother made it through the spring semester without having to resign. Although I never heard her say much about how she missed the classroom when she was out on maternity leave, it was obvious in her statement that "teachers are born, not made." I feel certain that if she had been forced to choose between having children and having a teaching career, she would have chosen having children. But I am equally sure that she needed both and could only feel fulfilled by both teaching and having her own children.

Her teaching career that extended to age 84 started when she had just graduated from DeLand High School in 1922. In those days, once a high school diploma was in hand, aspiring teachers took an exam and, after passing it, were given teaching credentials. Mother and her friend, Euda Massey, were roommates and taught in the elementary school in Samsula, a small community between DeLand and New Smyrna Beach. Like so many first-year teachers, their diet frequently consisted of Saltine crackers and peanut butter. The position in Samsula was a foreshadowing for her much later return to the classroom in 1959 after she had earned her degree at Stetson University. Once again, she taught at the same school in Samsula.

In those intervening years between 1922 and 1954 or 1955, Mother had taken enough courses in summer schools to accrue about two years' worth of credits toward a bachelor's degree. Standards were eventually set, and the requirement for a degree curtailed her being able to resume her career after Richard was born. She did manage to do some work as a substitute teacher and usually taught a Sunday School class. She frequently was the principal of Vacation Bible School and director of the Christmas programs at church. I think she viewed her role as a parent through the lens of a teacher. That may be said of most parents, but whereas many mothers think of themselves primarily as a care-giver, Mother thought of herself as our teacher, and sometimes our preacher.

Mother's diary is a folksy narrative of people of modest means during the time right before the United States entered World War II. In addition to presenting what life was like for my family, it also includes other families on the same block. Some of the neighbors were relatives; all were friends. Grace Avenue is on the north side of DeLand and was the hub of families who wanted to live close to Lake Molly, which was a convenient distance for biking or walking. Other friends or relatives lived one block over on Anita Street.

Lake Molly was a small lake—just a little larger than Lake Johnson, where about eight years later, we would swim when we lived out on Mockingbird Hill in the DeLeon Springs area. Even after we no longer lived close to Lake Molly, we would sometimes return for a swim or a Sunday school party. Houses eventually were built around it, but for many years, there was still public access. There was no diving platform and not much of a beachside area—just the constant invitation to cool off and practice relaxed floating and various swim strokes.

Someone had abandoned a small fishing boat, which served as an oversized toy for us or a table for cutting watermelon. The trick was to entice a newcomer to swim under the bottoms-up boat to experience breathing in the air pocket that existed between the top of the water and the floor of the boat. Once the swimmer was under the boat, we would pound on the bottom of the boat to see how long it would take for the novice to come out. It was almost like a rite of passage for visitors or newcomers to the area. Our adolescent brains thought it was funny to rap our knuckles on the boat to tell the person underneath that it was time to rejoin the rest of the group. Little did we care about the aural assault as the rapped sound was amplified as though the wood of the boat were the sound board of a piano.

Mother noted in my baby book that I walked before I was nine months old. She told me that I learned to swim in Lake Molly before I learned to walk. No wonder I still miss the lakes of Central Florida, especially those of West Volusia County.

In terms of picture-post-card beauty, Lake Winnimissett was the most beautiful lake in the DeLand area. Located a few miles east of DeLand just off the road leading to New Smyrna Beach, it was the destination of many residents in search of a cooling breeze and a beautiful view. It was one of the larger lakes for swimming and welcomed visitors with a narrow picturesque public road around the entire perimeter. The road allowed residents who could not afford lakeside property the opportunity to enjoy the beauty and practicality of a natural means of reducing the unpleasantness of air heavy with humidity and generously warmed by Florida's sunshine.

At Lake Winnimissett, there was a small public beach area at one end of the elongated circle—the perfect spot for a picnic or a nap after a swim. Visitors to the lake could drive out in time to watch the sun set over the water. With the sound of the water lapping at the edge, the sun setting, and the moon rising, birds singing and insects chirping, it could be a very romantic place.

Mother often recalled how, when she was a young girl, Gramma Skilton would sometimes allow her to stay home from school and would take her out to Lake Winnemissett for a picnic. When she talked about her childhood, she frequently reminded us of how much less developed DeLand was in those days, reminiscing about the side streets being simple lanes covered with pine straw that blew into the sandy ruts. Most of the buildings had a hitching post out front. She sometimes marveled at the ease with which we could travel anywhere we wanted for recreation. In her early years, a trip to DeLeon Springs (eight miles) or to Daytona Beach (20 miles) was an infrequent luxury. Even though Ole Betsey was old, it was dependable and still beat a horse and carriage like her parents had used. Since Lake Winnimissett was only a couple of miles from Mother's childhood home, it was *her* lake.

Daddy and Mother would often take a drive out to Lake Winnemissett to cool off before going to bed on those nights when high temperature and humidity threatened to give them a restless night. During the summer of 1944, the lake was even more important to them when they sought a cool lake breeze in the evenings when she was pregnant with my brother, who was born on August 30th. Mother often said that was the most uncomfortable summer of her life. Because of the proximity, she and others from the Grace Avenue neighborhood gathered at Lake Molly in daytime hours, but for early evening drives, Lake Winnimissett was the lake of choice.

Typical for the time, Mother remained hospitalized for a week or so before she and I went home in an ambulance. Daddy reminded me every year that I had been the best birthday present he had ever received because his birthday fell on October 26th, just three days after mine.

Mother had many friends from the community, church, and school. Even though I was the third child, her friends gave her a couple of elaborate baby showers as she and Daddy and Margaret and Mary anticipated my birth. The reasoning must have been that after eight years since Mary's birth, a completely new layette and other items were needed for the new baby. With a mother's pride, she told me, "Honey, you had the best of layettes available in DeLand at that time. We were completely ready for you."

She saved a few of those treasures, which I still have and occasionally take time to look at and wonder at my ever having fit into that little dress and shoes. One of the items she saved was a homemade wash cloth made out of cotton flannel as would have been used for a receiving blanket. Of significance is the hand embroidered border that includes both pink and blue thread. Whoever made it had both gender possibilities covered.

Mother filled out two baby books for me. When she passed them on to me, she explained that she had received two—one at each of the showers. She felt that she must use both so as not to hurt the feelings of one of the two givers. She would never have exchanged one of the baby books for something else because in that small town, word would have gotten back to the giver. Risking hurt feelings was something she adamantly avoided, even if the risk was more perceived than actual. That sort of concern taught me how sensitive she was. I later encountered other women who showed me that not everybody would be quite that sensitive.

So—I was born into a very modest household, but one that was financially stable and full of anticipation at the prospect of having a baby once again; into a community that would prove to be of critical importance to me when I later faced the most painful and potentially destructive period of my life.

I never heard anything about whether Margaret and/or Mary rode home with Mother and me in the ambulance, but about 34 months later, my earliest memory would take root in my brain when I rode home with Mother and my new baby brother, Richard. I have no conscious memory of my own birth, of course, but I distinctly remember riding in the ambulance with Mother and Richard when it was time for them to come home from the hospital. One of the reasons that very early memory stuck in my brain is because the ambulance was the fanciest automobile I had ever seen. I remember the velvety upholstery on the front seats. It seemed like the entire interior sparkled with new luxury and light—far different from the dull monochromatic olive-green drab of Ole Betsey.

There was a built-in pull-down bed that stretched along one side of the interior. Women often wore a bed jacket instead of a bathrobe back in those days. Although I do not recall the color of my mother's bed jacket, I do recall that she was lying down on the ambulance bed, and the jacket was tied together with a couple of shiny ribbons. It bothered me that my very active mother appeared to be sick. I certainly was not used to seeing her lying down in a nightgown and bed jacket. The mother I knew and loved was active. She wouldn't hesitate to put me into the basket of the bike and pedal me to Lake Molly for a swim. Never a bench-warmer, by her own admission, she was in her element when she was a big fish in a little pond. And now, she couldn't even wear regular clothes or sit up. My toddler's mind and heart must have felt conflict that had no immediate outlet.

Mother, along with the rest of the family, had prepared me for my baby brother's arrival as well as anyone could. Of course, the gender of an expected child was not known prior to birth back then, but I had to have been aware that the family was hoping for a son/brother. Margaret and Mary rode home from the hospital in the car with Daddy. Because they were almost 11 and 14 years older than our brother, I feel certain they were willing co-conspirators in the attempt to maintain my feelings of worth as I adjusted to Richard's presence in our lives.

The most vivid part of this memory is the white wicker bassinet that was placed on the opposite side of the ambulance from the bed. There were no seat belts in those days, and I was allowed to stand and walk between Mother's bed and Richard's bassinet. The part of the ambulance that I found most intriguing was the decorative chrome that was installed along the ceiling, where crown molding would have been placed in a house. I was not tall enough to see over the top of the bassinet, but by looking up at the chrome, I could see the reflection of my baby brother's face in the curve of the chrome as though it were a mirror. Mother often told this story and always included my less-than-clear enunciation, "Look! Dare's my 'Vichy Booce'!" ("There's my Richy Bruce.").

I have no recollection of wondering why he looked so *funny*, but the curve of the chrome must have reflected a distorted image. All I knew was that the big day had finally arrived and I was happy to be taking my baby brother home and for Mother to be coming home.

Bringing a son/brother home from the hospital was a big deal. Along with the family story of how I talked to and about my baby brother on the way home from the hospital, whichever parent was telling the tale always included the part about their longing for a son and the long wait from the time they married in 1926 to the first live birth in 1930. Both parents went out of their way to assure me that they were ecstatic when they first saw me, even though I was the third daughter, reassuring me of their delight at finally having a child with Mother's coloring. They reiterated how they had counted every little finger and every little toe and rejoiced at the hint that my eyes would be dark. Even though their inclusion and repetition of these details might sound as though they were compensating for some residual guilt for perhaps being somewhat disappointed that I was not the son they longed for, they succeeded in making me always feel special because I was the only child who had Mother's red hair and brown eyes.

As I think about this very early memory, I am thankful that my parents were sensitive to a young child's feelings. Since Mother was a teacher, I feel certain that she was aware of the natural sibling rivalry that might show itself in my behavior if I were not ready to accept a baby into our family and to adjust to the fact that the baby was a boy. She must have identified with my being the youngest daughter, just as she was the youngest in her family. She also had only one brother, although he was older than she.

Later on, my brother and I did experience some ordinary sibling struggles. When I recall those years when I was in elementary school, I feel an urge to thank him for not nursing resentment toward me for my impatience with the normal differences in our development. Wanting to have a playmate, I took it upon myself to try to force him to do things that I did that he was not big enough to do. Beating him at rural pastimes such as throwing rotten oranges at each other or green oranges no larger in diameter than a quarter gave me undue satisfaction. By the time I was in upper elementary school, his marksmanship was catching up to mine, and the force of the spin he learned to put on those small green oranges made me decide to limit that type of activity to the spring-green frogs that called the hickory nut tree home. Mother's reminder that we were wasting the new crop also played a part in my turning away from the green oranges.

Once I entered high school and he entered junior high, we became close friends and had a lot of fun together. Standing six feet, two inches tall, my baby brother has been my big brother since he entered high school. In a far more profound sense than a number on a yardstick, he is now the strong patriarch of our large extended family that includes five generations. Although he is also a tender man, he is a rock to all who know him. My "Little Vichy Booce" is quite a man!

And so it went, that after waiting eight years for my birth and almost another three years for Richard's birth, Mother and Daddy completed their family with us two postscripts. Mother often said, "It took us eighteen years to complete our family, but you were all worth the wait."

*Margaret, Sue, and Mary*
*(Grace Avenue or Adele Avenue, DeLand, FL)*

# CHAPTER 3

# LITTLE SISTER

*Give a little love to a child, and you get a great deal back.*
John Ruskin
(1819-1900)

My older sisters frequently saw me as a typical bothersome little sister. At the same time, just as Mother had been, I was the darling of the family, the one they had waited for the longest, and the only sibling with Mother's coloring. But the trap of trying to act as grown up as my sisters were despite the eight- and eleven-year age differences between us put me into an emotional bind that chaffed and blistered. An allure of age progression was inherent in the constant reminders to act mature. At the same time, though, that attraction was in friction with the equally strong counter-balance of age regression as I struggled with the effects of the opposition between acting mature and feeling infantile. The label of *little sister* produced both pride and envy in my age-appropriate immaturity.

To an extent, the attraction/repulsion syndrome of toddlerhood and adolescence is typical emotional conflict between the desire to be independent and the need for continued attachment. But I believe that my birth order exacerbated my feelings and skewed my self-perception. It seemed to me as if something were wrong with me because I didn't always want to act more grown-up than I was. Yet, I knew that if I didn't try to do that, I certainly would be denied privileges that Margaret and Mary readily received. I didn't want to wait until I was eight or eleven years older to receive the more generous freedom bestowed by additional birthdays. The emotional wheels that I felt spinning alternated between being mired in confusion, doubt, and pressure. It was something I couldn't label—something unsettled and unsettling.

When I heard the community statement in reference to a special needs child—*He ain't right in the head.*—I thought perhaps I was not *right in the head.*

For as long as I can remember, I didn't want to take naps, and I fought going to bed at a prescribed time. Ours was a family of night owls, and I associated late nights with food and fun. Yet my parents never seemed to have a problem with early-morning alarm clocks. Late night visits and snacks typically occurred in our home on Sunday evenings after church. Sometimes, though, we would go over to a relative's house in the evening on our way home from church if we were not expecting visitors at home.

For a while, one of Daddy's brothers, Uncle Banks, and his family lived near us. Visits to their home were always a respite from the disorder of our home. Aunt Vi did not allow clutter to accumulate; she cleaned regularly; and she took unusually good care of her family's clothes. I recall with great fondness how secure I felt as I fell asleep on their sofa and how protected I felt when Daddy would gather me up into his tire-wrench-muscled arms and carry me to the car when the visit was over. It felt like he was the strongest man on earth. That I couldn't stay awake as long as I wanted to was an admission I did not want to make.

Not long after the end of World War II, Mother called me down out of a tree in the back yard and asked me to meet her and Mary and Margaret in the kitchen. After putting their school books down in the living room, they joined us at the kitchen table. Mother's mood was high-spirited with anticipation of the treat. The tenderness in her heart leapt from her brown eyes that were a little darker than mine as it found its way into my own heart. "We have a little extra sugar," she said with delight.

Even though I was only about four and a half years old, I understood that having extra sugar was a luxury because it had been rationed during the war. My palate began to anticipate chocolate pudding, but when I sat on one of the farmhouse style chairs at the white wooden table, I didn't see any sign of pudding.

To stretch the small amount of sugar equally between all four of us, she gathered the loaf of bread from a cupboard, a small jar of mayonnaise (really salad dressing, but we called it mayonnaise) from the ice box, and the small Mason jar of sugar from the pantry. Rather than letting each of us make our own sandwich, she went ahead and started making them herself. With meticulous care, she spread a thin layer of mayonnaise on two slices of bread for each of us and then spooned out the white granulated sugar and sprinkled a little onto one slice of bread for each sandwich. Being true to her self-image of a born teacher, she demonstrated how to hold one slice of bread on the palm of each hand and to slap the plain slice onto the sugared slice. That way, we wouldn't spill many of the granules. Her face beamed with a mother's joy as she anticipated how thrilled we would be to have such a rare treat. When I bit into my sandwich, despite the tenderness I felt for her, in obvious displeasure, my lips curled.

"What's wrong, Honey? Have you forgotten how good sugar is?"

"No. I just like it when it's cooked. It's too gritty like this."

"Okay. Why don't you try two more bites? If you still don't like it, I'll finish it for you."

If my negative reaction to the supposed treat hurt Mother's feelings, she didn't let on about it. At least I was communicating with words, which I seldom did at that age.

Many times on Sunday evenings, some of Margaret's and Mary's friends would come home with them from church for teenage socializing. It seemed like such get-togethers occurred every week, but probably really only happened once a month or so. One of their favorite things to do was to make fudge—another special treat if there was enough spare sugar for it. Even though it was no longer rationed, sugar still was an extra on the grocery shopping list because Daddy was still looking for a job.

Making fudge was the perfect alternative to spending the evening singing around the piano. The kitchen was large enough to hold six to eight people, and it gave a focus to the time and relieved any teenaged social awkwardness. I wanted to be able to stay up, help stir the fudge, and eat my fair share of it. Often, I would find the fudge-caked pan the next morning with enough dried particles for me to scrape a taste of the candy. A few years later, at about age ten, the first recipe I learned to use was the one for fudge on the box of Hersey's cocoa. It is difficult to believe that Margaret and Mary, their friends, and perhaps our parents would have eaten the entire batch of fudge, but I have no memory of ever eating a piece of the candy soon after it was made or even the next morning until I started making it myself.

The gnawing in me that was stronger than the hunger for my share of the fudge, of course, was the need for inclusion and attention. I was no longer the baby, but I was not nearly as mature for my age as Mother and my sisters tried to make me believe I was. The admonitions to act mature were so pervasive that I felt like I had to become an actor to convince them that I truly was mature for my age. Awareness of expectations frequently reminded me of the unsettledness that was becoming my norm. But problems can't be fixed without awareness of their existence, and I was far too young to go beyond vague intuition.

Fudge also had played a part in our spring ritual of being treated for pinworms, a parasite common in Florida that Mother said we got from sitting in the sand. One time, Mary was perfecting her fudge-making skills when it was time for me to take the tiny purple pills that would declare war on the pinworms. My only motivation for even attempting to swallow the pill was my vivid image of worms crawling around inside my body. Not yet familiar with the sight of squirming maggots in the bottom of an outhouse, I still conjured up a vivid image of the tiny worms using my young body as a host. But even though I hated the idea of having worms in my body, I was never able to swallow the pills. Mother and my sisters had to figure out some way to sneak the pills into my food and hope I would swallow quickly without biting into the mouth-painting purple pill.

Mary happened to make a batch of fudge that didn't quite *fudge*. It sat like a puddle of thick chocolate syrup on the margarine-coated platter somewhere in the middle of No-Fudge-Land right between Syrup and Frosting. Having a brainstorm about getting the pinworm treatment down to my stomach, Mary said, "Come on, Suzie. I made some fudge, but we have to eat it with a spoon. It just won't get hard enough to cut into pieces. Here. See if you think it tastes good."

I trusted her and ate the fudge from the spoon. That improvised trick led to several years of Mary's deliberately putting a little too much milk into the fudge in the spring of the year so that they could get the pinworm pills down my throat.

By the time we settled in the Miami area, I was allowed to help make the fudge by squishing the margarine to make it turn yellow. It came in what probably was a one-pound clear plastic bag of what looked like white lard, accompanied by a little ball of amber color that made me think of a yellow eyeball. The first step in the process was to squeeze the amber ball to burst the outer coating so that the color could spurt and be absorbed by the white lard. The bag material must have been very thick and just as stubborn as I because it seemed like I squeezed and squooshed for half a day to get the margarine to be uniformly yellow. One of Mother's teaching maxims was, *If a job's worth doing, it is worth doing well.* A marbled look in the faux butter was not acceptable. She had never heard the maxim common today: *Don't let perfection get in the way of excellence.* So, perfectly uniform yellow margarine was the goal.

As Margaret and Mary outgrew their desire to play with dolls, I too announced that I was not going to play with dolls any more. But once, before they had put their dolls to rest, I managed to borrow Mary's favorite doll, Boots, and took it outside to play. Florida sand looks almost white, but when it gets rubbed into skin or fabric, it becomes very dark, almost black. Not only did Boots lose her head that day, she also acquired a layer of Florida dirt all over her nude body. When Mary saw the headless doll I brought inside, I think she felt the most anger toward me she had ever felt. Even though she was giving up playing with dolls, she had planned to keep Boots forever. Always the peacemaker, Mother intervened and assisted Mary in squelching her anger and gently lectured me about respecting other's things and getting permission to play with Mary's or Margaret's possessions.

In Miami, Margaret worked in the same small grocery store where our father was working as butcher. I was in the room when she told

Mother that she had bought an *L-L-O-D* for me for Christmas, thinking she had found a way to outsmart my inquisitive ears. I spoke up. "But I don't want a doll. I'm too old to play with dolls. I'd rather have a teddy bear." There was no hesitancy about expressing a preference for what I wanted. That hesitancy would develop later from hearing Mother's consistent message that expressing preferences was not very thoughtful and was, in fact, selfish. She and Margaret were chuckling as Mother said, "You can't use that trick any more. You'll have to think of some other way to tell me a secret or wait until your little sister is not within earshot."

I don't know how either of my sisters felt about the way Mother and Daddy disciplined me at that point, but they later told Mother in my presence that their treatment of me was unfair because I was allowed to get by with things that they would never have been allowed to get by with. Such was the luck of the birth order. But the latitude accorded me also reflected Mother's great wisdom in dealing with each of her children as the strong individuals they were. She knew that if she butted heads with me, it would be an immediate power struggle, and a struggle she did not want to take on. She said to me many times, "Honey, you are so very stubborn. I think it comes with the red hair because I'm the same way. You must learn to channel the stubbornness into something worthwhile, and you'll go far in life."

Mother tried to guide Mary and Margaret into a more patient attitude toward me and my behavior. For example, after we had moved back to DeLand/DeLeon Springs at the end of my second grade, I was feeling unusually grateful to Mary for the help she had given me regarding dental hygiene and hair care. I was old enough to be left alone while Mother and Mary made a short trip into DeLeon Springs for a few household items. While they were gone, I decided to show my appreciation to Mary by cleaning up her room. She was sharing the room with Katy, a friend from Miami, who was on an extended visit in our home. Before we left Hialeah, Katy and Mary had plastered the shower stall with Squirt (a drink similar to Sprite) decals, so I always thought of Katy as a prankster.

Mother and Daddy had bought sixty-five acres out on Spring Garden Ranch Road, and Mother named the acreage Mockingbird Hill.

The farmhouse sat pretty far off the road at the edge of what had once been a thriving little orange grove with one grapefruit tree near the driveway. Margaret and Peggy, her daughter, slept in the back bedroom; Mary and Katy had the front bedroom; Mother and Daddy slept on the sleeping porch, and Richard slept in what was meant to be the dining room. I slept on the sofa in the living room until Katy returned to Miami. Then, for a while, Mary and I shared her room.

Mary and Katy's room was not in terrible shape, but I thought I could make it look pretty. So I made the beds, swept the floor, and put the dirty clothes in a stack by the door. When they returned home, Mary and Katy saw that I had rearranged the items on the dresser they shared. I caught the *Oh no!* look that flashed between them. When Mary raised her voice and started scolding me, I burst into tears. Mother heard the commotion and came into the bedroom. Flustered in the face of controversy, she said to Mary, "Why are you so upset? They're only things, for goodness sake. Her feelings are far more important than combs and brushes and the placement of doilies. You must let her know that you appreciate her efforts or she'll never want to try to help again."

"All we want is for her to leave our things alone. Can't you make her do that?"

"I'll talk to her, but you also need to apologize for hurting her feelings. I'll make it clear that she is not to disturb anything on the dresser again."

"Yes, ma'am."

It took only one more incident for me to give up on trying to beautify the house. Richard and I were both home without supervision. There was not even a telephone yet. I had been spending some time at a girl friend's house in town. She was taking piano lessons and hated to practice. I was wishing I could take lessons and that we had a piano. In all the uprootedness, the piano had been sold when we headed to Washington. My friend's house was a small cement block house behind the little general store where *Aunt* Lonnie Mae and her husband had occasionally babysat Richard and me.

It was my good fortune that my friend let me practice on her piano. She showed me her piano books and attempted to play some of the pieces for me. I knew the rudiments of reading music because I had always been curious about it. While in the first grade in Miami, I asked Mother how the choir learned new music. Recognizing the teaching opportunity, she took a prized book out of a small trunk and told me that her father had taught voice and directed choirs using that book. I sensed it was one of the few material objects Mother really revered. She helped me do some basic sight-reading and told me she would show me the book any time I asked to see it.

At my friend's house, between my music reading skills and her letting me hear how she thought the pieces were to be played, I could figure out how to play them. The thing that I loved most about her house, besides the piano itself, was the gleaming hardwood floors. She had a room of her own that seemed like a princess lived there. In retrospect, the room was pretty, but not extravagant. It was clean with a closet just for her things. I asked her mother how she kept the house so clean. "It really isn't hard. There's just the four of us, and we all help a little. Since I don't have a job away from home, I make sure that things are put away before I go to bed at night, and I do a few chores each day. That way, I don't have a big cleaning job."

"How do you make the floors look so pretty?"

"The builder put a good coat of varnish on them, and I just dry mop them several times a week."

"Can you make old wood floors shine?"

"I think so. You just have to get the right varnish or polish and put it on. It might be a hard job, though."

"Oh. I wish our floors were as pretty as yours."

With that minimal understanding of putting a finish on hardwood floors, I made a mental note that I would surprise Mother sometime by polishing the floors while she was gone. There was no doubt in my mind that she wanted the house to be pretty, too, because she often talked about how beautiful the house her parents had built in DeLand was and how much she had loved it. According to her reminiscing, it was an idyllic place in which all seven children were musical, conversation around the dinner table often included word games with their father, and her sensitive mother read original poetry. She often said,

"Our home was filled with books, music, words, and love." No wonder she missed it so much, even though there had to have been some of the ordinary challenges and complexities of a large family living in the first quarter of the twentieth century.

The opportunity to work on the farmhouse's unfinished floors didn't wait long to present itself. I knew that Mother had gone to DeLand that day rather than just to DeLeon Springs, so I would have perhaps a couple of hours to work. I recruited Richard and explained what we were going to do. We would just do the living room that day. The need to move the furniture, gather the right supplies, and find instructions for making the finish shine had not crossed my nine- or ten-year-old mind. All I was certain of was that I was going to do my best to make the floors look pretty.

There was a small bottle of Old English furniture polish in a storage bin under the stairs. Dust-coated and about half empty, it may have been among the stash of stuff left behind by the previous owners. It seemed to be what I was looking for to do the trick. It was odd, though, that we even had any furniture polish because we didn't have any unpainted furniture. The beds had iron headboards and footboards; the kitchen table was painted white, and the only wooden bedroom furniture was the dresser in Mary and Katy's room. By then, I knew not to mess with that piece of furniture or anything resting on it.

Rich and I squatted down in an open area that approached the archway between the living room and eat-in kitchen. I told him I would pour out the polish and he would have to start rubbing right away to spread it around and make it shine. I looked aghast as the black Old English furniture polish soaked into the unfinished wood as though it were a sponge. "Oh no! It shouldn't be black! We have to get it up."

"How?"

"I don't know. Just keep rubbing. Mother's really going to be mad if she sees this black circle on the floor."

We almost rubbed our fingers raw, but the black stain remained. The unfinished wood drank that little bit of black liquid and begged for more. The spot on the floor was about a foot in diameter—not easily disguised or overlooked.

Typically, Mother did not resort to yelling because she knew it would do more harm than good. Rather, she said, "Martha Sue, you know I have told you it is okay to try to improve how things look. But you must wait until I am here to supervise and help you. We can cover up this mistake with a small area rug, but I do not want to have to cover up any more mistakes. I know your intentions were good, but this is the last I want to see or hear of any such attempts. Do you understand me?"

"Yes, ma'am. I just wanted to make the floors look pretty."

"And one more thing—do not get your brother involved in any more of your schemes. You must set a better example for him to learn about helpfulness and responsibility. Let's make sure that this is the last of any such incidents."

"Ok. But when I'm in 4-H, can I sleep in the dining room and make my room look pretty? I've heard that they have projects for things like that. I could help Daddy paint the walls and I could get a bedspread and a throw rug. I know just the shade of green I'd like for the walls."

"We'll see. It's too soon to know who will be living with us a year from now, but we'll think about it. Where would your brother sleep if you took the middle room?"

"After Mary and Margaret move out, he could have his own room and I could have my own room. I hope they both get married soon and move out."

"Now, now. Don't be critical of your sisters. They are doing the best they can."

"When I'm their age, I'm going to be in college. I'm not going to quit school. And I'm not going to have a baby right away."

"I hope your dreams come true, Sweetheart."

"Don't worry. They will."

Sure enough, a year or so later, I joined 4-H. Mary had married Daniel McDonald, and they were living in North Carolina while he completed his military obligation. Just as I had anticipated, Daddy readily agreed to paint the walls a light shade of green that complemented the green linoleum on the floor. He always let me help him paint, which I loved to do because it gave me such an immediate sense of accomplishment in my quest to make our home look pretty.

Aunt Betty, Uncle Ruric's wife, was trying to establish a business by selling merchandise out of her station wagon. She would drive all over West Volusia County, knock on doors, and give her sales spiel with great enthusiasm. Mother did not escape the sales pitch. Aunt Betty noticed the fresh paint and complimented us on how nice it looked. With almost breathless enthusiasm, she gushed about having the perfect comforter that would set off the room. Mother agreed to pay for what amounted to an extravagant purchase over a time span of three months. It was disappointing that I didn't get to pick out the color of the comforter, but I knew not to complain and to show proper gratitude for getting one at all. When we made a later trip to McCrory's, I did get to choose the green throw rug. To this day, my favorite color is green.

When Daddy dragged home after work that evening, I couldn't wait to show him the addition to my room's décor. When he saw the elaborate comforter, the small muscles around his mouth tightened as he fought his urge to lose his temper. "It looks nice. Did it come from your Aunt Betty's store?

"Yes, it was the only one she had, so we decided to buy it so we wouldn't have to wait for a different one."

By then, Mother had joined us and was mildly agitated at Daddy's tone of voice. We always knew when she was tense because her face developed red blotches that I now believe was rosacea. My own symptoms of rosacea (diagnosed by my dermatologist) are prone to pop out when I am under stress. "Alice, you know Betty knows every sales trick in the book. We could have caught a good sale at Penny's or Sears."

"It's alright, Dear. She gave me ninety days to pay for it."

"I just wish you could learn to say *No* when you need to."

Neither of them raised their voices, but the tension between them crackled like static electricity as it shorted out the spirit of joy I thought I had found. I went to the piano and started practicing the piece I was learning. Daddy came up beside me a minute or two later and said, "You already know *Humoresque*. Could you play that for me? It always makes me feel relaxed. Your room really is pretty. I didn't mean to make you feel bad. I'm just worried about money."

Accepting his words of apology, I flipped the page to *Humoresque* and tried not to cry as my fingers relied on muscle memory to play the familiar piece.

## CHAPTER 4

# BREMERTON OR BUST
# AND BACK AGAIN

*The use of traveling is to regulate imagination by reality, and*
*instead of thinking how things may be, to see them as they are.*
Samuel Johnson
(1709-1784)

When war rations were imposed, Daddy said that he was in a situation where he had to either go on the black market or get out of the service station business. It was never clear to me whether he owned an interest in the station at that time or if he was managing for someone else. I assume, though, that he was the manager and someone else was the owner. He knew some men who worked for Florida Power and Light Company and was hired to collect bad debts for the company. It put him in a position of having to go door to door demanding that the light bill be paid if the customer wanted the service to be maintained. He said that he typically had to talk with the lady of the house, who often had several children hanging onto her skirt. His tenderness was much stronger than his ability to turn off the lights if the woman was not able to pay immediately. To him, turning off the lights for a family with young children was immoral.

I was never sure whether Daddy told his boss that he could no longer work as a debt collector or if perhaps the boss told him that he needed to work in some other capacity. They came to terms with Daddy being assigned to one of the light pole crews. His favorite part of the story about that part of his work was the time they were out in the woods in sandy soil with palmettos covering both areas beside the trail. His friend, Elmo, was leader of the line crew and was going through the area too fast for Daddy's comfort. He said to Elmo, "Watch out, there's a rattlesnake nearby."

"How do you know? Did you hear the rattles?"

"No, I smell it."

"How does it smell?"

"Like a rotten watermelon."

From then on, Daddy was the lead man and Elmo walked behind him.

With financial strain hammering at them and relatives on both sides of the family pulling at their heart strings, Mother and Daddy decided to solve their woes with a literal drastic move. Many times, they recalled how they sat down at the dining table in the house on Adele Avenue in DeLand—the largest and nicest house they had owned at that time— and studied a U.S. road map. Having relatives in Connecticut, Mother initially suggested they could consider moving to New England. "Just think, Honey. We could enjoy the hills and fall colors Mama always talked about."

"Yes, but we'd still be too close to relatives. Let's go some- where where we don't know a soul—a place that will have decent job openings."

Mother asked him if he had talked to his brother, Uncle Ruric, about the possibility of his moving at the same time. "Yes. He had a good suggestion."

Daddy explained that Uncle Ruric had said they should look for work in a war-related industry. One of them soon heard a radio report that ship-building companies in Bremerton, Washington, were hiring. It was the summer of 1945, but neither Daddy nor Uncle Ruric had any concern that the war would soon be over.

When Mother told the story about how she and Daddy had decided where to move, she recalled that they tied the end of a ball of twine to a tack, placed the tack where DeLand sat on the map, and swung the twine out to see how far it could reach. The farthest spot was the Pacific Northwest. Bremerton was almost three times farther away than cen- tral Connecticut. That firmed up the decision. Their spirit of adventure complemented their need to escape the infringement of relatives on all types of resources, and the job prospects gave Daddy hope. About to turn 43, he had expressed concern that just as he was too old to serve in the war, he might be too old to be hired. But hope and need outweighed fear. In her words, they sold everything but the car and kids and took off.

Uncle Ruric and Aunt Betty decided to caravan with us. None of the four adults had expressed any reservations about looking for work in the ship yards. As usual with my parents' major decisions, a large portion of their thought process got sucked into rationalization. They became swept up in the thought of how educational the trip itself would be, particularly for my older sisters, Margaret and Mary. They would see first-hand different types of land formations that until then had been mere words in text books describing gray-shaded photos. They would find out just how big this country is. And maybe the close quarters in Ole Betsey would teach them a thing or two about getting along more congenially.

The constant climb from near sea level on the Atlantic coast to a pass through the Rockies and on to another coastal region near sea level on the Pacific coast took two weeks. Daddy liked to brag about how faithful Ole Betsey had been. In all those miles and long hours, she never faltered, and only once balked when a T-bone out of a steak punctured a tire. The tires must not have been anywhere near new if a T-bone could pierce one of them.

We were approaching the half-way point in Arizona when V.J. Day (Victory over Japan) turned the country into a frenzy of relief and joyful celebration. A young couple on a motorcycle heading east saw us and started frantically waving their arms and flashing the two-finger victory sign. Thinking they might need some help, Daddy stopped the car. Uncle Ruric pulled up behind us on the shoulder, and the motorcycle stopped in the middle of the road. Daddy asked, "Need some help?"

"No. We just wanted to be sure that you've heard the news."

"What's that?"

"The war's over!"

After expressing elation and gratitude, Daddy and Uncle Ruric thanked the couple for stopping and gave each other a *What now?* look.

We all got out of the cars and stretched our legs while the grown-ups huddled. The motorcycle motored on.

Realizing that the ship yards probably would be closed immediately, Mother and Daddy faced the choice of either returning home to the same situation they had left or forging ahead with trust that Daddy could find work in Washington. Uncle Ruric and Aunt Betty turned around and went home. Their toddler son was not adjusting well to the rising elevations, which gave them a rationale that they could accept for themselves and sell to others.

V. J. Day occurred on August 15. It must have been the sixth or seventh day of the trip, which put the Bremerton arrival day around September second, the day the formal ceremony of surrender was held in Tokyo Bay aboard the USS Missouri. As expected, the ship yards were no longer hiring. Daddy looked for work in Bremerton and began working his way south in each of the small towns leading through Tacoma and beyond.

With Mother and Daddy resigned to the probability that his chance of finding work was small, we reached Chehalis on a Sunday, thinking we were on the way home. After filling the gas tank and checking the oil before pulling out of town, Mother and Daddy decided to attend church. When Daddy shook hands with the minister after the service, the minister asked him where he came from. Daddy answered, "Florida." The minister probed further.

"Have you always lived there?"

"I was born in South Carolina, but my family moved to Florida when I was just a boy."

"That's it! I knew it was somewhere in the Deep South."

Assuming that the minister probably was looking for possible new members, or at least regular visitors, Mother explained that we were on our way home because Daddy had not been able to find work. The minister asked, "What's your trade?"

"I've been an automobile mechanic most of my life."

The minister then instructed Daddy to go to a service station in Centralia, the next small town back to the north. He said to be sure and let the proprietor know that he had sent him.

"The owner of that station is crazy about southern accents. He just might hire you."

Open to the minister's suggestion and eager for an opportunity, Daddy found the service station and was hired on the spot. We found a two-story house just big enough, rented it, and moved in.

My fourth birthday was approaching soon after we got settled in Centralia. Margaret was almost fifteen; Mary was almost twelve; and Richard turned one near the time we arrived in Bremerton. For two weeks on the road, Mother held Richard or let him sit between Daddy and her. She let me sit on her lap some of the time, especially when I was the only one who needed a restroom break. I would straddle one of her thighs while she bent over to pull back the floor mat.

When Daddy had inspected the car before we left DeLand, he discovered a rusted area in the floorboard on the passenger side of Ole Betsey. Rather than waste time stopping every time I had to urinate, he methodically tapped the rusted metal loose and increased the size of the opening enough for it to hold a child's potty like a countertop holds a sink. He put a floor mat over the dropped-in potty, creating my own built-in toilet. We were traveling slowly enough so that Mother could empty the potty (liquid only) before pulling the mat back over the one-holer. Richard was in Chux disposable diapers, a fairly new convenience at the time. Margaret and Mary took turns teasing Mother. Margaret said, "Watch out, Mom. Don't ruin one of your shoes."

Mary would chime in, "Mama, be careful. Your foot might go all the way to the pavement."

In addition to my own potty, I had my own bed in the car. All of the household linens that had not been sold or given away were neatly layered in the back floorboards so that they were level with the seat, making an ever-ready bed or seat for me. The climb between the front and back seats gave me some practice for climbing trees everywhere we lived.

When colder weather than we were used to set in, Daddy took us to what felt like a huge store and bought each of us a heavy winter coat. Mother also bought woolen blankets, including a Jack Frost blanket, which lasted for many years. Funded by cash from the sale of the house in DeLand, that is the only family shopping spree I recall Daddy being present. His new coat was a brown leather bomber's jacket, which he wore for at least fifteen years. About five years later, when we lived out on Mockingbird Hill, Richard and I would sometimes look at the jacket hanging in the closet under the stairs. I wondered why he didn't buy another nice jacket. By then, the smooth and supple texture had become stiff with crinkles and cracks that gave it the appearance of extremely dry brown skin. The original scent of soft leather had been taken over by the lingering aroma of Prince Albert pipe tobacco and traces of Old Spice aftershave.

Persistently prone to quarrelling, Mary and Margaret sat on opposite sides of the back seat with their legs folded. When willing to exercise patience and cooperation, they could take turns stretching out their legs without tangling them or crowding me out of my space. When they inevitably started squabbling, Mother would start singing a Gospel song with clear signals for them to join in. We covered that 3100+ mile long road twice with many repeats of "On the Jericho Road."

Mother used every counting trick her teacher's mind could think of to keep my own mind busy and focused—license plates from other states, mesas in the distance, mountain peaks, light poles, fence posts, horses, and on and on. My favorite thing about the trip itself was learning to recognize some words. It seemed like I was reading and made me feel more grown-up. Words I started recognizing were: café, eat(s), motel, gas, vacancy, and no vacancy, along with some traffic signal signs. Eager to show my reading prowess, I competed with Mary and Margaret to see which of us would announce the signage words first.

On one of my last visits with Margaret before her death, we talked about the trip to Bremerton and the return trip to DeLand. She verified that we stopped at a park on the way out to Washington. There was an indoor swimming pool in the basement with rough stone steps leading to it. An odor of mold or mildew mixed with chlorine fills my nostrils when I recall that stop for recreation. Margaret and Mary raced laps while Mother held Richard and watched me in the shallow end of the pool. Daddy stayed up on the street level and talked with the manager about the best routes from there to our destination.

My fourth birthday hit not long after we were settled into our new location. It was the first birthday I remember. Undoubtedly, the trip itself, being away from Grandmother, and getting used to a different climate helped to mark that day as memorable. A girl my age lived a few houses down the street from our house. While I was outside that morning, she came up to me and asked if I could play with her that afternoon. "No."

"Why not?"

"It's my birthday; I have to be with my family." She asked me if she could come to the party.

"There's no party, but we'll have cake and ice cream."

"You're a liar. It's not your birthday if you don't have a party."

Defending myself, I told her I was telling the truth and that she could not be my friend anymore because I didn't like being called a liar. We parted with a tongue-sticking contest and me in tears. If I saw her outside after that, I don't recall. With cooler temperatures setting in along with gray skies and frequent rain, I probably didn't spend much time outside after late October.

Two events that occurred near the time of my birthday stand out in my memory. There was a small grocery store a block or two from our house. I can't say whether Mother let me go to the store by myself as a reward or as a change-making lesson; or perhaps she needed to have a few minutes alone with Richard. Whatever the motivation, she gave me a nickel and told me I could buy two pieces of penny candy. She stressed the importance of my being responsible with the change that the clerk would give me. I felt no fear and took off on the candy-buying mission. I wonder if perhaps she lad let the store clerk know to look for me and to make sure I headed home in the right direction. At that time, there was no hint that my sense of direction would be just as unreliable as Grandmother's, but it seems likely that Mother would have used some general caution before sending me on that short trip toward independence wrapped in the persona of being mature for my age. It may have been a matter of trying to get me to eat something, even a little bit of candy, because I was slipping into a habit of eating very little.

Within the same time period, I climbed the small apple tree that was in our back yard. Depending on the variety, apples may ripen any time between August and November. That tree must have produced one of the late-ripening varieties. I proceeded to try to fill my hunger by eating so many of the small green apples that stomach cramps set in. Uncharacteristically, I yelled for Mother to come outside and get me out of the tree rather than retrace the route that placed me too high to jump down. I probably had seen Granny Smith apples at some time and had assumed that the apples were supposed to be green. But they were not Granny Smiths. Associating eating with intestinal discomfort may have reinforced my emotional refusal to eat.

Once my birthday was celebrated, it was time to turn our attention to Halloween. It was never a big deal in our household, and whatever celebrating there was took place primarily at school. Margaret and Mary would have given a nod to Halloween with their new church or school friends.

Of more importance and significance were Thanksgiving and Christmas. Once we were past Halloween, I had stood the separation from Grandmother about as long as I could. Around the time we would have been anticipating preparing for Thanksgiving, my sisters and parents became concerned about my refusal to eat. Grandmother Orrell had been my primary caregiver while Mother taught school. I believe I suffered separation anxiety and deep sadness. Still in my possession are a few cards that Grandmother wrote to me while we were away from her.

Grandmother was an outstanding cook. In her prime middle years, she had owned and managed a boarding house in DeLand. All of her children had to help in some way. Being the oldest son, Daddy often helped in the kitchen. He enjoyed cooking then and for the rest of his life. Mother was also a good cook, but had no passion for it. She usually was in charge of the Thanksgiving turkey and the occasional Sunday dinner roast, but getting a regular meal ready was no more than a burdensome task for her. If any baking or dessert making was done, Daddy was the one to whip up a pie or custard.

More often than not, dessert was a store-bought Merita seven-layer cake, which had seven layers of yellow cake with chocolate fudge frosting between each layer. Rather than being a complete circle, it was sold in half-cake packages. In the summer, we sometimes had ice cream floats. According to the diary Mother kept while she was pregnant with me, relatives occasionally brought dessert in the evening; more often, though, they showed up just in time to let Mother or Daddy know the servings had to be adjusted to accommodate the guests.

When I quit eating normally, each of the family members—except Richard, of course—joined the campaign to get me to eat. Each of them offered what they thought would be a tempting suggestion. "Want some ice cream?"

"Cake or cookies?"

"How about some fish like Daddy used to catch?"

Taking his turn, Daddy said, "Honey, if you don't want any of the things your mother and sisters have mentioned, just tell Daddy what you want. I'll get you anything you want to eat. You need to eat so that your bones and muscles will keep growing and be strong. What is it that you want?"

Trying to squelch or ignore my tears, I looked into his blue eyes and said, "Just plain old grits, Daddy." I don't know if he or I fought harder to contain our tears.

"Alice, I don't care what it costs. Send a telegram to Mother and tell her we need five pounds of grits for Suzie and to send the package the fastest way possible."

They had already discovered that grits were not stocked by any of the grocery stores. All of the family missed having grits for breakfast and sometimes even for supper, but I was the only one who had gone into a tailspin over the issue.

With hindsight, I believe grits were the tangible connection to Grandmother and that what I really missed was her presence in my life. Her little wildcat needed her understanding, her rocking and cooking, and her gentle expression that told me I could do no wrong that she couldn't make right or forgive. Her face was the epitome of an idealized depiction of what every child should visualize when they hear the word, "Grandmother."

There was never any apprehension about being branded Gramma's little wildcat because I felt only love and longing for her. The understanding of my characteristics gave me a sense of pride in the nickname she chose for me. As self-awareness developed, I relished the notion of being wild enough to be me—independent, stubborn, inquisitive, and committed to ideas and ideals not entirely shared and often disapproved of by my family and community.

I must admit, I probably missed being the only child in the house when I was with her, or at least the only mobile child since Richard would not have been walking before we left DeLand. With limited mobility because of an accident that left one of her legs stiff and having the site of the break never heal due to diabetes, I expect that someone else—probably Aunt Bessie—was in charge of Richard's care while Grandmother watched me and rocked me when the nap time I always fought came around.

The major holidays were approaching along with the longer winter than we were used to. Considering how little room the trunk of Ole Betsey had, I am amazed that Mother was able to hang on to the objects that meant the most to her. She must have kept them all together in the small trunk that followed us on every move. In it, she kept the few pieces of Skilton memorabilia in her possession: the published genealogy; books her father used when he taught voice; a hand-written volume of poetry by her mother; a miniature china tea set from her mother's childhood; a few linen doilies with crocheted edges crocheted by her mother; and an ivory napkin ring that had been hers at the Skilton dining table. The number 2 was etched on the outside of the octagonal napkin ring.

Mother's childhood and heritage had been reduced to this small stack, along with a volume of the predecessor to "Ladies' Home Journal," which had belonged to her mother. In her purse or in a dresser drawer, she kept a coin purse with some of the coins left on the dresser after one of her parent's death; in total, a few tangible items that represented and summarized her early years. They served as her emotional lifeline to the heritage and history she profoundly grieved.

When it was time to decorate the Christmas tree, we found the few treasured Christmas items in the same box where the mulberry vase and brass candlesticks had been packed. No matter where we lived, if we had a fireplace, the vase and candlesticks always sat in the place of honor on the mantle. They were considered precious because they were wedding gifts from some of the relatives in Connecticut—a tangible tie to Mother's parents and to her own birthplace.

Our Christmas decorations were not abundant, but we felt content with sparkly garland, a new string of popcorn, and a new string of cranberries. There were also a few ornaments and a star for the treetop. I wanted us to make a paper chain of green and red loops, but Mother explained that Mary was too sick for that and we would have to decorate the tree quickly so that Mary could get back to bed. When Mother saw my face droop, she assured me that we could make the chains for Easter with pastel colors.

In the last couple of Christmas seasons prior to the one in Washington, Mary had been in charge of decorating the tree. Even though I wanted to do the same things that my older sisters did, I was afraid to be the one in charge of the Christmas tree. Mother finally talked everyone into helping to get Mary's cot into the living room near the tree so that she could still supervise the operation without getting overly tired. As I recall, I wound the garland as high as I could reach; Margaret took care of the ornaments; and Richard sat on Mother's lap or stood at her knee. I got Mary's approval before placing anything on the tree.

Mary's illness was some type of bladder or kidney infection. Without a doubt, she felt miserable, ran a fever, and was lethargic. Whether Mother took her to a doctor or not is unclear in my memory, but I would assume that she did. Regardless, Mary's condition was not improving. From the remarks I later heard from Margaret and Mother and Daddy, it seems likely that Mary may have had some convulsions when her fever spiked.

Mother typically described her church affiliation as staunch Methodist. Her preoccupation with church attendance and involvement seemed to set in either right before or right after we ended up in Miami after leaving Washington. She described the search for a church home in Washington as frustrating because there were so many off-shoot churches.

One of the neighbors in Centralia attended a church that practiced faith healing. She invited Mother to attend a prayer service with her. Mother took Margaret, Mary, and me to the service. It had to have been a vulnerable time for Mary. She and Margaret had been taken away from family and friends over 3,000 miles away and were expected to fit right in to a new school and to make new friends. And just when she needed to work her magic on the Christmas tree, she was too sick to do more than the minimal toward that end.

Not long after attending the faith healing service, Mary was running a high fever and had a dream which, in her mind, was a divine vision. She believed she went to heaven and met Jesus and that He told her to come back to Earth. She further believed that He told her she was to be a submissive wife when she grew up.

Never one to question or overtly disagree with someone else's opinion, and suffering from false guilt from a similar experience, Mother (in my opinion) failed Mary by not only allowing her to believe the dream was real—a deeply spiritual prophecy and blessing—but also by perpetuating the fallacy to the point of turning it into family lore and writing a poem to honor it. In my view, Mary's belief that being submissive was Jesus-mandated eventually set her up for a life of misery with the man who took full advantage of her outlook and willingness to be his doormat.

As the holidays wound down and Mary's condition slowly improved, Daddy finally said, "Before we have to take one of us home in a box (coffin), let's go home."

That was just the rationalization they needed to turn their backs on the rain and wintry gray skies and head back to the Sunshine State. But this time, we would be crossing the Rockies on the northern route in winter without snow chains. Ole Betsey had rallied to the west-bound trip admirably, but her performance in snow and on ice was unknown, and neither Daddy nor Mother had any experience driving in those extreme conditions. They had already established that Daddy would be the main driver because if Mother was driving and exclaimed about how beautiful or interesting the view was, Daddy was ready to crawl through the roof. Mother relieved him only if he was desperate for a nap or a break. On the way home, though, he did all the driving. He had a way of nursing the car along and squeezing a few more miles out of each tank of gas. Mother was more patient with potty patrol, changing diapers, and refereeing quarrelsome teenagers, while Daddy was better at coaching Ole Betsey and keeping us on schedule.

There was no dramatic national event such as V.J. Day as we crawled toward home—only unending miles that disappeared just fast enough to remind us of how many more there were to go. The trip was uneventful until we drove through Rabbit Ears Pass into Steamboat Springs, Colorado. There were no reservations, of course, and I spotted every "No Vacancy" sign on motels as we searched for shelter during a severe snow storm—maybe even a blizzard. Daddy finally gave up and stopped at a motel even though the sign should have been turned off since there were no rooms available.

Relieved to be off the road, he went into the office of the motel and spoke with the owner. He explained that we had been in treacherous weather all day; we were hungry; and we needed a room for the night. We really needed two rooms, but he offered for Mother and him and Richard to sleep in the car if the owner could just get the three girls into a room. Standing by his first declaration of *no vacancy*, the owner expressed concern and said that he wanted to help us, but that all of us would have to sleep in the car. He loaned us enough blankets for each of us to have one and one for the radiator. Not knowing what Daddy did for a living, he cautioned him about the need to keep the tailpipe unclogged to avoid poisonous gas getting into the interior of the car. Gracious to a fault, Daddy didn't inform the man that he was a mechanic and knew about safety issues. Rather, he simply smiled to himself and assured the motel owner that he would check the tailpipe periodically.

The owner's wife made peanut butter and jelly sandwiches for us and told Mother that we were welcome to use the restroom. Hot pots of coffee and cups of hot chocolate kept appearing whenever one of us had to go inside. None of us really slept, but Daddy got enough rest so that he could face the next day of driving. He rationed out the use of the car heater during the night as he watched the gas gauge creep ever closer to the empty mark. The blankets the proprietor loaned us were Army surplus olive drab wool and were even scratchier than the similar wool fabric of Ole Betsey's upholstery. For those dark hours interrupted by the flashing neon lights, we tolerated the scratchiness with gratitude for the owner's concern, hospitality, and generosity.

The first time I had to use the restroom, Mother bundled me up in one of the blankets. Daddy opened the front passenger door and hoisted me up onto his shoulders. His shoes were no more waterproof than mine, but they were Daddy's shoes, and they could take us anywhere. Riding up on his shoulders, I had to look up to see the tops of the shoveled snow banks. Lights from inside the motel's office blinked, and the neon sign showing a steaming cup of coffee bid us welcome, if only to use the restroom. Rather than scaring me, that short trek into the shelter of the little motel assured me that even in an unusual situation, I could count on Daddy to be the hero. Riding piggy back was a special treat because he was not home with enough energy to offer it very often.

The next morning, Daddy filled the gas tank, checked the spark plugs and oil, and wiped the windshields before we left the motel. After leaving the severe weather behind, for one of our lunches, Margaret suggested that we could have chili for lunch because it would be a good meal for cold weather. Mother and Daddy agreed, so we started looking for the sign. Margaret wrote the word, "chili," on a piece of paper and told me to start looking for it on signs. "It's funny," she said. "Chili sounds like it should be a cold meal, but watch out—it might be hot."

When the waitress brought the small bowl of chili to me, I didn't like the taste or the burn that travelled to my stomach, but I tried to be brave, and ate it. It felt like it was fighting my insides. That was one of the first clues that I would have to avoid hot spices my entire life. I topped off the chili with several saltine crackers because Mother said they would absorb whatever was bothering my stomach.

We had not gone far after lunch when I stood up behind Daddy's head, tapped him on the shoulder, and began to ask him to stop the car. I felt sick. With every word I tried to say, another wave of nausea swept over me. The words didn't get out, but the chili did—right down his shirt collar with dribbles on the upholstery. He pulled over and opened the door for me to get some fresh air and to make sure all the chili was accounted for with no more threatening to come up. I apologized and attempted to explain that I was trying to tell him I was sick.

He said, "I know—just—please, if this ever happens again, try to let me know sooner. Why don't you walk around a little bit while I get a clean shirt out of the suitcase?"

Mile by mile and state by state, we made it back to the DeLand area with no other unfortunate events. So far as I know, Mary was doing fine by then.

Mother maintained a nostalgic desire to retrace the 1945-46 trip route and especially wanted to see Steamboat Springs again. At age eighty-four, she finally was able to do that when she was a widow and I was divorced. We made a ten-day road trip in my car from her home in Missouri to Colorado up the eastern side of the Rockies, across Rabbit Ears Pass, and down the western slope. She walked on top of Pike's Peak at the Visitors' Center and got close to the suspension bridge over Royal Gorge. On the round trip steam engine train ride between Silverton and Durango, we counted water falls until we lost count. The engineer gave his talk about the communication signals used by the whistle, and we recalled how Daddy had loved to sing train ballads he probably had learned from his father.

On the western side of the Rockies, Mother counted road kill (mostly deer) and squinted to make out the letters on the motel signs, hoping to find *Vacancy* waiting for us. Her failing eyesight limited her ability to help with reading maps, but she still enjoyed the sights and had no trouble spotting the ears of Rabbit Ears Pass as we approached Steamboat Springs. I wanted to see the motel lobby where I had cried to be allowed to ride a rocking horse, but, of course, there was no spotting it. Although she didn't opt to hike to the ruins at Mesa Verde, she sat at a picnic table and watched the deer that were almost domesticated while I made the short trek to see the ruins more closely.

Our 1989 trip was vastly different from the family's trip back in 1945-46. I could almost wish that the family had never gone to Bremerton, but I could never wish that Mother and I had not retraced the Steamboat Springs section of the trip.

## CHAPTER 5

# MOTHER HOLMES' ARBOR

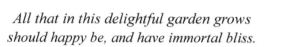

*All that in this delightful garden grows*
*should happy be, and have immortal bliss.*
Edmund Spencer
(1552-1599)

There is a green thumb somewhere inside of me, but you wouldn't know it by looking at my yard. I see with my internal green thumb's eye and envision how my yard would look if Mother Holmes lived here. She had been our neighbor prior to the trip to Bremerton and also was our neighbor when we rented the house across from hers when we returned to DeLand from Washington. Her yard was so much smaller than mine, but its soil supported vignettes of miniature landscapes. Color and texture ran like threads woven by design, dappled or burnished by Florida's aerial gold, the surrounding air binging on fragrance.

The historical and cultural ambiance of central Florida during my childhood was a setting unto itself—too northern to be deep south and too southern to be true north—but some of the southern customs were adopted by visitors (*snowbirds*) who wintered in Florida, many of whom stayed indefinitely. Honorific titles such as *Mother*, *Aunt*, or *Uncle* often were assigned to friends of the family.

Grandmother Orrell and Mother Holmes were strong mother figures for my mother. In their own way and in their own time, each of them took up where Mother Telford left off. When one of my uncles started to tell a mother-in-law joke Mother said, "You might as well forget about telling mother-in-law jokes around me. They aren't funny, you know. I adored Mother Orrell."

When we first returned to Florida from Washington in early 1946, we rented a small house in DeLeon Springs. I believe it was owned by Mac Bessinger and that we had lived in that same house for a little while right before we left on the trip to Bremerton. It sat in the middle of a large corner lot that never cried out for a lawnmower. Dust chased me inside when cars passed by during a dry spell.

Three memories from those few months stand out in my mind. I can't account for the reasons behind it, but I had one bout of choking on food and two episodes of swallowing non-food objects that could have produced choking. The first I recall was a coughing fit when I swallowed bacon before I had adequately chewed it. There was a bit of connective tissue that my teeth had missed. The piece of bacon with sinewy strings still attached wouldn't finish its trip to my stomach, and the remaining piece in my mouth couldn't reel in the dangler. As I coughed with increasing gag reflex, making my eyes bulge, my sisters were agitated with fear that I would choke to death. Remembering that Mother was outside, I ran out onto the front porch. She had heard my coughs and my sisters' calls to her. She rounded the corner of the house about the same time that I reached the top of the steps. Mary and Margaret were right behind me and said in unison, "She's choking on bacon."

"Here, girls, I'll take care of this. Since she can't seem to get the bacon down, I'll just have to pull it back up."

With that announced determination, she reached into my mouth and began pulling the attached portion of the bacon that I had swallowed. As she gently pulled, the swallowed portion came up. It tickled my throat and exaggerated the gag reflex before I finally spat out all of it onto the ground. It was years before I tried to eat bacon again.

When a little older, I learned that Mother could get so worked up over something that appeared to me to be unworthy of the emotional stew. But in my early years, there were at least as many times when she simply took matters into her capable hands to quickly and quietly solve a problem. I would learn a few years later that she would become frantic if one of us swam under water longer than she thought was normal. Somewhat to my surprise, I later found that I also share her bent in that direction. That is, I also have the tendency to handle emergencies with total restraint and efficiency. I don't think, though, that I work myself up into a tizzy over small matters.

Not long after the bacon incident, Mary and I were playing marbles in the sandy front yard. Actually, she was teaching me how to play and helping me practice using her big shooter. My beginner's finger strength and aim were no competition for her, but she was patient. Before we finished the game, I swallowed one of the smaller marbles. She ran inside to tell Mother, but Mother showed no great concern. She said to Mary, "Is she choking?"

Mary said, "No, she just told me she swallowed it and I wondered if we need to do something."

With nonchalance, Mother said, "No, I guess 'Mother Nature' will take care of that."

A few weeks later, when I swallowed a penny, Mother was more concerned. I heard her tell Margaret and Mary that she was afraid the size and shape of the penny might make it more likely to get stuck in the digestive tract and cause a true medical emergency. But, again, she reminded me that "Mother Nature" would take care of it. She gave me a slice of white bread to eat to help force the penny along its way. I didn't like the idea of checking to see if or when the marble and/or penny were expelled, but within a few days of each swallowing event, they both were accounted for.

After just a few months, we moved to a two-story house in DeLand across the corner from the house Mother and Daddy sold when we moved to Washington. Mother Holmes' white stucco house stood directly across from the rented house and diagonal to our former residence. We were in DeLand long enough for Daddy to find there were no jobs available before his youngest brother, Uncle Bob, told him he could work as a butcher in Miami. Uncle Bob was already managing one of his father-in-law's neighborhood grocery stores, and he knew that Daddy could pick up whatever skills he needed in order to become a butcher.

Because of Daddy's employment search and outcome, our stay across from Mother Holmes' place did not last nearly as long as we would have liked. Yet, the memory of her house on the corner across from our rented house is as strong as though she and her yard had always been a part of my family's collective long-term memory. The entire impression of Mother Holmes and her yard was strengthened by my associating her appearance and manner with Grandmother Orrell. Grandmother lived across town and was already seriously ill. Daddy visited her regularly, but he usually stopped to see her when he had additional reasons to go to town. That made my visits with her infrequent, and my fears of her approaching death constant.

So far as I know, Mother Holmes lived alone and did most of her own gardening. My favorite part of her front yard was the white arbor arching over the sidewalk just inside the gate of the picket fence. As I think of it now, I realize that the yard could have been right in the heart of the Cotswolds in England. The arbor supported climbing roses that made the archway the focal point of the yard. It was a beckoning welcome to all who entered the gate; a filigreed shelter from sun, and a light-weight brace from showers.

There was also a small rose garden for long-stemmed roses and what she called an English cutting garden. A vibrant butterfly garden was tucked away in a corner. I always wondered why the butterflies didn't land on me. Viewing her space through 4 1/2-year-old eyes, I sometimes felt sad when she cut flowers because I missed them when they were no longer on their stems. The in-town air around Mother Holmes' yard was as fragrant as country air when orange trees blossomed.

Mother and I sometimes walked toward the junior and senior high schools to meet Margaret and Mary as they walked home from school. No other yard in the neighborhood had the gently persistent call of invitation to stop, observe, inhale, and relax as did Mother Holmes' yard. Just beyond the arbor on one side of the sidewalk leading to her front door, there was a concrete bench used for garden gazing. I can still feel my short legs swinging back and forth as I sat there, reciting nursery rhymes to myself, feeling as though I was in a completely different world that was in sync with my tempo and rhythm.

Mother Holmes sometimes babysat Richard and me in her home. It's odd that I have no memory of the back yard and very little memory of the interior of her home. But the image of the front yard with the rose-laden arbor is as strong today as though I had entered the gate, stood beneath the arbor, and breathed in the beauty just yesterday.

Most of the houses in the neighborhood were wooden frame Victorian, Craftsman, or Southern Vernacular architecture. But Mother Holmes' house was Southwestern. As I picture the rough texture painted white and the arches that matched the arch of the arbor, the Southwestern stucco façade reflected her sense of style, beauty, and grace. The English garden seemed completely at home in that Central Florida town.

The few months spent in that location were enough to cement a bond between Mother Holmes and me. Then, when we learned we would be moving to the Miami area, I again faced the fact that trips to visit both Grandmother Orrell and Mother Holmes would be infrequent. I wondered if either or both of them would die before I got to see them again. Already aware that Mother's parents died when she was a teenager and that Daddy's father also had died before I was born, it seemed that I had been really unlucky when it came to grandparents.

Although I could not articulate it, with hindsight, I believe that I suffered from separation anxiety from the time we moved to Washington and that it took decades for me to grow into a willingness to put myself in emotional harm's way to any significant extent. Physical distance triggered emotional distance as a means of coping with the ongoing pull-up and move-out cadence of our geographic mobility.

Moving to Miami left my emotional roots tangled in an airborne grasp at solidity like a hardy succulent tossed into the breeze on its way to an unknown landing. The absence of Grandmother and Mother Holmes in my life was far more important than anyone around me realized.

After the disappointing fourth birthday in Washington, I was not expecting much on my fifth. Not long after we settled in Hialeah, it was time to celebrate. It is the only birthday, other than the fourth birthday out in Centralia, that I remember prior to my twelfth. The fourth one stands out in my memory as the first birthday I remember, and the fifth stands out because it was an unusually happy day for me.

Knowing that I liked to be mobile and had an excellent sense of balance, Margaret had saved enough money from her meager earnings to buy a pair of roller skates for my birthday gift. I had not been expecting them and when I opened the package, couldn't wait to try them on and try to skate. She was a pretty good skater, and I had watched her at the roller rink and wanted to learn to skate. Mary may also have skated at the rink, but I don't recall seeing her there.

The skates were silver metal and were in a big box. The key that was used to adjust the length and width of the skates hung on a shiny red satin ribbon. Margaret explained that having the key meant that I could use the skates for years before I would outgrow them. I also could let someone else use my skates even if their feet were larger or smaller than mine. Margaret helped me put them on and tightened the leather straps to a snug fit. She and Mary held each of my hands as I tested my balance.

My parents often speculated that my extraordinary sense of balance was accounted for by my unusually long second and third toes. Nobody was surprised when skating seemed easy to me. It didn't take many trips up and down the sidewalk before I was ready to try skating on the road. Mother reminded me that I was not to skate in the street unless an adult or one of my sisters was with me. The sidewalk was smoother than the street, but I wished it was a lot longer. I knew that Margaret had her own pair of skates that looked like boots on top of wheels and that she carried them to the rink when she went to skate. She told me that I could get a pair like that when I was older and had stopped growing.

Margaret and Mary went inside when Mother called them to help get supper ready. Daddy came home from work soon after they left me with instructions to stay on the sidewalk. He was beaming when I greeted him. I showed off my new skating skills, and he said, "Is that all you wanted for your birthday?" I told him that I had hoped for a bicycle, but I was happy with the skates. He said, "Why don't you run inside and tell the rest of the family to come outside with you?"

He had figured out how to get the bike home from the grocery store without having me see him haul it out of the car. He had been making the repairs and refurbishing it without letting me suspect a thing. Uncle Bob likely helped him with the project. Making sure it was a surprise was a large part of his delight in finding the bicycle, repairing and refurbishing it, and presenting it to me with all the joy of a father proud of what he could offer his youngest daughter.

When I went inside and told everyone that he wanted them to come outside with me, I could tell that Mother and Margaret and Mary exchanged knowing looks. It seemed like they were in on a secret that I knew nothing about. For a flash of a second, I felt left out, but quickly focused on leading them outside.

As soon as I stepped onto the small stoop, I saw that Ole Betsey's trunk was open and Daddy was rolling a silver-colored bicycle toward me. To my five-year-old eyes, it could have been pure sterling. It was the fanciest bike I had ever seen, and I never suspected it had been used by someone else. I screamed with delight and ran the few steps to meet up with him. He said, "Do you think this might be the right size for you?"

I squealed, "Yes! Is it mine?"

"Yes, my Darling. It's for you and for the little boy I once was. I always wanted one too. With your sense of balance, you won't need training wheels."

He patted the seat to tell me to hop on and told me he would help keep it steady until I knew how to steer it. I lost count of how many times I ended up in the bushes alongside the fence to the pasture where the neighbor's Palominos grazed. He kept up the bike patrol/control for a while, then asked Mary if she could take over while he went inside. She would push me off and see how long I could hold the wheel steady before heading for the bushes. Once I could stop the bike without crashing into the bushes, she declared that I knew how to ride and didn't need her help any more. She reminded me, though, that I might need some help again the next day. Meanwhile, Margaret had put the skates back into the box. It was time to go inside for supper and cake and ice cream.

That was the happiest, most memorable birthday of my childhood. It was not just the unexpected gifts, but the accomplishment of learning to skate and to ride my bike on the same day that lodged the memories so deep in my heart and mind. I later learned that the bike was not new, but I couldn't tell it was used and didn't care when I found out. What mattered was that Daddy had found a way to provide what seemed like an extravagant gift and had painted it and made sure it functioned and looked as good as new.

The elation of the fifth birthday celebration was short-lived. When around my cousins, the age differences between my parents and theirs was a constant reminder that my family didn't indulge in high-energy activities unless we were with Uncle Bob and Aunt Ruth. When Santa Claus lavished the cousins with what seemed to be abundant gifts, I wondered why he didn't do the same for us. At the same time, though, I was aware that I was not supposed to feel that way; rather than jealousy or envy, I was supposed to feel gratitude.

During the years in the Miami area, I identified more with Mother's family although most of the cousins on her side were considerably older than I. In my compartmentalized observation and thinking, I wanted to take on Mother's family's value of education, but also wanted to absorb and take on the attitudes toward recreation that I saw in Daddy's relatives. Of course, I couldn't articulate these desires or even identify them, but I sensed the differences between the two sets of relatives and sought comfort by not allowing myself to take sides emotionally. Inevitably, though, it was just a matter of time until I would be forced to side more with Daddy's attitudes than with Mother's. I compartmentalized Daddy's family as fun-loving, outdoors types of people and Mother's as educated, serious types. While I couldn't find or adhere to some sort of neutral ground between the two family backgrounds, I was able to use the fear of detachment as a reinforcement against tight attachment to either side of the extended family.

Three of Mother's sisters made appearances in Miami, but did not spend enough time with our family to completely soothe my longing for Grandmother and Mother Holmes. But each of them certainly affected my long-term connection to them and generated my gratitude for what they meant to me, both then and always.

Aunt Jessamine was married to Uncle Stuart (Gould), a Doctor of Osteopathy, who was trying to set up practice in the Miami area. I am unaware of most of their history and only recall seeing them a few times while we lived there. They had strong family ties in Orlando and in the north. By the time their children were born, they were established in Michigan. We visited them in their apartment once or twice before they moved. What impressed me the most at their apartment were the curtains at the windows—a luxury unfamiliar to our home. In the back of my mind, I added pretty curtains at the windows to my mental list of wants. The correlation of more education with more pretty things was not being lost on me, although it was at an intuitive level and couldn't be articulated until years later.

Aunt Helen and Uncle Alden (Boor) visited us several times, but lived up north. He was a professor of chemistry and eventually retired from the University of Chicago. The visit I recall most vividly is the one when Aunt Helen asked Mother, "Where are Martha Sue's books?"

Mother responded, "Oh, we don't have books at home. I tell her bedtime stories every night, and sometimes Bruce tells her stories. She also looks at library books when we take the older girls to the library."

Being one of the older sisters who had helped take care of Mother when she was a young child, Aunt Helen announced with the voice of authority, "Alice, this child must have some books of her own. Let's go. I'm going to get her first books right now."

I still have the two books that survived my childhood and were shared with several others in the family: Goldenbooks' *A Child's First Dictionary* and Robert Louis Stevenson's *A Child's Garden of Verses*. Aunt Helen was so wise to buy those specific books for me. Robert Louis Stevenson is still one of my favorite poets. The connection between higher education and valuing nice, pretty things, such as books and curtains at the windows, was being set ever more firmly as I made unconscious decisions as to what I would value and what I would ignore.

Aunt Miriam had a large family and had moved to Miami when her husband, Uncle Sam (Stone), thought he could find work there. Following in their dad's footsteps, two of their sons became plasterers and had already found the job market improved in the Miami area. The greener grass of construction called to Uncle Sam as he followed his sons' lead to Dade County. Their youngest daughter, Christine, was a couple of years older than I and crushed me when she confirmed what I had suspected—Santa Claus was not real. The previous year, I had been looking in the coat closet for something when I spied a couple of bags full of something half hidden behind the coats. I had just opened the top of one of the bags when Margaret came in from the kitchen and intervened. "Martha Sue, what are you doing?"

"Nothing," I said.

"If we catch you snooping in that closet again, Santa Clause will not bring you anything for Christmas."

I couldn't yet put it all together, but I sensed that there was something, some sort of secret, about Santa Clause that I was not supposed to know.

By the time we were living in Hialeah in the Miami area, I was getting more suspicious. Margaret swore me to secrecy when she showed me what she had bought for Mary as a Christmas gift. When we went over to Aunt Miriam's apartment, I told Christine about seeing what Margaret had bought for Mary. She said, "Do you still believe in Santa Clause?"

Sensing that it was a loaded question, I quickly shifted mental gears from wanting to believe to wanting to act mature so that Christine would see me as an equal. "No."

"Santa Claus is really just your parents pretending to be Santa."

"I thought so."

I wanted to cry, but put on my big girl face and wished she had not told me.

The constant push/pull I felt between wanting to claim the innocence of childhood and the acceptance that I had to act mature churned my developing psyche into a haze of confusion and anxiety. Despite shattering my childhood belief in Santa, she and I remained friends and later would be roommates on a trip to a church camp in North Carolina.

Mother had always said that Aunt Miriam had forgotten more about piano performance than Mother had ever known. Aunt Miriam was only seven years older, so had been the one most closely tied to Mother in a more sisterly than aunt-like or motherly way. On the surface, Aunt Miriam showed a sense of humor, with Mother sometimes referring to her as the "family clown." Knowing that Mother's doctor had recommended that she wear a corset or girdle with firm support for her lower back, if Aunt Miriam noticed that Mother was not wearing one, she would tease her and tell her that everyone was going to see her rear end jiggle as she walked if she didn't wear the proper undergarment.

The worry about bodily jiggles didn't seem to go along with Aunt Miriam's mildly scolding Mother when she came for a visit and saw that Mother was walking around the house wearing only her underwear, which included a full slip. Besides trying to get some relief from the heat, it was likely that Mother was waiting for the dress to dry or to iron it before putting it on.

I was not yet at an age when talking to someone about my confusion between acting mature and acting my own age was an option. I had heard Daddy say that he discovered that he learned a lot more if he was quiet and listened than if he talked more. I took that remark, which he repeated with some regularity, as an instruction that I would be better off to stay quiet. Reinforcing that notion was the reminder by both parents of the cultural admonition that "children should be seen and not heard." I feel certain that taking in these misguided assumptions led me into emotional stagnation with vague unsettled feelings of isolation and a longing for the security I felt in the presence of Grandmother or Mother Holmes.

Perhaps the certainty that they would live in their respective homes until they died was the underpinning that I both needed and dreaded. It was simultaneously comforting to know where they were, but discomforting to know they could not leave their home to visit me. By the time we were in Miami, we had lived in six different houses in three different geographic areas, but I was aware that older people did not move around so much.

With two strong attachments needling me, I internally fought against emotional loss caused by uprootedness. I had no desire to make friends at school or church and took in minimal slights as though they were deliberately meant to hurt me. For instance, when my art work was not displayed on the bulletin board for an open house in the first grade, I asked Mother to ask my teacher why my picture was not displayed. The teacher responded with a very rational answer and pointed out the good things about the drawings that were selected for the display. But I didn't need or want to know why those pictures were so good. I wanted and needed encouragement to try harder the next time. On the way home, I asked Mother why my teacher didn't like me. She tried to sell me the idea that all teachers like all of their students equally. That was too big a stretch for my heart to accept.

I never saw Mother Holmes again; Grandmother died while we were still in Miami. All the while, I absorbed the message: act mature. Big girls don't cry.

*Sue in First Grade (Hialeah, in dress made by Mrs. Stanley)*

*Bonnie (cousin) and Sue in Tubs*
*(Hialeah, Flood, 1947)*

# CHAPTER 6

# SETTLING INTO SCHOOL

*Education is not preparation for life; education is life itself.*
John Dewey
(1859-1952)

Mrs. Whaley welcomed me to her first grade class in Hialeah Elementary School. She was young, had a pretty smile, and made me believe that she really was happy for me to be in her class. Like at least half of my classmates, I had not attended kindergarten, but unlike most of them, I would not turn six until late October. When Mother took me to school to register, she assured the principal that I was ready for first grade. At the same time, she let him know that she was available for substitute teaching. Despite feeling eager to attend school, I was self-conscious because I couldn't pronounce my last name very well. Mrs. Whaley had to ask me to repeat it. With a pleading look into her eyes, I delegated that task to Mother.

After saying a quick *goodbye* when Mother started to leave, I looked around the room before noticing the playground equipment just beyond the large open windows. Turning my eyes back to the class-room, I saw that several classmates were crying and clinging to one of their parents. Why anyone would cry about starting school baffled me. With my thickest persona in place, a smug feeling of superiority came over me when I realized that I was acting the most *mature* of anyone in the room. I didn't even want to cry. The dress that my cousin's grand-mother had made for me felt like the most special dress I had ever had. Mrs. Stanley had asked about my favorite color and selected a teal green fabric with small white flowers that looked like daisies woven into the fabric. The short sleeves puffed out, and the full skirt swished around with just a hint of a twist in my walk. Margaret called it my *swishy-tailed* walk.

Being around so many books and school supplies, sitting in connected desks that looked just like the larger ones in Margaret's and Mary's classes, and knowing I was on my own socially boosted my big girl image. The day passed far quicker than I could ever have guessed it would. After I got used to attending school, I was to walk home, but someone would usually drive me to school in the mornings.

On that first day, Mother picked up Margaret and Mary in Ole Betsey before driving on to the elementary school. Mrs. Whaley told a couple of classmates and me to wait at the monkey bars because someone from our family would be there to pick us up. Not waiting for the others, I ran all the way to the climbing structure, hoping to be the first one there so that I could scamper to the top. I wasn't about to waste time standing around and waiting while I could be climbing. The structure was similar in shape to a pyramid with decreased circumference in each tier. It called to me with just as strong a voice as the trees I loved. Only one student beat me to the spot—a boy who looked like he was probably a year or two older. He had already climbed to the top—the same spot I had assumed would be mine.

At the very top, there was room for only one child. Rung by rung, I didn't hesitate to aim for the top perch. When I was several rungs below the top, I asked the boy when he was going to drop to the ground. He must have felt a turf-guarding urge. He said, "I got here first. You can play down there."

"Can't we take turns?"

My resolve never wavered, but my mouth fell silent. He gave a dismissive cold shoulder shrug and stared back toward the building. More slowly, I eased up to the second tier from the top. He started stomping my knuckles. Forced to let go, I dropped to the ground—unhurt, but as mad as my five-year-old red-haired temper could flare.

Meanwhile, Mother had parked the car, and she and Margaret and Mary were watching the scene play out. Not knowing they were there, I left the climbing structure and stood just beyond it with my hands on my straight hips, back turned toward the street, and waited for the bully to come down. When he saw his ride, he dropped to the ground and came out into the open area. I lit into him with both fists and chased him as he turned tail and ran for his car. Margaret started calling me and Mary started running toward me. "Martha Sue, get yourself over here right now and leave that boy alone."

"He wouldn't let me climb all the way up, and he wouldn't take turns. When I got close to the top, he stomped my knuckles."

Margaret took my hand in hers and marched me over to Ole Betsey. When we walked through the gate and were on the sidewalk, she showed me how to pick hibiscus buds and suck out the nectar. Mary joined us at the car. Mother explained that if anything like that happened again, I should go back into the school building and let the teacher handle it. Mary said, "Didn't you notice that the boy's bigger than you?"

"Just taller. I'm faster and stronger."

By the time the day for taking school pictures rolled around, I had a frizzy perm, compliments of Mrs. Stanley. It wasn't that I wanted to have short hair and a perm, but it was thrust on me by the boy who sat behind me in the row of heavy oak desks joined by iron connections bolted to the oak floors. They still had the cup for liquid ink, and the boy had managed to bring ink to school and pour it into the ink well. On the morning a couple of days before the scheduled photo day, he grabbed one of my pigtails and dipped it into the ink well. The tip of the braid barely got stained. Mrs. Whaley gave him a stern scolding and made him help clean the ink out of the well. The problem seemed to have been taken care of.

That afternoon, with even more determination, he practiced his scissors skills on the same braid. Perhaps he thought that would solve the issue of my telling my mother about how my braid had turned black or blue on the end. I'll never know what his motivation was, but I went home with no ink-stained braid; in fact, I then had only one braid and a stub of the other one. I think the boy received corporal punishment at school and was changed to a different seat.

When Mrs. Stanley, Uncle Bob's mother-in-law, saw me and heard the story, she volunteered to cut off the other braid and give me my first home permanent wave. All the adult females in the family and extended family sold me on the notion that my hair would be beautiful—curly or wavy. Her heart was good and in the right place, but I doubt if Mrs. Stanley had had any experience with giving permanent waves, especially to little girls. She was a skilled seamstress, though, and always had a sweet treat for me when I visited in her home. But my hair was not ready for the onslaught of chemicals meant for adults. I didn't have another perm until I was in high school. By then, the "very gentle" formulas were on the market. I also never had braids again.

Instead of attending kindergarten, I had sat with Mother as she tutored an adult who was illiterate, our pastor's wife. The lady asked to speak privately with Mother one day after the church services were over. "Alice, I know you are a school teacher, but have you ever taught any adults?"

"No, but I expect I could. Who might be looking for a teacher?"

"Well, you know, when you teach the adult women's Sunday School lesson, there is someone in the class who always makes an excuse about not reading from the *quarterly*."

When Mother told this story, she reminded us that she had noticed that the minister's wife never seemed to want to read, but she had assumed that she was just trying to encourage others to take part in the reading. As the potential student's eyes misted over, Mother realized that she was referring to herself. "You don't mean yourself, do you?"

Unable to speak, she merely nodded and took out a fine linen hanky from her purse. "Most people don't know it because he is so smart, but my husband also didn't go to school. He is mostly self-taught and hopes to go to seminary before too long. I don't know what I'll do when I get around all those educated people and I can't even read and write. Can you help me?"

With a warm embrace, Mother assured her that they could work together and that she could teach her to read and write and to do basic arithmetic computations.

Mother was excited about the opportunity to teach in a new way and told me that I could sit in on the lessons. Equally excited, I viewed it as my private school and looked forward to the lessons. By the time I entered first grade, I was reading at second grade level, but my lack of interest in math had already set in.

When Mother announced that it was time to end the reading and writing lessons and turn to math, I would excuse myself and go outside to skate, ride my bike, or climb trees in the back yard. Green grasshoppers waited for me to chase them, and the wispy Australian pines stood ready for my nimble feet. Apparently, my mind was primed and ready for reading and writing—probably at least in part because of the rudimentary reading skills I had developed on the Washington trip—but I had no interest in computational skills. As a result, the skew between verbal and quantitative skills was set as a stumbling block until I had completed the Master of Music degree and finally decided to conquer the imbalance by taking undergraduate math classes. It was a point of great satisfaction to me when I no longer feared math.

After the uprootedness of leaving DeLand, traveling diagonally across the country to Bremerton; staying there for just a few months, returning first to DeLeon Springs, then to DeLand, and finally to Hialeah, it felt good when we were settled into a brand new little house. Not knowing to call it stability, I heard Mother and Daddy tell others about buying the house and absorbed some of their own satisfaction at being able to buy their own house.

The tiny structure built by Mr. Alf was part of a new housing vogue—a subdivision built primarily for veterans who would be able to get loans through the government. Daddy was not a veteran, but he and Mother managed to find a way to get the house financed. It must have measured about 24 x 20 feet with each of the four rooms being 12 x 10 feet, giving a total of 480 square feet. We had to walk through Mother and Daddy's bedroom, which they shared with Richard, to get to the bathroom.

Mary and her friend, Katy, had tried to decorate the shower stall by slathering it with Squirt logo decals. In my pseudo maturity, I thought the caricature looked silly and didn't understand why they wanted to have so many decals on the shower stall walls. Daddy asked Mary, "What in the world did you go and do that for?"

Mother softened the tone of his words, "Oh, Honey, they were just trying to have a little fun and decorated the shower stall. We can take the decals off after they get tired of them."

My sisters and I were able to squeeze into the living/dining area for sleeping. They slept on the sofa bed, and I slept on a cot in the dining room. The cot stayed under the front window and was the source of more than a few arguments when Mother or someone else would try to get me to take a nap. The possibility of missing out on something made me want to stay awake, and I just never felt sleepy in the afternoon. Turning my back toward the room so that I could look out the window, I spent most of those nap times wondering if I would ever get to ride a Palomino horse like the ones in the pasture across the street. The rhythmic tick-tocks of the alarm clock only increased my wakefulness and lengthened my perception of time.

The front and back yards were disproportionately large for that sized house. On one side, the property line was marked by mature Australian pines. In retrospect, I can see that I categorize each house we lived in by the tree(s) I climbed. In my baby book, Mother noted that I loved to climb at a very young age. Perhaps that was a foreshadowing of a more symbolic climbing I would have to do throughout most of my life.

Much of the new year (1946) was weathered in what I intuited as family upheaval. I sensed the lack of stability that had marked our trail of addresses. From Grace Avenue to Adele Avenue in DeLand; a two-week trip in an already old, small car to the Seattle area in search of a job for Daddy in the shipyards of Bremerton; V. J. Day catching us on the road in Arizona; determination pushing us farther and farther toward the Pacific Northwest; shipyards closed; Mary's illness and glorified *vision*; rationalization to return to Florida; another two-week road trip; crossing the Rockies in January; Daddy's settled belief that he was old at 42; Uncle Bob's solution and offer; DeLeon Springs rental house; Adele Avenue rental house; and finally the one-bedroom house for a family of six in the little subdivision of track houses beside a horse pasture a block or two away from a canal in Hialeah. In an age-appropriate way, and to an unusually sensitive child, it was all about me.

Before the family joined Daddy in Hialeah, he made several trips between Miami and DeLand. Since he had left Ole Betsey with Mother, he had to fly. Even after we were all living in Miami, he still flew up to DeLand to see Grandmother occasionally. The sound of the *singing bridge* still rings in my ears when I think of riding out to the airport in Miami to meet his plane. When I asked Mother what the sound was, she explained that the tire treads grabbed the surface of the bridge and made it sing. Hearing her musical spin on the sound changed it from annoying noise to soothing lullaby. From then on, I would often ask her if we could drive over the singing bridge, even if we didn't need to go to the airport.

On one of the trips to the airport, Mother noticed that I was crying. When she asked me what was wrong, I said, "I'm so afraid the plane won't come down and Daddy will be stuck up there forever."

Mary started giggling, which made me cry harder. Tears dug their heels into every cell they reached, but once they started, they needed time to calm down and retreat back to where I kept them stashed while practicing my act mature persona. It was perfectly normal for a four-year-old child to cry, but I didn't want to let my tears announce that I was only pretending to be mature for my age. Mother said, "You musn't laugh at your sister. She just needs to learn a little about how planes work. We'll come out with Daddy and watch the planes take off and land some time. Would you like that, Honey?"

"I guess so. I just want Daddy to get down out of the sky and be home with us."

We went up to DeLand, a distance of over 260 miles, every couple of months. Both Mother and Daddy had family in the DeLand area, but the primary reason for the trips in Ole Betsey was to visit Grandmother. By then, she was bedridden and was steadily getting sicker due to complications of diabetes. She was so sick that each time we went to visit, either Mother or Daddy would prep us for how she might look or how she might not be awake very much. Her room was at the top of the stairs in the house where Aunt Bessie and her family had cared for her after we went to Washington. Before the adventure to Washington, Grandmother lived with us at least most of the time and took care of

Richard and me while Mother taught. During the school year, I probably spent more time with her than with Mother.

About two years previously, Grandmother tripped over a cat on the steps leading up to the front porch, fell down, and broke her leg. Daddy was there and told me about how awful it was to see his mother's broken bone sticking out of the skin and piercing the dirt. He took care of getting her to the doctor. Because of diabetes, the wound and break never healed completely. Her doctor wanted to consider amputation, but she would not agree to that drastic treatment. Her mobility was limited from then on.

Aunt Bessie was a Licensed Practical Nurse and, once we left for Washington, was the primary caregiver for Grandmother. She rigged up a warming brick to help warm Grandmother's feet. It also kept the heavy quilts off her bad leg in the winter time. There were several times when all the family gathered around Grandmother's bedside and sang hymns for her. I wanted to leave the room when they sang such songs as "When We All Get to Heaven" because it made me feel sad and confused. I thought that singing should be happy and not make us think about Grandmother dying. My young brain was still too literal to latch on to the figurative imagery of the song and connect with the theological implications. All I understood was that my family had moved away from Grandmother twice and she was about to die. While she was still using the upstairs bedroom at Aunt Bessie's, the aroma of Lifebuoy soap, Bluegrass perfume, and Yardley's Lavender potpourri announced, *This is Grandmother's part of the house.*

Not long after one of the trips to DeLand from Hialeah, I asked Mother if she would take me to see Grandmother. As usual, I didn't want to settle for a vague *We'll see* answer. My intent was to make firm plans that minute to hit the road as soon as Daddy got home from work. When I realized that no amount of pleading would make Mother promise something that she could not deliver, I found one of Daddy's handkerchiefs and tied a few coins that were on the dresser into one corner of it before tying the opposite corner to the end of part of a broken fishing pole. With that, I was ready to head off on my own to walk to Grandmother's house—all 260+ miles.

There's no telling how or where I had picked up that image, but I knew that was what you did when you ran away from home. My ability to judge distances is still much less than accurate, and my sense of direction is, at best, on the exact opposite end of accuracy. But my determination and confidence were high. Years later, when I became a fully licensed driver at age 16, most of the family would just laugh when I would call from a couple miles away from the house to find out how to get home. I had no trouble walking, but driving at night was likely to produce some degree of mystery and dependence on someone else's sense of direction.

Believing that Grandmother missed me just as much as I missed her, I was on a serious mission. She always ended the cards she sent me with *Come see me soon,* so patience for the family's next trip to DeLand was not an option in my thinking. Her smiling face and welcoming arms stood in front of me like a rainbow of calm after a storm. Her white wispy hair would be blowing in the breeze, and her bright blue eyes would be watching for me. And she would never remind me to act mature.

Mother caught on to what I was up to and waited until I was a little way beyond our property line as I headed toward the main road that bordered the canal. She came outside drying her hands on her apron and called to me, "Martha Sue, you know you are not supposed to be walking on the road. Where do you think you're going?"

"I'm going to see Grandmother right now."

"I've explained that we don't have any extra money now, and your Daddy has to work. He can't just take off whenever he takes a notion."

"He goes when he wants to go. Why can't he go when I want to go?" That was bordering on punishable sass, but my pitiful tone saved me.

"Come back to the house and put your things away. We will go to see Grandmother as soon as we have money for the trip and Daddy has a day or two off from work. It's not safe for little girls to walk so far, and I don't want you to get hurt."

"Ok. But when will we go?"

"I'll have to talk with your daddy about it and see if we can make some plans."

"But she's so sick. What if she dies before I get to see her?"

"We will pray that she gets well and that we all get to see her many more times."

With sad resignation, I handed the pole to Mother and walked back to the house with her.

"Why don't you get your skates out and do some skating?"

"No. I'll just go into the back yard and climb one of the pine trees. The wind sounds so pretty when it blows through the feathery branches."

"Alright. I'll watch through the window to see how high you can climb."

And so it went—Grandmother died on February 20, 1949 shortly after that aborted trip. Mother asked me if I wanted to go to the funeral. I declined. A babysitter had taken me to a tragic double funeral for two teenage girls who had drowned in the canal near our house not long before Grandmother's death. We sat in the back of the church, but I could see the open coffins and hear the keening grief of the parents. The babysitter tried to make me sit still on her lap, but when my curiosity got the best of me, I stood up on the pew to see as much of the "show" as I could. I wanted nothing to do with any more funerals, least of all the one for my grandmother.

After finishing the first grade, several impactful events took place. Following the unpleasant introduction to funerals, I started paying a little more attention to the sermons at church. With a constant attitude of *Oh, yeah?* or *I'll show you*, I looked and listened for statements and role models that made sense to me. One of the two ministers at our church preached on the concept of unpardonable sin. I understood the idea to mean that the only thing God would not forgive was if a person cursed him or denied him in some way. Out in a small tree in the back yard of the grocery store, I chanted to myself, *God is the devil, and the devil is God.* For good measure, I repeated it several times at a quiet volume for fear that Mother might hear me. I feared her disapproval much more than I feared God. When I found that God did not strike me dead instantly, I felt relieved and comforted. As far as I was concerned,

I had proven to myself that the preacher did not know what he was talking about.

That year, two hurricanes hit South Florida with little time between. The ground was still soggy from the first one when the stronger of the two hit. When the water started rising, we evacuated to bunk in with Uncle Bob and his family in the upstairs apartment over the store. Water was rising there too, but the grownups felt that we would be safe in the second story. There may have been two small bedrooms in the little apartment, but there were two teenagers and Richard and me in our family and two cousins near my and Richard's ages plus an infant in the other family. We had pallets all over the living area. I remember enjoying listening to music on the radio.

On the night when we went to stay in the apartment, Daddy took me upstairs on his shoulders just like he had carried me into the motel when we spent the night in the car in Steamboat Springs, CO. "Look, Daddy! What are those black things crawling on the building?"

"Don't let your hand get near them. They're scorpions, and their sting is pretty bad. Just keep your hands on my head and you'll be okay." There must have been hundreds of scorpions climbing toward the eaves of the building. It was as though someone had splashed the side of the building with black paint.

The next day, when I saw fish jumping in the front yard, I asked Daddy why he didn't catch some so we could have fish for supper. He explained that they were mullet—bottom feeders—and were only good for bait.

When Mother told the story of the flood that affected our house, she reminded us that the hardwood floors looked like the hills of a potato patch in a garden. The water had not entered the house, but it lapped the underside of the floor boards and warped them so badly that it took thirteen weeks for the boards to dry and for the budget to stretch to include floor repair.

We had gone to DeLand in June of 1948 for Margaret's wedding. She had had second thoughts about marrying that person, but when she informed our parents, Daddy told her that she had made her bed and would have to lie in it. Always concerned about what people might think of how we looked, acted, or talked, he would not face the embarrassment of a broken engagement. To his dying day, he fully admitted that that was his biggest regret. It probably accounts for his going along with Mother's allowing Margaret and Peggy and, eventually, her second husband and second child to live with us quite a while.

Margaret's daughter, Peggy, was born on March 14, 1949, less than a month after Grandmother's death. Soon after Margaret was married, she discovered that her husband had a sadistic streak, and she became afraid to be alone with him. Reversing the assumed roles for herself and me, she asked Mother if I could spend some nights with her. At first, it was fun—a type of adventure in a real apartment with a Murphy bed for them and a cot for me. Margaret and I were looking at one of my books that Aunt Helen had given me when her husband came into the living room and sat down in the chair near the exterior door. As soon as he sat down, I noticed a look of frozen fear on her face

Distracted from the joy of the book and the satisfaction of being alone with her, I snuggled closer to her. Fear spread from her to me, and I wondered what was happening and what I should do. Although I did not yet know the alarming circumstances of her life in that apartment, I could feel the tension that her husband's presence caused. When I looked up and started to ask her what was happening. I caught a glimpse of the gleam of sunlight that bounced off the blade of a knife he pulled out of a case that hung from one of his belt loops. Margaret saw the coming question and whispered through the side of her mouth, "Don't move a muscle, and he won't hurt you."

When the knives started landing near her feet, Margaret gently pressed her palm against my thigh as she felt me flinch. When she saw how scared I was she said to him, "You can aim for my feet all you want, but leave Sue alone."

My thoughts were racing as to how I could get out and run for help, but there was no exit without going right by the knife-throwing brother-in-law. He finally said, "You tell her if she or that brother of yours keep acting like brats, I'll give them more than a whipping, and they won't forget it." I concentrated on becoming a statue and focused my attention on the tree outside the window, thinking that I would be safe if I could just climb to the top of it.

Then I knew. That's why she told Mother she had to sleep with one eye open. She was afraid in her own home. She and Mother had built up my visit as a chance for me to help her, but I was clueless that part of my job would include sitting perfectly still and quiet enough so that his aim wouldn't escalate from proximity to direct hits.

Mary told Mother that the brother-in-law had tried to rape her a few days after the knife-throwing event that I witnessed. Mother asked our pastor to come to the house and help her decide how to respond to the situation. After the pastor left, Mother got in the car and went and got Margaret and everything they could take that belonged to her and brought her home. Through it all, Daddy was mum, but did agree that she should get out of harm's way.

That was the first time I saw Mother become really angry. Although I was not completely informed about the attempted rape, I was aware that he had done something really bad and that it was so bad that Margaret was going to move back home.

About twelve weeks after the wedding, Margaret filed for divorce. When he found her gone, he came over to our house and demanded to talk with her. Mother stood between them and told him to get his clothes that Margaret had ironed and leave immediately or she would call the police. That was the only time I ever heard her directly threaten anyone. And the number of times I ever saw her that angry was small.

When Peggy was just a few weeks old, we took her to the nursery at church for the first time. Word was out among church friends that Margaret had filed for divorce, which was still looked upon with scorn and sanctimonious judgment by many people, but close friends knew enough about the circumstances to offer support. Mother and Margaret were singing in the choir, and I was sitting in my usual spot on one of the front pews so that either one of them could give me their "behave yourself" eye if I became restless.

Looking around, I noticed that one of the nursery attendants had come to the side door and motioned to Mother. Since Margaret was sitting on the opposite side of the chancel, she only saw Mother get up and head toward the hall leading to the nursery. Margaret followed. When they got to the nursery, they saw the soon-to-be ex-husband arguing with the other caregiver. He was trying to convince her that he had visitation rights and that she had to let him hold the baby. Scuttlebutt proved to be a good thing that day. The nursery worker kept Peggy held tight in her arms while he ranted. Margaret sometimes had a sharp tongue and didn't hesitate to use it in case of perceived danger or strong disagreement. She said, "You can either leave right now and never come back here or anywhere else where we are, or you can talk to the cops right across the street." He chose to leave rather than risk talking with the police. I never saw him again after Mother confronted him at our house.

That scare on church property prompted Daddy to contact the man who owned the Standard Oil service station on Woodland Boulevard in DeLand to see if he needed help. It was a busy station because Highway 17-92 was the major north/south route along the Atlantic coast without being within sight of the ocean. The interstate system was a futuristic notion not yet on the maps beyond the developers' minds. Lou Skillman was glad to hear from Daddy and offered him the job. He needed Daddy to manage the station while he tended to other business matters—a win/win situation. By then, picking up and moving with little planning ahead had become the norm for us. Once I knew that Mrs. Mosier had written a nice remark about me on my report card, I was resigned to the move, but still felt as though my feet knew only shifting ground.

Many years later, my heart went out to Margaret more than ever. She had been 18 years old, had dropped out of high school, was married to a sadist, had a child on the way, and was facing the stigma of being a young divorced woman in a judgmental cultural climate. Her future looked bleak, and her attempted outreach for comfort and possible help was her seven-year-old sister.

*Sue holding Peggy beside Ole Betsey (March, 1949, Hialeah)*

*Mary, Sue, Richard, Peggy*
*(Mockingbird Hill, 1950-51)*

# CHAPTER 7

# FROM MIAMI TO MOCKINGBIRD HILL

*All our geese are Swans.*

Robert Burton
(1577-1640)

It was such a different world then in post-World War II. Today, if a comparable threat existed, moving less than 300 miles away would hardly be viewed as a safety net. Even back then, there was still an undercurrent of concern that Margaret's ex-husband would find us and cause trouble. Thinking about the possibility that Peggy's father might try to steal her added more kindling to the ember of fear stoked inside me.

Visiting other homes often gave me a fleeting sense of what living in a safe environment must be like. Seeing peaceful, fearless homes reflecting care and warmth also validated the accuracy of my perceptions. I knew something was wrong, and I knew I could not fix it. I also knew I wanted more, better, and different living conditions when I grew up. Learning to handle the guilt that came with the *Blessed are the poor* reminders from Mother would take much longer to reconcile.

Peggy was about as much younger than I as Mary was older, so our early relationship was more like sisters than aunt and niece. I loved helping to take care of her and was intrigued by how she learned things, especially her motor development and language acquisition. Being around an infant when I was still a young child myself would later give me an ease in teaching young children and filled some emotional gaps for me.

When we arrived back in the DeLand area after leaving the Miami area, Mother and Daddy bought 65 acres of land out in the country in DeLeon Springs, about eight miles north of DeLand. I completed the last six or eight weeks of second grade in DeLeon Springs Elementary School. Our place was located off of Highway 17-92 on Spring Garden Ranch Road out beyond the ranch itself. In those days, Spring Garden Ranch Road was a very narrow, sandy road with ruts that kept tires out of the deeper sand that would grab at them like a vacuum and hold them in a grip that required another vehicle to pull the stuck car back into the well-worn ruts. I would later learn that it was almost like getting stuck in the sand on Daytona Beach, but without the sound of the surf and the view.

On days when we received substantial rain, the road turned into a washboard of ridges with sharp pieces of oyster shells that could puncture a bald tire. The road crews of the Volusia County Department of Transportation could not keep the sand off the oyster shell road bed, although they occasionally scraped the road in an attempt to make it more passable. Either way—dry sand or wet oyster shells—my sense was that the road threatened to make us have to stop and wait for someone to help us, and I didn't know anyone who was available for that sort of help. It seemed that the ground that should have been so supportive as to be taken for granted was neither safe nor dependable.

My apprehension as I thought about entering the school we had passed only a few minutes before turning off the highway became exaggerated as I heard Mother tell my sisters that we had just passed the famous Seven Oaks tree. The road made an S-turn as it avoided the well-known landmark. Mother told us that it was the location of hangings back in the days when *Negroes* were lynched. I immediately looked out the window to see if I could see any blood left on the bark of one of the trunks that accounted for the tree's name.

Between DeLeon Springs Elementary School (now named the Louise McIinnis Elementary School) and the right-hand turn onto Spring Garden Ranch Road, Mother pointed out the area of the sand pit on the same side of the road as the school. She warned me that children sometimes tried to slip away from the playground and explore around

# 84    CRIES OF THE PANTHER

the sand pit, but that I must never do that because it was a very dangerous place. She told me the story about how one of her close friend's
young son was playing on or around a large pile of sand near their home
and the sand collapsed and suffocated him. This was out of character
for her and showed how terribly upsetting that death had been for her.

In general, Mother encouraged us to explore and didn't mind if we
or our clothes got dirty in the process. She let us play in the rain as long
as there was no lightning. She let us climb trees and swing on the vines
that surrounded the bottomless sinkhole on the property to which we
were enroute. She was not a fussy mom, not over-protective, but her
fear of the sand pit was set firmly in her mind. I feel certain that some
of her students at DeLeon Springs had been along on one or more of
those secret excursions away from the playground area.

How could I work up any enthusiasm about enrolling in that school
when all I heard and observed shouted *danger*? I was absorbed in the
notion that I must act mature in order to get some of the privileges ap-
propriately granted to my older sisters. It was mental quick sand. I was
certainly not in a positive frame of mind to start the end of the school
year in a new environment after leaving Miami almost in the dark of
night.

Unlike much of the land in Florida, West Volusia County is not
completely flat—at least not every acre. As we continued our ride in
Ole Betsey, out to the home that Mother would almost immediately
name Mockingbird Hill, I became more and more concerned that we
would never reach our new home without some major problem. I was
already missing the niceties of town and city. About half-way between
Highway 17 and our new home, I saw a truck coming from the opposite
direction. I asked, "Mother, how are you going to let that truck pass us
and not get stuck in the deep sand?"

She said, "Oh, Honey, I guess he will know what to do. His tires are
bigger than ours, so I think he will move over and let us pass."

"Is it the garbage truck?"

Giggles from Margaret and Mary brought Mother's *Skilton Stare* to
the rear view mirror. She said, "Girls, you simply must stop making fun

of your little sister. It is a perfectly reasonable question. No, Honey. We won't have a garbage truck out here."

"Then, what will we do with the garbage?"

"Daddy will have to dig a hole and bury it. In fact, there will be one hole for things like empty cans and bottles and another hole for kitchen garbage such as vegetable and fruit peelings. There will be a cleared area with a metal barrel so that trash can be burned safely."

Taking time to elaborate on the ways of the old days, she told me that Daddy knew a lot about living in the country because he grew up on a farm not too far from DeLeon Springs. "By the way, I need to tell you that we also will not have an indoor bathroom, and the only water in the house will be cold water at the kitchen sink."

After alerting us to the fact that there would be no electricity, she went on to say that we would be able to have electricity in a year or two. "The people who sold us the place told Daddy and me that the REA (Rural Electric Association) will be installing the lines and poles for electricity in one or two years. While we wait for that, we will use kerosene lamps. We'll have a fireplace for our heat when it's cold, and there will be an iceman who will bring us ice for the icebox. You older girls will get used to the flat irons that the previous owners left. It's going to be such fun to live out in the middle of peace and quiet."

"But Mother, how can we not have a bathroom?"

"Don't worry, Honey. Daddy will bring home some of the large oil drums from the service station. They have tight-fitting lids and are large enough so that we won't have to use the outhouse during the night." She went on in her verbalized dream, telling us what a wonderful adventure we were going to have. "I can't wait to taste the water we'll pull up in the bucket at the well. This is how things were when your daddy and I were little. You'll get used to it."

In my seven-year-old mind, I could not give internal articulation to what I felt, but it was like my entire world was not only being redefined, but disintegrating in the process. Tears were throbbing against my eyelids, but I didn't dare give in to them. Wishes were popping up, making me wonder if we would ever live where we would have an indoor bathroom and a paved street again. How long would it be before there would be a sidewalk for my bicycle and skates? The entire move seemed useless to me because Grandmother had died. Why move back when we couldn't see her anymore? Sensing the lack of agreeable answers to my questions, my whole body sighed and settled into the itchy fabric on Ole Betsey's seat.

As we drove past Spring Garden Ranch, I noticed the large groves of some type of tree about a city block before we could see the buildings of the ranch. Seeing no oranges hanging, I said, "I thought we'd have oranges on the trees out here in the country."

"We will in due time, but those are not orange trees. That is a tung oil tree grove. They use the oil from the fruit to make turpentine. You know—the smelly stuff that Daddy uses to clean his paint brushes. That type of fruit is not edible." She went on to say that she remembered learning about the tung oil industry when she was a student at DeLand Senior High School.

My attention and that of my sisters was drawn more immediately to the horses we could see off in the distance. Spring Garden Ranch was and still is the winter home for many harness race horses. On several of my more recent visits to DeLand, I noticed a restaurant near the track on the ranch. Visitors could enjoy breakfast or lunch while they watched the harness racing trainers in action.

Other than relatives, Uncle Ted and Aunt Mable (honorific relatives) were our most frequent visitors. One of their daughters was close to my age, and their other daughter was closer to Mary's age. Their son was older than the daughters, and there were also two older sons of Uncle Ted's by his first marriage. I recall the heavy dark furniture they had when they lived in one of the caretaker houses on Spring Garden Ranch.

Later, Uncle Ted started working for the Florida Forest Service, and they moved to a house on the same property as the fire lookout tower. It was always fun to see how fast I could climb to the top of the tower and to tease Saralyn by coaxing her to look up at the clouds. She may have just gone along with my childish prank to please me, but I thought I was showing how much more mature I was by not being afraid to see the optical illusion of the tower toppling over as the clouds' movement created the false perception. Since she was older and taller, she usually beat me in the race to the bottom.

Sometime within the first year of our total of five or six years spent living on Mockingbird Hill, Mother told the family that one of her friends, Marge Lastinger, had warned her that it was about time for the panthers to wander through West Volusia County. "Don't be alarmed if you hear blood-curdling screams that sound like a woman is being murdered in the middle of the night. It will be the **CRIES OF THE PANTHER**, a common occurrence this time of year."

Mother said, "Oh! That explains what I saw just a couple of days ago."

She told Marge that she had been on her way to town and had just made the turn onto Reynolds Road. "Something came barreling out of the woods from the left and crossed the road in just a couple of leaps. You know, my eyes are not what they used to be, so I didn't get a good look at it. I thought it was the biggest wildcat I could imagine. But it was black—not spotted like a wild cat."

As Marge listened with a knowing nod, Mother went on to say that the animal's long leaps were powerful and graceful, but that at the time, all she could think of was keeping the car in the ruts and trying not to hit it. "No, Alice; that couldn't have been a wildcat. It had to have been a Florida panther leaving the woods near your house and probably heading for Lake Hires. Some of them are black. Just don't corner one or get too close, and they'll stay away from you."

Being seven or eight years old when that happened, I lumped wildcats and panthers into the same category—big cats on the prowl for food and territorial rights. Much later, I learned of the panther's strength, beauty, and power.

Eventually, I heard the cry of the panther in the middle of the night as I lay on the couch in the living room. Wrapped, and warped, by the mantra to act mature, I could not bring myself to call out to Mother, even though she was not far away on the sleeping porch. When I had called to her on other nights, she had told me that big girls could find their way to the chamber pot by themselves.

It wasn't the dark that I was afraid of, but the roaches that had full range of our floors at night. I didn't want to step on one or feel them crawl over my feet as I sat on the chamber pot. So, I lay perfectly still, hoping the urge to urinate would go away or that I could work up the courage to cry out for Mother's help. Even worse was the fear that she would hear me and not answer at all.

The thing that gave me entertainment and, eventually solace on Mockingbird Hill was the huge hickory nut tree that grew closer to the sinkhole than to the back yard. One of the branches hung low enough for me to jump up and grab the branch, make it bend far enough toward the ground so that I could swing my feet up on to the "Y" of the branch, and then shimmy upside down to the main trunk. Once there, I could flip over and move up or out on whichever branch I set as my target. By the time we moved to town, I probably could have made the climb to the top of that tree in the dark or blindfolded.

Since Richard is three years younger than I, he could not jump high enough to reach the branch to bring it down to his level. One of the meanest things I ever did to him was to place a ladder against the trunk of the hickory nut tree and encourage him to climb up the ladder and get into the tree. Once he was in the tree, I kicked the ladder away. In my childish brain, I was doing him a favor by forcing him to learn to imitate my climbing skills. I never accounted for the difference in height and climbing experience, though. I can still hear him yell, "Mother! She's done it again."

Mother did not have to wonder what he meant. She would call from the back yard, "Martha Sue, get down out of the tree and put the ladder back for your brother. Don't make me have to come do it myself!" I knew not to push the issue any further.

And so it was that we moved back in time and space from suburbia to the country. Margaret's personal problems served to give Mother and Daddy the justification they needed to return to their favored part of the state. The use of marginal or negative circumstances as a means to an end became their common approach to solving problems regardless of rational arguments against the rationalized decision.

With more than 260 miles separating DeLand and Miami, the school calendars did not match. Schools in Volusia County started two or three weeks earlier than the Dade County schools. Mother said it was because of the hotter climate in Miami. With different start dates, I had just been introduced to the concept of borrowing in subtraction, but the students in the new school were well on their way toward mastering the application of that concept. The idea of borrowing as part of the operation of subtraction made no sense to me.

The expectation that I act mature caused corrosive anxiety and self-doubt. To me, asking a question would be admitting that I couldn't do what I was supposed to be able to do and would mark me as dumb. When the teacher asked if I understood the explanation about borrowing, I said that I did. But I had a complete lack of understanding why my computation answers were wrong. I would guess that I couldn't even form a question because I had no basis from which to navigate the math maze. As a result, I was branded as lazy. *Try again* or *try harder* were the directions I received. It was baffling to me that I could feel so smart in reading and so dumb in math.

Since it was less than two months until school would be out for the summer, buying additional school supplies was not high on Mother's *to do* list. My pencils were short, and the erasers never lasted as long as the wood and lead. After the eraser was worn flat, I would bite the metal rim that encased the eraser in hopes of squeezing a little more useable rubber out of the encasement. If a tooth was loose or missing, I had to be careful not to use part of my bite. I feel certain that I was not the only student who did that, but I wonder why the teacher didn't notice and provide an eraser when one was needed.

My math papers were ugly with smudges and sometimes holes where the metal had shred away the wrong answers. Any right answers on my math papers were like the proverbial blind pig sometimes finding an acorn—just enough for the teacher to say, "Yes, you're coming along."

On top of being viewed as lazy, the unsightly papers added sloppy to the impression I gave. But I wanted everything, even my math papers, to be pretty. The second grade teacher at DeLeon Springs Elementary

School was a friend and former colleague of Mother's, which drove my fear of appearing to be dumb even deeper.

The girl who sat across from me had a big pink eraser that caught my eye. On a day when I was almost in tears of frustration and embarrassment, I took her eraser off her desk when she went up to the teacher's desk. It felt like a miracle of high technology to have that reliable tool at hand. She noticed that her eraser was missing and asked, "Where'd you get that eraser?"

I lied, "My mother bought it for me."

"I'm going to ask the lady at the store if that's true."

"You can't."

"Why?"

"Because she bought it in Daytona." Stating that Mother had gone right out and bought something I had requested was much more fantasy than reality.

Already standing to go back to the teacher's desk, the classmate said, "I'm going to tell. You stole my eraser."

As soon as she turned her back, I slipped the eraser into her desk under some papers. The teacher headed my way. She asked, "Martha Sue, do you have her eraser?"

"No, ma'am."

"She did have it," my classmate said.

"Perhaps you misplaced it. Why don't you look in your desk to make sure it's not there?"

I will never know whether the teacher was simply trying to avoid a classroom spat or rescuing me from a terrible situation. It must have been obvious that I had made some clean erasures farther down on the page than the smudges and holes.

It was a despicable thing for me to steal an eraser and then sneak it back into the owner's desk. When the lie accompanying the theft worked, I was petrified that the classmate's mother would come up to school, make a scene, and force me to confess.

The fear that my classmate would see the dishonesty on my face and in my eyes made me avoid playing with her at recess. Caught up in my own defenses, my frustration with not understanding subtraction, and being afraid to admit my lack of understanding, I bided my time for the remaining few weeks of the semester and hoped that she would forget about it over the summer. She could have nailed me if she had asked how I had made the clean erasures on the lower part of the paper. But to her credit, or perhaps with luck on my side, she didn't badger me about the eraser. My own internal discomfort ate at me every day, though.

The classmate and I avoided each other on the playground for the rest of that year. With only one class per grade level, we remained classmates for three more years before we went to junior high school in DeLand. Despite what appears to be a lack of pedagogical skill regarding helping me learn the rules for subtraction, the teacher stands out in my memory as kind and forgiving. While those qualities are admirable, the math deficit that developed in those few short months haunted me for more than twenty years before I worked up the courage to fill that gap.

In my thirties, I took college algebra and introduction to trigonometry and earned high grades in both. To prepare for those courses, I bought an arithmetic review text and a copy of the book, *Overcoming Math Anxiety*, by Sheila Tobias. The first chapter I studied in the review text was the one that covered the rules for borrowing when solving a subtraction problem. About twenty-five years had passed between the end of the second grade and finding the courage to face the fact that despite having a good reason for having the math deficit, there was no acceptable rationale to not eliminate it. Finally, I could claim a more balanced view of myself and my aptitudes. At long last, I understood the concepts and had the requisite skills to successfully approach math problems logically rather than waste my time in the pit of math despair.

# CHAPTER 8

# THE SINKHOLE ON MOCKINGBIRD HILL

*Below the surface stream, shallow and light,*
*Of what we say and feel—below the stream,*
*As light, of what we think we feel, there flows*
*With noiseless current, strong, obscure and deep,*
*The central stream of what we feel indeed.*

Matthew Arnold
(1822-1888)

Like a baited trap, the sinkhole sat in stagnant silence; tight spring jaws hinged like an alligator's, itching to snap. With superficial false innocence, it called to water lovers and adventurers alike: *ignore the lore; jump right in; trust me; you'll have fun.*

For a child in search of independence and entertainment, the lure of the invitation was almost as strong as the lore of warning. Set with a mind-numbing mixture of innuendo, shady activity, and false impression, the trap came close to ensnaring me.

To her Connecticut relatives, Mother described the sinkhole on our central Florida property as a woodland pond—perhaps an unconscious reference to Walden Pond of literary fame. But the sinkhole on Mockingbird Hill was no Walden. Mother's prism of shaded tunnel vision enabled her to see the pinpoint of potential without the peripheral of reality. Neither of the extremes persuaded me to accept her point of view. Words in her mind could clothe the lowliest of land formations or the shabbiest of non-chic appearances into the tone and texture of finely woven lace. With unadulterated late childhood honesty, my 20/20 vision blazed through the scrim of her rose-colored prism.

No matter how many times she swooshed up unfolded laundry off the sofa and almost threw stacks of dishes into the farmhouse sink when we heard an unexpected car in the driveway, the temporarily improved appearance of the living room and kitchen did not take on an air of permanence. In her determination to give a sanitized description to friends and relatives, she passively clued me in to the reality of denial and the depth of her shame. Our house was not presentable, and the sinkhole was not a woodland pond. Sinkholes are sudden accidents of nature; woodland ponds are more subtle in appearance, yet deliberate in purpose when created and cultivated by individuals. A sinkhole thrusts itself upon the environment; a woodland pond is planned and created with intention.

Our sinkhole was not very large, but by the time my family lived on Mockingbird Hill, everybody we knew seemed to know and accept the assumption that it was, indeed, bottomless. It might as well have been bottomless in actuality, just as it was in our minds, because of its power to mobilize fear and to immobilize curiosity. To a child, then, the sinkhole's being bottomless meant that if a person could dive in and swim all the way to the origin of the sinkhole, they would be on the other side of the world, vaguely identified in my mind as China. On hot summer days, I would stand near the edge, wishing I had the courage to belly flop into the water, but the creepy leeches that lurked at the edge and the ooze of the unstable sand between my toes reminded me that I would probably regret taking such a reckless action.

Although West Volusia County is not as hilly as some other areas in Florida, it certainly has its share of gently rolling hills, including the one that held the footprint of our dilapidated old farm house. From the back yard, the path leading down to the sinkhole was more or less level as it curved its way past the chicken coop and gradually switch-tailed back to dodge the hickory nut tree. From there, it made its short descent to the sinkhole's edge. The slant was so slight that it looked as though there were a large invisible cylinder buried far beneath the ground's surface where underground water rose and rain water fell into the murky pool.

The diameter of the sinkhole must have ranged between 40 and 50 feet, depending upon the amount of recent rainfall. The lore about its depth was based on a rumor that previous owners had tossed a very long length of weighted fishing line into the sinkhole and never felt it reach bottom. A number was never assigned to the length of the weighted line, and, just as the size of a fish grows with each telling of the story about the catch, so the depth of the sinkhole deepened with every speculation.

I often recalled my first sight of the sinkhole on the first trip to Mockingbird Hill. When I saw the tree trunk that jutted out and spread its branches over the water, I thought of how much fun it would be to have a rope hanging from the limb and to swing out over the water and drop in. That thought served as a momentary diversion from the sense of personal deprivation that had begun to set in as soon as we approached the property.

Thinking immediately of the sinkhole as our own private swimming hole gave some momentary hope that there would be something very special about living on Mockingbird Hill. Maybe being able to swim at home would make up for no electricity and no indoor plumbing. When I learned that it was not a place for swimming, it felt like something enticing and pleasant had been jerked away from me. Mother so often said, *You can't fool kids;* her attempts to glorify family fun within the context of deprivation could not fool me.

There was another sinkhole on someone else's property across the road from our house. But the temptation to explore that area didn't hook me, although I typically wanted to investigate areas near where we lived. In Miami, the nearby canal where two teenaged girls had drowned piqued my curiosity, but traffic between our house and the canal curtailed my wanderings. Mother and Daddy had instilled in all their children a deep sense of honor and trust that their parental concerns were based on love for us and that if they told us not to do something, it was for our benefit. An absence of arbitrary rules, such as a definite bedtime or study hours, led me to trust their judgment more than if *because I said so* had been the only justification for their guidelines. They resorted to that exhortation at times, but usually gave a reason when my inevitable question, *But why,* popped out. So, I accepted their clear *off limits* regarding the property across the road.

For me, water always held an immediate attraction. Whether I was on, in, or near it didn't matter. My ears magnetized aquatic sounds and channeled them throughout my body. The same element that served as my source of recreation gave me a sense of serenity mixed with excitement and anticipation. It could have been any one of the numerous lakes in West Volusia County, one of the myriad natural springs in Central Florida, or the *World's Most Famous Beach,* Daytona Beach, just twenty miles east of DeLand. (That marketing slogan is still plastered across billboards and banners.)

Swimming or jumping waves, helping Daddy row the borrowed bass fishing boat, or simply lying on a towel hoping my freckles would merge into a tan all provided equal contentment for me. At the beach, as soon as I heard the background sound of the surf blending with the agitated rhythm of the sea gulls' chatter, I ran to the swells, ready for them to lift me up with elongated undulation that my imagination likened to a pony's ups and downs.

As my confidence grew, I ventured farther out to ride the breaking waves back to shore. If someone else were with me, I would coax them into going out beyond the breakers to find the sand bar that I knew was there. The challenge was to get from the drop-off depth to the sandbar without tiring or panicking when our feet no longer could find the tide-stirred bottom.

Lake water hypnotized as it lapped against a dock or a boat, lulling a permanent message into my heart: *I will hold you. I will wait for you. I will entertain you, and I will not hurt you. Come and play.* Water was kind. Water was joyful. Water rocked me when I was too old and too proud to let myself be rocked, when rest was put off and sleep was denied. Even though I knew that water could be dangerous, I trusted it. Its intent never was to harm, and I would not be so bold as to tempt it to overwhelm me. Knowing its dangers, I respected its power. But I longed for frequent exposure and engagement in the various activities it offered.

The presence of the sinkhole on Mockingbird Hill was a different matter, an exception to my usual bent. Rather than attraction, it provoked caution and fear. With an odor of musty decay and water stained brown by tannins leeched from leaves and other vegetation that fell daily, that small pool of water held no promise of entertainment. Swirling tendrils of gray Spanish moss hung from the limbs hanging over it. A whisper of breeze scattered moss threads across the water and into the woods, looking as though specks of dust caught in the glint of sunshine through a window had flown outside.

At times, the leaves on the ground at the edge of the water were so thick that the leeches I feared were able to find sanctuary as they sat like miniature brown bullfrogs on green lily pads, poised at-the-ready for succulent hosts. Mosquitoes flitted over plant debris in the water, and lightening bugs wore bright-colored sports coats as they sporadically lit pinpoints of evening air. Incessant chirps of insects mixed with bullfrogs' burps and the songs of birds to set the air a-shimmer. Occasionally, the distant crack of a rifle interrupted the reverie when someone hunted small game for supper or reduced the size of the rattlesnake population.

Mockingbird Hill's sinkhole was somewhat like Robert Frost's woods . . . *lovely, dark, and deep* . . . more dark and deep than lovely, though. The longed-for banks dressed in azaleas that Mother nurtured in her mind never materialized. When I reflect on that landscape, I wonder at the lack of sunshine sparkling on the water. In my mind, the sinkhole was in perpetual shadow, shrouded by moss-cloaked oak limbs, invasive bamboo, and vines that crisscrossed into tangled loops of inviting swings. Just as Frost had miles to go before he slept and, therefore, could not stop to enjoy the wintry woods, so I would learn in only a few more years that those days of childhood would be cut short, and I eventually would endure decades of restlessness before I, too, could truly sleep. I would learn that, just as the sinkhole could initially get my attention by appealing to my already-formed associations of water, so too, a person could beckon with attractive offers, only to prove that the offers were more toxic than the polio virus incubating within our community.

Although we never had lived in luxury, using kerosene lamps for light and tolerating five-gallon discarded oil drums for chamber pots were new experiences. And never before had we worried about the water level in a shallow well.

Because there was no electricity for miles around, the dark nights made star-gazing and lightning-bug-catching special pursuits for adults as well as for children. On evenings when we gathered a safe distance from the sinkhole to enjoy such twilight pleasures, we felt the night settle down as whip-poor-wills serenaded us and each other. When morning dawned, with windows open to catch a breeze, the calling song of the Bob White quails greeted us. Mockingbirds were always symphonizing sounds as they celebrated the honor of being the State Bird of Florida. No wonder Mother affectionately named the acreage Mockingbird Hill. No wonder she used the beauty of stillness and the potential for upgrading as a buffer between the comforts of her own childhood and the realities of her adulthood. Perhaps the sinkhole's greatest purpose was to salve her perception and feed her dreams of beauty being birthed out of elemental lowliness. Perhaps her denial eased the feeling of pride-mocking living on Mockingbird Hill.

Snapping turtles felt welcome in the sinkhole and readily set up residence there. Seeing their snouts protruding from the water's surface added to the eerie mystique of the area. The community's widespread lore that snapping turtles would maintain their iron-jaw grip on a human body until thunder rolled added to the sense of foreboding. Those self-appointed sentinels made sure that no human hands or feet dared to invade their space. But their successful guardianship backfired on them by making the water so fear-filled that they never got to taste our fingers or toes.

On one of Uncle Bob and Aunt Ruth's visits, the older cousins and Richard and I were playing near the edge of the sinkhole. By then, Bonnie and Bobby had been fishing with their parents many times. Bobby said to Richard, "I wish I had brought my fishing pole. Maybe we could catch some fish for supper."

Richard said, "We don't fish here because the sinkhole is bottom-less."

Bonnie spoke up, "I was hoping that we could go swimming. We didn't bring our swimsuits, but we could swim in our underwear."

I said, "We're not allowed to swim here because there is no way to get out of the water. There's just a straight drop-off with no slant like the bottom of a lake would have. I was so happy when I first saw this water; I thought it was a small lake until Mother told me it was a sinkhole."

I suggested that we could use the tangled vines as swings and pretend to be swinging through the jungle like Tarzan and Jane. I was worried because Bobby and Richard were getting too close to the edge and hoped that the suggestion would get them to move back toward the vines.

They came to where Bonnie and I had found a couple of vines that were anchored to the tree branches enough so that we could take turns swinging on them. When the boys joined us, one of them tried to sit beside her on the vine. It pulled loose and sent both of them down into the underbrush. I think it was Bobby who had tried to sit beside her. I was hanging onto the vine I had shimmied up, then blistered my palms as I slid to the ground. I remembered the time when we were living in their apartment over the store after the hurricane of 1947 and Bonnie had shimmied up the rain gutter and had fallen and had to go to the hospital.

"Bonnie, are you hurt?"

"No—just a few scratches."

"What about Bobby? He's not in the water, is he?"

"No, he's right here—just a little winded from landing on his back."

I urged them to head back toward the house and to stop at the hickory nut tree for the rest of our climbing that day. That may have been the last time I ever played on the vines at the sinkhole.

The hint of invitation when rain water pooled on the slight slope outside of the drop-off served as a reminder that we could not trust the wet sandy soil to support us in our attempt to enjoy the fresh, cool rainwater. It made me recall that some of the natural springs in Central Florida had areas of quick sand. That made me wonder if the area surrounding the sinkhole was turning into quick sand. Danger seemed to be hiding in plain sight everywhere. Superficial appearances passed as the bearers of safe invitation, but all the while kept weaving the net that would tangle feet and trip those that got too close. No matter what verbal spin Mother used, wished-for reality could not be activated by her combination of denial and positive attitude.

If we had dared to jump in, we would have taken the risk of hitting a submerged object—even though we thought there was no bottom to support anything. At one point, I wondered if the sinkhole had swallowed trees or farm equipment and what would have happened to them if the depth were bottomless. Without some sort of barge or at least a large innertube, anyone trying to swim in the sinkhole would have felt fatigue set in quickly. Nothing about the sinkhole's invitation could override the undercurrent of foreboding resignation.

The sinkhole's characteristics ultimately managed to alienate itself from everyone's active interest, creating an arm's-length relationship; it was something to be avoided, worthy of fear—unsafe and unforgiving. It was a fascinating topic of conversation, though, especially when friends or relatives from up north visited us.

The thought of our property somehow being connected with China also played in my mind as I watched Daddy dig garbage holes back behind the house between the two-holer outhouse and the edge of the woods. When I saw that the subsoil was golden yellow not far beneath the surface, that was proof to me that our property was connected to China—I had learned in Sunday School that Chinese people were yellow (. . .Red and Yellow, Black and White, They are precious in His sight. . .).

And so, the sinkhole proved to be useless as a body of water. It certainly couldn't increase the appraised value of the property, even with landscaped beautification. Maps of sinkholes in Florida show they tend to exist in clusters. Prospective buyers of Mockingbird Hill would be justified in their concern about the possibility of other sinkholes opening up. So far as I know, that has never happened on the 65 acres that made up Mockingbird Hill. But like Daddy's warning about rattlesnakes stated—Where there's one, there's two—so it often is with sinkholes. It just so happened that the other one in the same area was on someone else's property.

The internalized sinkhole is much stronger, more powerful in the abstract, than the external sinkhole on Mockingbird Hill ever could have been in reality. The bearer of such memories and fears must be stronger than reality and abstraction combined in order to rein in the negative influence and conquer the sense of foreboding that the sinkhole produced. A commitment must be made to find the scarce sunshine even if its rays are dimmed by shrouds of fear-filled memories. If, at times, such memories intrude like crashers at a party, they must be expelled. If they nag like a gnat, they must be swatted. If they shift suddenly and scream their narcissistic demands, they must be quieted, and their potential for control must be neutered. In time, they will be put to rest so deeply vaulted that they meet their rightful demise and free up space for love, joy, and fulfillment.

# CHAPTER 9

# BRIEF MOVE TO DELEON SPRINGS

*Keep a green tree in your heart and
perhaps the singing bird will come.*

Chinese Proverb

We had lived in the farmhouse on Spring Garden Ranch Road only a matter of months before one of Daddy's brothers needed a place to live. As a rising third-grader, I was mystified as to why my family had to move once again to a different house so that Daddy's brother and his family could move into our house. It was probably a matter of Daddy helping his brother financially, but it seemed so convoluted and unnecessary to me. Of course, I was seeing the move through my own prism, mostly concerned with how the move affected me. For once, though, Daddy appeared to be the leader in that decision making. He and Mother discussed the pending move, but it was clear that his mind was made up.

The good thing, though, was that we would be living in a two-story house just a block or two from the elementary school, so I could walk to school, as I had in Hialeah. If I was lucky, no dogs would chase me. Riding my bike to school would be an option that had not been available out on Mockingbird Hill. Once again, I would be able to skate on the sidewalk and street. We would have more room, indoor plumbing with a bathtub, and even electricity.

The house on Mockingbird Hill had a large attic, but the small area that was floored with rough boards was filled with leftovers from the previous owners. In the living room ceiling near the door that led to the intended dining room, there was a sizable circle of beaded boards that didn't match the rest of the ceiling boards. It looked as though the former owners had been content to patch the hole where a large person or object had fallen through the ceiling. It had to have been a strong force to carve the circle in the wood. The mismatched boards served as a reminder that the attic was not a safe place for play or exploration. I was always sure-footed with very good balance, but I didn't dare try to walk across the beams in the attic for dread of opening up another hole in the ceiling.

In the Sapp house, there was a true second story that held all the bedrooms. There may have been an attic, but if so, I was not aware of it. My bent toward exploration was tempered by the knowledge that it wasn't really our house. We were just renters. A full bath was off the downstairs hall, and a half bath was upstairs.

My favorite place on the corner lot was the camphor tree in the front yard. Large enough to provide needed shade, yet small enough to let me reach the top limbs quickly, the shimmering leaves sent out the invitation, *Come and play*. It took very little breeze for the pleasant aroma to flavor the air.

When I was home on rainy days, I would stay out on the front porch and watch the traffic on Hiway 17. It tended to be heavy nearly year-round as people who wintered in Florida came in the fall and left in the spring, and as summer vacationers added to the thin local traffic. I hoped that a lot of the cars would buy gas at Daddy's station.

Watching the stream of cars and trucks from the porch was sort of like walking on the Boulevard in town and window shopping on nights when Mother had kept Ole Betsey after taking Daddy to work that morning. If we got to town with time to wait for Daddy to close the station, we would walk and look in the shop windows and dream about what we would buy if we had money. Mother usually preferred to look in the Sears or J. C. Penny windows, but even in elementary school, I drooled over the pretty clothes in the stores we didn't expect to visit.

When I watched the traffic, I noticed the picture of a ship painted on the sides of one of the trucks that travelled in both directions, seemingly every day. The pictures looked just like the one of the Mayflower we had seen at school. I puzzled over it many times before I finally asked Mother, "Why don't we ever get to see the Mayflower? I know it's important."

"There may be a replica of it in Plymouth, Massachusetts, where it landed, but we would never be able to make a trip up there just to look at it."

"We don't have to go there. The truck just needs to stop at the school and let all of us see it. Maybe it only stops at big schools."

"What in the world are you talking about? What truck?"

"You know—the big yellow one that goes by all the time. It has a picture of the Mayflower on both sides. Don't they haul the old Mayflower around and let kids see it?"

Now, Mother was the one who had to stifle laughter, just like she told Margaret and Mary to do. She chuckled a little, but soon put her arm around me and said, "Oh, no, Honey. Those trucks don't haul around the ship. They are owned by the Mayflower Moving Company. That's why the picture of the ship is on the sides of the trucks. If they stopped and unlocked the door to the trailer, you would see furniture on its way to a new home or an empty space if the truck had just unloaded the furniture for a family."

"Oh. I wish they carried the ship and we could see it."

The red chow dogs that had chased me on my walk to and from school in Hialeah had put me on alert for dogs roaming around looking for a chase. Was it my red hair that flaunted a challenge the chows couldn't resist? I felt lucky when I found there were no mean dogs near our rented house. Mother often mentioned missing the peace and quiet of Mockingbird Hill, but to me, the Sapp House offered a sense of contentment and tranquility that I had never experienced out in the country. The panthers and their blood-chilling cries stayed in the country; my squelched cries found honest rest, buried by the superficial advantages of in-town living.

With Margaret already divorced and with a toddler and Mary eager to quit school and start a family, dating was a top priority for them. Church was the most likely place to find suitors. But in such a small town—population around 1,000—the dating pool was small. Since Mary was still in school, that would have given her more social opportunities than Margaret, who worked full-time as a cashier at Winn Dixie, but Mary's fanatical religious views served to shrink the possibilities for dating companions. Her self-imposed moral superiority ruled out most otherwise eligible young men who also became cautious toward her attitude.

Nevertheless,both Mary and Margaret soon had steady boyfriends. But before those relationships had developed, there was a boy near their age who sometimes attended our church. Neither of them wanted to date him, but he was slow to take "no" for an answer. At church, he would ask first one, then the other, if he could walk them home. Neither of them would accept his offer, but would make up an excuse as to why they had to ride home in Ole Betsey. On at least one occasion, he probed further, "Well, if I can't walk you home, can I stop by your house for a visit?"

Mary said, "I don't think that would be a good idea. We have to help Mother get school clothes and lunches ready for Sue and Richard."

There was a rumor going around the community that the boy was *not quite right in the head*. When I asked Mary why she didn't want to go on a date with him, she said, "That boy? He's nutty as a fruitcake and twice as crummy."

Mother scolded her, "Mary Alice, you know you are not to criticize others, especially those who may not be as able-minded as we are." She followed that reminder with the saying that we all heard many times, "If you can't say something nice about someone, say nothing at all."

The remark seared itself into my mind as a rule that Mother would not allow to be broken. Yet, at the same time, it seemed to me that Mary's remark was not so bad. When I asked Mary why she wasn't allowed to say what she did about the boy who wanted to date her, she explained, "It's because Mama's afraid that if he really isn't *right in the head*, he might try to hurt me if he ever finds out who made that remark. It has to be a secret, okay?"

Eager to press for more detail and to understand all the implications of adult talk, I asked her how he might hurt her. She went into detail about how he could climb one of the larger trees opposite the camphor tree and get into the bedroom through the window—more danger lurking just a block away where he and his mother rented a small house across the highway from us. I wondered what I should do if he knocked on the door. Dread replaced curiosity and strengthened my growing sense that I lived in a dangerous environment. The notion of feeling completely safe and secure was a fantasy no more likely to happen than any other childhood wish. Still the internalized tape played constantly: act mature; keep the secret; don't tell.

Mary's steady boyfriend soon became her serious boyfriend, an honorific big brother to me. His name was Charles Holloway. Since they knew each other at church, they seemed comfortable with each other. My little sister syndrome was in full force a considerable amount of the time, but I felt happy to be living in the little town and appreciated Charles' sweet attitude toward me. He came from a large family who lived out in the country not far from Mockingbird Hill.

On one occasion, when Charles came to pick up Mary for their date, I ran to the door to let him in as soon as I heard the car stop out front. He got out of the car and sauntered around the front fender, heading up the short sidewalk to the front porch steps. As I went to the edge of the porch, instead of taking the steps down to the sidewalk, I took a split second to gauge his considerable height and quickly calculated how far and how high I would have to jump for him to catch me in his arms. "Charles," I called.

Aiming my flight toward his shoulders, I pounced. He wasn't expecting my jump, so didn't have his arms extended to catch me. And my jump was not nearly as far or as high as I thought it would be. He was close enough to reach, though, and my jump was successful enough for my hands to grab his shirt at the pocket level—not bad for such a screwball spontaneous notion. As a result, I grabbed the pocket of his white dress shirt and ripped it as I shimmied back to the ground. Feeling horrified as I heard and felt the stitches rip, I turned loose quickly as he broke my fall and gently set me on the ground. Like a limp, wet flag, the shirt pocket flapped against the body of the shirt, still attached by just a few stitches along the bottom of the pocket. Being from a large family with sisters, he took it good naturedly and told Mary not to get me in trouble with Mother. "She was just trying to have a little fun. I'm sure my mom or one of my sisters can sew the pocket back on."

A family who lived down the street from us had a sugar cane processing outfit in the yard. I felt sorry for the tired old mule that had to spend its life walking in circles to stir the cauldron of boiling cane juice to make it turn into syrup. Even though it was a semi-rural environment, it was unusual to see a large animal right in the middle of the little town. There may have been a barn behind their house, or perhaps they pastured the mule out in the country when they were not making syrup.

Meanwhile, Margaret and Daniel were dating. Margaret told me that it didn't take long for Daniel to realize that he didn't want a long-term relationship with her because she would not put up with his domineering personality. She spoke up when she disagreed with his ideas and called his hand on inconsiderate behavior and dismissive verbiage. He soon switched his interest to Mary. I was never privy to the announced reasons for the breakup between Mary and Charles, but I missed him when he no longer dated Mary.

By the time we moved back to Mockingbird Hill, Mary was dating Daniel and Margaret eventually started dating Bill. I had the impression that some thought Margaret was unusually kind to sing at Mary and Daniel's wedding because they saw her as the jilted party. In retrospect, I view Margaret as the healthier, more independent sister whose ego was strong enough for her to function with much more emotional integrity than Mary's weak ego ever allowed.

In the spring of that school year, about the same time as the pin worm treatment was launched, the school nurse informed Mother that I needed dental care and a lice treatment. Dental care was not a part of the limited household budget, but there was no option but to treat the lice infestation. So far as I know, there was no additional cash outlay for treating lice because the recommended treatment used kerosene, which we always had in a tin can on the back porch.

Richard also had his own share of critters living in his blond hair. One of the families down the street had several children who were treated for the same problem at the same time. Mother assumed we had caught the critters from the other family because we had played at their house recently, and their yard was mostly sand.

Even though Mary had strawberry-blond hair, she was never known as a redhead. She described her hair color as orange, but it was a light shade. Being a redhead was my distinction, and was the only part of my physical appearance that I considered pretty. I was horrified that my red hair had been invaded by the creepy-crawly insects that made me scratch my scalp into multiple sores with large scabs that itched as much as the crawling, biting lice. But it took the school nurse to discover the problem.

The remedy was to pour kerosene through the hair and rub it into the scalp. It stung and stank and clung pore by pore and strand by strand. My cries and tears brought about Mother's reminder that I was mature for my age and shouldn't have to cry for such a simple thing. The treatment was only half over, but it was the worse half. The next part was to get the stink out of my hair. It must have taken at least half a dozen shampoos to get the odor level to a point of tolerance. The rest of the aftermath of the infestation was to wait for the sores to heal and to figure out whether the itching in those areas was from the scabs healing or from another infestation. From then on, I was very careful to have my own comb and not let anyone else use it.

Taking a personal interest in me, Mrs. Godbee, my third grade teacher, discovered that I loved to try to play the piano. When she asked what kind of piano I had at home, I told her that I didn't have one. "I go over to my friend's house about once a week and practice on her piano. She hates taking lessons, so she lets me use her books."

Soon after that conversation, Mrs. Godbee informed me that she knew I was smart and that my mother would help me with the math facts. "Why don't you go into the auditorium and practice your piano pieces while we do the math lesson? I know you will memorize the times tables. They'll be easy for you." She had not noticed that despite being able to memorize things easily, I did not understand mathematical operations necessary for even simple calculations.

In my class, I was branded the class musician; Gladys was known as the class artist, and G.G. was the athlete. By the end of the year, I

.

was playing somewhat more advanced piano pieces, but I still did not know the math facts. Nor did I want to learn them.

When the fourth grade teacher, who also was the principal, discovered that I was so far behind in math, she also told me to go to the auditorium and practice piano. Going even farther, though, she loaned me some piano books that her daughter, who was one or two years older than I, had already finished. Mrs. McInnis was an accomplished pianist herself and would occasionally come into the auditorium when I was still practicing piano while the class was working on math problems. She talked to me about the importance of correct fingering. At that point, she also passed on a book of pedal exercises because she knew I was trying to figure out how to use the pedals by myself. It took over twenty years to overcome the math deficit, but I am grateful for the nurturing from both teachers who recognized my strength and helped me develop that interest.

Our stay in the Sapp house lasted less than that school year, but it left life-long impressions, some cherished memories, and a point of comparison regarding country versus town living. For me, it tipped the balance of preference to town living, although I still enjoy time in the country.

In addition to remembering her help with my interest in piano, I recall a time when I accidentally embarrassed Mrs. McInnis. She informed the class that a supervisor would be visiting the school that afternoon to evaluate one of the programs. Students looked forward to seeing that person because she had a collection of seahorses, which she usually brought with her and let us pass around the cardboard flat that held them. She cautioned us not to touch them, but we could get a close look. We sometimes called the supervisor the *Seahorse Lady*.

Her area of expertise was the teaching of reading. Because of that, I knew she would expect to observe us using phonics to sound out new words. Soon after the supervisor arrived at the portable building where our class was housed, she announced that she had the seahorse collection with her. I walked up to her and asked her if I could use the restroom before she started talking about seahorses. After receiving permission, I rushed to the main building.

On the wall of the stall, I saw the word, fuck, for the first time. It was completely foreign to me, but I sounded it out in my mind and hurried back to the portable building, thinking I would surprise Mrs. McIinnis and Mrs. McCauley with my phonics expertise. I sat down, saw that Mrs. McCauley was just starting her remarks about the lives of seahorses, and raised my hand. She called on me. I said, "I know that we are not supposed to write on the walls in the restroom, but I saw a new word there. I don't know what it means, but the letters make the sound of fuck."

"I beg your pardon."

"I said that there is a word on the bathroom wall and the letters say fuck."

I was embarrassed—not because I had uttered a vulgar word, because I did not know it was vulgar—but because I apparently had not spoken clearly. It reminded me of the first day of first grade when I couldn't pronounce my last name clearly enough for Mrs. Whaley to understand me. Mrs. McCauley responded, "Martha Sue, Mrs. McIinnis will see to it that your mother has a talk with you." Her scowl and strident tone told me that I was in some kind of trouble, but I had no idea why my remark and attempt to make Mrs. McIinnis look good for teaching me phonics so well had triggered such an unpleasant response from the school's visitor. There was probably also some desire on my part to be able to show off my reading skills.

That afternoon, not long after the school bus dropped Richard and me off, we heard a car approaching. I looked out the front door and told Mother that I thought it was *Aunt* Jane, Daniel's mother. Thelma, one of Aunt Jane's nieces, whom she was raising, was with her. Thelma was in my class, but was a year older.

Aunt Jane seemed nervous. Thelma hung her head and acted like she was in trouble. When Mother greeted Aunt Jane, she said, "Alice, you're going to have to talk to Thelma about that word Martha Sue used at school today. I can't bear to talk about those things."

"What's that? I haven't heard anything about this. Martha Sue, what's this about?"

I proceeded to relay the story to Mother. When I said fuck out loud, she and Aunt Jane both gasped.

"What's wrong with that word?"

"It is considered a vulgar, dirty word."

"I didn't know it was a cuss word." She went on to explain that it wasn't exactly a curse word, but that I must never use it because it was a word that referred to something perfectly natural, but some people used it in an ugly way. I was beginning to catch on since euphemisms were used for anything to do with body functions or reproduction. With sisters who were teenagers, I was aware of menstrual cycles and that they had something to do with getting pregnant.

"Go on, Alice. Explain it because I can't. Since Thelma is a year older than Martha Sue, she needs to know about the birds and the bees."

Mother set in with the explanation of sexual intercourse. "When a man and woman get married, there is a God-given way for the man to make the woman get pregnant. He places his penis in her vagina, and if a baby is conceived, they will know it pretty soon because the woman will stop having menstrual periods."

She went on to explain that it was possible for this to happen before marriage, but that it would be very displeasing to God if a girl or woman let that happen. Thelma's head remained bent with no eye contact. I was not able to completely squelch a giggle or two. "There's nothing funny about this. If you can't control yourself, I'll know you are not mature enough for me to finish the explanation."

"I didn't mean to laugh about it. I just started wondering what would happen if the man had to *wee-wee* while he was doing that." Seizing the moment to transition back to Elementary Anatomy and Physiology, Mother went on to say that there was a liquid that came from the man and carried sperm that joined an egg from the female to make a baby begin to grow.

So far as she specified, I clearly understood that it was something that a man did to a woman without even an inference that the female would have any interest other than the hope of making a baby. There was not even a hint that such action also produced great excitement and both physical and emotional passion. It was presented as a God-given function for procreation, a wifely duty, and something for me to avoid. Perhaps that was all we needed to know at ages nine and ten, a wise representation of the physical act of sexual intercourse, but she never elaborated or intimated that there was more to it other than to remind me when I was in high school that she had not always been in her fifties and could remember when a suitor wanted her to sit on the front porch swing with him.

Without a doubt, the most fun-filled and meaningful experiences at school were the music classes. In both Hialeah and DeLeon Springs, we didn't have a music specialist on campus every day, but only occasionally as the multi-school schedule rotation allowed. In both schools, each class went to the school auditorium for sing-alongs and basic instruction. Even in the first and second grades in Hialeah, I recall the pleasure and pride I felt when the music teacher helped us improve our diction so that we would sound better. She told us she was helping us sing like a choir. That made sense to me, and I could hear the difference in the sound when we followed her instruction.

In DeLeon Springs, Mr. Webber was the itinerant music teacher. He came to our school about every two weeks. We had music books in each grade level. I was most intrigued with a piece by Mozart that was in the sixth grade book. It was in three vocal parts, and the text was in Latin—*Ave Verum Corpus*. Mr. Webber noticed that I had memorized all three parts. He had started letting me play some of the songs when we sang after he made sure I could follow the chord changes.

One day, Mr. Webber asked me to stay after class so that he could tell me about an opportunity I should think about. He said, "You know, you could possibly get a college scholarship in piano accompanying if you keep taking lessons. That means you would play accompaniments when vocalists or instrumentalists sing or play on recitals. You would have to keep improving in your playing, but I believe you could do it. Think about it and keep practicing every day. Let me know if I can help you."

I thanked him and latched on to that bit of encouragement as I finished sixth grade and prepared for junior high school.

In about the third grade, I had noticed that Margaret called our mother *Mom* and Mary called her *Mama*. I decided to call her *Mother*. Both sisters called our father *Dad*. I decided to call him *Daddy*. Since the *act mature* mandate related primarily to my relationship with Mother and Mary and Margaret, it never dawned on me that I was choosing a childish name for my father.

I do not recall ever thinking of Mother as *Mommy*. I loved thinking of myself as *Daddy's Little Girl* and felt no conflict between acceptance of that role and the one of pseudo maturity. What a paradox: I called the parent who readily took us swimming and thrived by entertaining others by the more formal moniker and the parent whose only play was solitary or with a few others as he fished by the informal childhood moniker. Perhaps the imposition of emphasis on my grown-upness was others' attempt to change my status from the baby in the family to the older sister role when Richard was born. I feel certain that Mother's intent was positive and based upon her best understanding of loving and parenting children. But I can't help but wish that she had understood the difference between behavior that was not age-appropriate and true childhood issues.

*Grapefruit Tree (Mockingbird Hill, October 25, 1953)*
*Richard, Sue, Judy on limb; Pastor's children*
*in foreground; other cousins in tree, barely visible*

# CHAPTER 10

# BACK TO MOCKINGBIRD HILL

*It's an adult myth that childhood is idyllic*
Malcolm Forbes
(1919-1990)

Moving back to Mockingbird Hill meant that I would no longer be able to ride my bike to school or skate. Returning to a house with no indoor plumbing was an even worse come-down than when we first left Miami. In the Sapp house in DeLeon Springs, we had become used to the comforts of indoor plumbing and running water. I had especially enjoyed being able to ride my bike to school and walk to the drug store and to my friend's house.

Not long after getting re-settled on Mockingbird Hill, Richard was looking for Daddy's oil can in the closet under the attic stairs. He often busied himself by tinkering with small toys.

Standing on a kitchen chair to get the spouted oil can off the shelf, he set it down on the floor. When he put his foot down, he apparently lost his balance and stepped on the tip of the spout. As he felt it against the bottom of his foot, instead of shifting his weight onto his other foot, he must have placed his entire weight onto the spout. When he cried out in pain, I went over from the other side of the kitchen to see what had happened. The skin on the top of his arch was not punctured, but it was tented by the spout. Acting on impulse, I grabbed the bottom of the can and tried to pull it out. "Stop! It hurts!"

Mother was within ear shot on the back porch. When she heard his scream, she called out, "What's the matter? What happened?"

With a shaky voice, I said, "It's all the way through his foot."

Bursting through the back screen door, she said, "What do you mean? What's all the way through his foot?" Imagining an even worse accident, she was beside us in a matter of seconds.

"The oil can spout—I tried to pull it out, but I couldn't make it move. That's when he really started crying. I didn't mean to hurt him."

"The muscles have grabbed hold of it. I'll have to twist it out. Hand your brother that towel so he can bite it while I pull."

I tossed the towel toward her and left the room as my eyes finally filled with tears and my stomach churned. Mother was able to get the oil can out of his foot and tended to the wound with hydrogen peroxide and mercurochrome. She later asked me how I stayed so calm when I discovered what had happened. "All I knew was that I had to get the can out of his foot or get you to come do it, so I just did what I could. I didn't feel very calm, though."

Mother went to the drug store and bought an Ace bandage in an attempt to relieve the pain and to help keep Richard's foot from swelling. So far as I recall, she didn't take him to the doctor. When Daddy got home that night, he told Rich to keep his foot elevated as much as possible. He also melted an aspirin in a spoon of water and gave it to him. The foot healed with no permanent effects.

That year, my fourth grade, was a significant time for me because Mary and Daniel got married that spring. Thelma and I were junior bridesmaids. I liked having a fancy dress, even if it was an altered hand-me-down from one of Mary's friends. I liked having candles in the church. And I liked the notion of getting an older brother figure in my life. Maybe he would be nicer than Margaret's knife-wielding first husband had been. I had always known that my parents had lost a stillborn son less than a year after they were married and hoped that Mary's husband would become the big brother I had longed for.

"Just think," Mother would say. "If he had lived, your big brother, Robert, would be ____ years old now." That information became a declaration of loss for me as well as for my parents. I was not preoccupied with thoughts of my stillborn brother, but on his birthday, on January 1st of each year, Mother made the same remark and triggered the annual wonderings. She never went into sobbing fits of grief, but certainly let us know that she still hurt over the loss of their first child. She had no intent to transfer grief to me, but I couldn't help but feel her sadness.

I had seen very little of Daniel because he was in the Army for most of their courtship. Mary wrote many letters and showed me her secret code on the back of the envelopes: *SWAK*. That meant *sealed with a kiss*. Sometimes, she would spray cologne on the envelope.

When I found out about the planned wedding, I asked Mother what I was supposed to call the man who was to become my brother-in-law. She said, "His name is Daniel, but everyone calls him *Boy*."

"I know. That's why I asked you. I've never heard his real name."

"I imagine that his parents started calling him that when he was a baby and they just never switched to his name."

"Maybe so, but I'm going to call him his real name. I think *Boy* sounds silly, especially for a grown man."

At the time, he was only about twenty, but he seemed grown to me. Mary was about seventeen—a high school drop-out who had repeated fifth grade. Margaret was also a drop-out, divorced, and had a young daughter. The fact that I loved my sisters and niece dearly could not offset my sense of shame about their educational status. Getting a good education was already so important to me that I begged Margaret to go back to school. I knew she was smart and realized that she had to work to help support the family, but I had heard that the high school had some sort of special program for students who had been out of school a little while to return and complete the requirements for graduation. She told me she would look into it.

Daniel was the same age as Margaret, three years older than Mary, and eleven years older than I. In some ways, he became the older brother whom I had never known, but had always known about. There was no confusion on my part; I simply enjoyed having an older person who was younger than my father be a part of my life. Mary had mothered me in many ways. She naturally took over a lot of the nurturing that Mother would have offered. But Mother was so head-over-heels in her own activities at church and school much of the time that she welcomed Mary's help.

As soon as they were married, my sister and her husband moved to Columbus, GA, where he was stationed at Ft. Benning. Later, they moved to North Carolina where he was stationed at Ft. Bragg. They were gone for about two years. They had a daughter the first year they were married. From that point on, her husband believed that he was not in God's favor unless God sent a son. In an attempt to prove that God favored him, they kept trying to produce a son. They would ultimately have four daughters and many miscarriages while trying to have a son.

Soon after Mary and Daniel's wedding, I was overjoyed when Margaret came home from work with school supplies. I knew they didn't look like anything I would need, so I figured out that she was going to go back to school. Something happened that made her change her mind, though, and I once again was disappointed when she told me that she was not going to do it. Not long after that aborted attempt to rectify her former decision to marry and get pregnant, she announced that she was going to marry the man she had been dating—Bill.

By the time I was in the sixth grade, Margaret was expecting her second child. My teacher was a recent Stetson graduate who was a bachelor. I had a huge crush on him. His lessons were fun and often very engaging. I especially enjoyed his music listening lessons. He even gave us a few ballroom dance lessons. With hindsight, I do not recall his being particularly effeminate, but there were rumors in the community that he had lace on his drawers.

After the fourth grade episode with Thelma and the lecture about the word fuck, I felt like Little Miss Brave and didn't hesitate asking any question that I or one of my friends wanted answered. One day while we were playing baseball (yes, baseball with no glove, not softball), I told Mr. Leggett that I had a question for him. "Ok. What is it?"

"You don't have lace on your drawers, do you?"

I can see his smile and hear his laugh as though it were yesterday.

"Of course not. See?"

For proof, he separated the front of his shirt and pulled out the waistband of his shorts (*BVD's*) about an inch. "Do you see any lace?"

"No. I knew it was just a lie."

Because he had taught a unit on nutrition and we had cooked several meals in the classroom, I wanted him to come for Sunday dinner at our house. I had exaggerated on my report for the unit about how well my family ate, but I knew that we could have a reasonably good meal for him. He accepted the invitation to come for Sunday dinner in early January, probably the day before school resumed following the holidays.

Mother and Margaret both played piano at the local Baptist Church. There were even two pianos, although the building was very small. Mr. Leggett had declined the invitation to visit our church, but showed up at the house soon after we arrived home. I had made a huge bowl of butterscotch pudding for dessert. It was in the largest of the nested mixing bowls. Trying to impress him with my culinary and serving skills, I brought the bowl over to the table to dish out the pudding.

Margaret's due date was approaching, but it had become obvious to her that she wouldn't make it. She had already started timing early labor pains during the invitation hymn at church and was hoping to get through the meal before she would have to go to the hospital. I asked my teacher if he knew that Margaret was going to have a baby soon. He asked how soon. I said, "As soon as we finish eating."

He was so surprised and flustered that he swung around toward me. His elbow bumped the big bowl of pudding, and it hit the floor right at his feet. He jumped up and started trying to help me clean up the mess. Once Margaret saw that cleaning up the floor, picking up the shattered pieces of bowl, and sponging off his trousers would take more time than she thought she had to wait, she said, "You needn't worry about cleaning up the mess. Bill and I are heading for the hospital. Mom, will you and Dad follow us in case we run out of gas?"

I wondered why they ran out of gas so often and swore to myself that I would never let that happen to me. Mr. Leggett excused himself and took home more pudding on his trousers than he had tasted. My oldest nephew, Jim, the only nephew for about twelve years, was born later that day. It wouldn't be long before Daniel would be discharged from the Army and he and Mary and their daughter also would be living with us.

From the time of my first niece's birth, I was frequently on call to babysit. Taking care of and playing with my nieces and oldest nephew as I was growing up myself provided the impetus for my own nurturing instincts and gave me an excuse to feel more child-like, at least for a while, rather than trying to act mature beyond my years.

The lone grapefruit tree among the dozen or so citrus trees on Mockingbird Hill stood in the side yard. It was large enough to give some shade to Ole Betsey when it was parked beside it, but not large enough to compete with the hickory nut tree. It was the gathering spot for cousins, though, when Uncle Bob, Uncle Ruric, or Uncle Banks and their families visited us. The limb that served as a balance beam for would-be gymnasts jutted out from the trunk toward the road. In one of the pictures of the grapefruit tree, Richard and I and several of our cousins are in the tree. Some younger friends are shown standing around watching. The picture was taken in October, 1953, when Daddy and I celebrated our birthdays. That was the last year I spent any time in the grapefruit tree. By then, the majestic size of the hickory nut tree offered much more challenge, fun, and refuge.

When we were a little younger, a swing hung on the balance beam limb. Gnarled roots of the grapefruit tree were bare where our feet had chased away any hint of grass or even weeds. On one of my swinging episodes, the little toe on my right foot caught on one of the roots and became hyperextended at about a 45 degree angle. I hobbled inside to show Mother, thinking it was broken and that perhaps I would have to go to the doctor. I knew that some of our cousins went to the doctor more than we did, and I felt a little jealous of that attention they received.

Mother said, "You know, when Mary broke one of her toes, the doctor told me there is nothing they can do about a broken toe. It just takes a little time to heal. Go find one of your brother's socks and put it on. It will be tight and will pull your toe straight."

Because I was learning about health at school, I felt somewhat ashamed and confused by the fact that we never went to the doctor except for booster inoculations. Feeling both relieved and a little disappointed that something that hurt enough to make me want to cry didn't warrant a trip to the doctor, I followed her instructions. Sure enough, it wasn't long before I could graduate back to my own sock and have the little toe stay in place. I discovered, though, that I could no longer cross it over the fourth toe. To compensate, I started practicing that trick with the little toe on my left foot and soon mastered it.

The grapefruit tree planted two other painful memories, along with all the pleasant ones. The only time I felt the sting of a small scorpion was when I moved some scraps of lumber away from the trunk. It was nothing compared to the huge scorpion that stung Daddy in Hialeah and left him with wobbly knees for several days, but it taught me the lesson of caution outside. It's odd that I knew to shake my shoes before putting them on inside the house, but I didn't use equal caution outside until after the pain of the scorpion sting.

The grapefruit tree on Mockingbird Hill was the only tree I ever fell out of. I'm not sure what caused the fall, but I landed on my back and felt the air escape my lungs when the impact smacked my back. In hindsight, it sounded just like Mother's final breath. Later, I wondered if re-filling my lungs with air felt the same as a baby taking its first breath. By the time I got up and went inside to let Mother make sure I was alright, I had no trouble breathing.

A few years later, when we moved to DeLand, we also had a grapefruit tree that was in our back yard beside the driveway. It was one of the few citrus trees on that property that bore fruit. The one out in the country, though, never bore fruit. In addition to the freeze that all the citrus trees had suffered before we moved to Mockingbird Hill, they were not tended to after we bought the property. I expect that Daddy was aware of what they needed in terms of water and fertilizer, but that was a budget item that I never even heard Mother and him discuss. His financial concerns were the very basic needs of getting by from one pay envelope to the next, along with hopes for some tips during the week; Mother's main financial concern was that each of us had a coin or two for the Sunday School offering and that the household income was tithed at church. I feel certain that a less legalistic outlook toward church support would have eased their budget and Daddy's stress level considerably.

Near the same time as the oil can incident, Peggy, Margaret's daughter, went out the back door to play by herself. She was between two and three years old and loved to pick a flower and bring it to Mother. She would say, "Meemaw, this is for your heart."

She had apparently made up that statement because Mother so often told her, "Peggy, Dear, you are the southeast corner of Meemaw's heart."

On that day, Peggy didn't make it as far as the yellow allemande bush or the blue periwinkles. She had just reached the end of the ramp and was about to step into the yard when Tippy, the watch dog, started barking and hopping around in a circle. Peggy saw the snake and ran back inside to tell Mother, "Meemaw, there's a snake out there."

Mother always said that she wasn't sure if Peggy had ever seen a snake or not, so thought it might be something else—perhaps a land tortoise. When she stepped onto the back porch, Mother saw Tippy jumping and yelping around the entire circumference of the diamond back rattler coiled, rattling, and hissing.

Because she needed glasses, Mother was afraid to try to kill the snake. She called Richard to the back porch and told him to use the front door and go down into the field where some men were working in the watermelon patch. One of Daddy's friends had leased the land just for a season and had a large crop of melons almost ready for harvest.

Richard had a habit of speaking slowly, but he hurried to the workmen's location and said, "Would one of you gentlemen please come up to the house and help my mother kill a rattlesnake?"

Eager to help, two of the men ran through the rows of melons. Mother met them with Daddy's .410 shotgun in one hand and Richard's .22 rifle in the other. Meanwhile, Tippy maintained her dance of distraction, never giving the snake a chance to uncoil and escape. Mother told one of the men to stand on the ramp and not let the rattler go toward the house. The other man was to stand off to the right and aim the gun toward the pump house. The man on the ramp fired first. The snake started racing toward the pump house. The other man fired and hit the four-foot rattler mid-belly. The snake slowed, and both men walked toward it. One of them finally hit the head. Mother thanked them for taking care of the problem and for not hitting Tippy accidentally. "That little mutt may have saved Peggy's life."

It seemed that Mother's life was just as threatened as Peggy's had been, but on a daily basis. Appealing to my act mature role, she instructed me how to make her come around with smelling salts if she fainted. I only had to find the capsules and use them a few times before we found out the cause of her "dying away" spells. If her faintness was mild, she referred to it as wooziness; if worse, it was a dying away spell, and I had to find the smelling salts, break the capsule, and waft it under her nostrils until she came around.

Being on her feet sapped her energy and was the most likely trigger to her feeling faint. That meant that much of the laundry work either didn't get done or that Daddy had to do more of it than he ordinarily could manage with his limited daylight hours at home.

On one of their visits home while Daniel was in the Army, Mary discovered the huge blood stain on Mother's bed. She told Mary that she thought she was "going through the change" and that she had shown me what to do if she fainted. I knew that she meant that her periods were going to stop, but I was not ready to witness and remedy the effects of her hemorrhaging. It didn't make sense to me that instead of lessening, her periods were causing so much blood loss and were lasting so long that she had few days when she was not bleeding. I remember how white her face was when she tried to hang up the laundry on the clothes lines or when she would try to take it down and bring it inside. One of my jobs was to help fold the sheets before we took them inside. More often than not, the piles of clean laundry were dropped on a chair with little folding done except for the sheets and towels.

Mary insisted on getting Mother to see the doctor. He diagnosed uterine fibroid tumors and recommended immediate surgery. The lab report showed anemia so severe that surgery had to be postponed for two weeks while she followed a strict diet of iron-building nutrition and B-12 shots.

I was ten when she had the surgery. The new hospital, Fish Memorial Hospital, sprawled across a large footprint on the east side of town. I was allowed to visit her, but Richard was too young to go beyond the lobby. Daddy and I took turns staying with Richard while the other visited Mother. On several of the visits, Daddy lifted Richard up on his shoulders outside Mother's hospital window so that they could wave to each other.

With her robust general health, she fully recovered from the surgery after a couple of weeks at home, then spent some time with Uncle Bob and Aunt Ruth. I assume that they offered to help when they realized that I was the only one available to help at home. Margaret worked full time, Mary lived out of state, and Richard was only seven years old.

During those months when Mother was so weak, she sometimes resorted to delegating discipline to Daddy. The two things that could prompt either parent to use corporal punishment were sassy back-talk and outright refusal to do as we were told, especially when assigned household chores. I feel certain that I was sufficiently aware of Mother's weakened condition to push the boundaries and to try to get away with things that normally were not tolerated. The only times I recall Daddy using his belt as punishment were during those months when he found out that not only had I failed to be as helpful to Mother as she needed me to be, but I had sassed her when she tried to handle the problem(s). I only heard her say, "Your father will take care of this when he gets home," a few times, but when I did hear that remark, I knew to dread the outcome of my willful disregard for her condition. It seems likely that I was aware of her weakened condition and that I took advantage of it as an opportunity for me to exercise my bent toward establishing my own will as equally strong with her parental demands. It was a tossup as to which was worse—Daddy's belt or the peach tree switch she would have me get for my own punishment when she resorted to whipping me.

So—with daily readjustments and small adventures, we re-settled into rural living on Mockingbird Hill.

*Mother and Daddy, Mockingbird Hill*
*October 25, 1953*

*Immediate Family: Daddy, Mother, Margaret, Mary, Sue, Richard*
*October 25, 1953*

*Daddy's Sisters: Nell, Marian, Maggie, Bessie*
*October 25, 1953*

*Daddy and two of his Brothers*
*Bob, Ruric, Daddy, October 25, 1953*

*Daddy and Sue at Birthday Party*
*October 25, 1953*

# CHAPTER 11

# PROJECTS ON
# MOCKINGBIRD HILL

*You can safely assume you've created God in your own image
when it turns out that God hates all the same people you do.*
Anne Lamott (b. 1954)

One of Mother's dreams out on Mockingbird Hill was to build a
family business by becoming chicken farmers. She subscribed to a
couple of farming magazines and read an article about raising chickens
in cages—a new concept at the time. She also talked with the owners
of two feed and seed stores in DeLand. One of the feed and seed store
managers told her that an estimate of potential profit was $1.00 per bird
per year. Hoping that Daddy would agree to set up a chicken farm, her
mind quickly calculated a goal of 12,000 chickens. She told me about it
on the way home from the feed and seed stores and explained that a potential profit of $12,000 per year would allow Daddy to stop pounding
the concrete at the service station and also would provide much more
income than he could produce in any other way. In her typical optimis-
tic way, she romanticized the notion that it would be such fun to have
the entire family involved in the business of raising chickens in cages.

We certainly had plenty of room in the cleared fields for 12,000
cages. With twenty acres devoted to planted pines and five acres to
be deeded over to Margaret and Bill, a chicken farm would still fit
nicely. When she talked to me about it, all I could think of was 12,000
mounds of chicken manure—the word *shit* was not in my vocabulary
when this business speculation was on Mother's mind—that someone
would have to shovel. Gathering eggs and tossing out chicken feed
for a small yard-roaming flock was one thing, but shoveling droppings

for 12,000 fowl was off my radar. I wondered how many hours all of us would have to spend taking care of chickens, even if they were in cages. Despite having poor math skills, I understood the difference between a dozen and 12,000.

In his reputed way of being the Old Scotsman—his grandmother came from Scotland—Daddy would not even seriously consider the chicken farm proposal. He saw that it required too much initial capital outlay. With his eighth grade education, he had a firm grasp of business math and thought that there was far more to the pros and cons of chicken farming than Mother was considering. She saw the pros, and he saw the cons.

Remembering the experience of having grocery store debt following the Great Depression, it was easy for Daddy to vote against the chicken farm idea. So—he continued working at the station, and Mother continued reading the *Farm Journal* and the *Progressive Farmer*. She was as happy when the mail carrier delivered them as I was when the Sears or Montgomery Ward catalog arrived.

Not easily discouraged, a few years later, Mother came up with the idea of building a new house by tearing down the old house and salvaging materials from it. Daddy's face lit up in an *aha* moment of interest, and his mental wheels began turning when Mother first mentioned the idea. Because the expense would amount to a mortgage, his attitude was open, and he fully participated in the planning. He said to Mother, "I think I might know just the man who may be interested in such an unusual project."

The man had to have been either one of his customers or was referred by a customer because he was not a church friend. Daddy followed through and found that Mr. Norman would like to contract to build the new house. The only catch, though, was that he would not agree to tear down the old house. That would have to be a family project or be done by a different contractor. Mother and Daddy agreed with Mr. Norman that we would tear down the old house, salvage the lumber and as many of the nails as possible, and pay him for the rest of the building supplies and for his labor. Mother and Mr. Norman drew up the floor plans. The project and the summer began. I remember hearing

Mother and Daddy talk about the cost for materials and labor totaling about $3,600.

Not long after we started dismantling the old house, two car loads of people, mostly young people, from our church and one or two other churches in the area headed up to Ridgecrest, North Carolina. I had been to a Girls' Auxiliary Camp when I was ten and had planned to go to a 4-H camp when I was twelve, but I had to cancel the 4-H camp plans because of a bad sunburn. It was not the worst I had experienced, but it was bad enough so that I had to stay home.

The worst sunburn occurred when I was ten and attended activities held at Welch Pools in Daytona. We swam in the pool all morning, had a picnic lunch, and then competed in field races all afternoon. So far as I recall, I was the only one with severe burns. The doctor said they were second degree burns and that another hour in the sun would have caused third degree burns. He recommended a product called Foille, which was the consistency of warm syrup, and smelled like liquid Vaseline. We tried all sorts of home remedies, but the Foille was the only thing that helped. The blisters were an inch high and covered my chest, shoulders, and upper back. To this day, I have to stay out of the sun or my dermatologist will fire me.

Located near Ashville, Ridgecrest is a beautiful campground used by various church groups. It was my first trip to the mountains other than the crossing of the Rockies. We were too engrossed in the Blue Ridge scenery to even realize we were not homesick. My cousin, Christine, went with me, so I had a buddy and was able to go into her classes with her—one more opportunity to act mature—since she was a couple of years older than I.

She and I enjoyed the activities and responsibilities of shared living in a cabin with the others. That was the first time I became aware that I really hated to have to get up early enough to have a cooked breakfast and to take time to make my bed. The mountain water was so cold that I couldn't stand to brush my teeth, and the hot water was in short supply and slow to find the sink. I don't recall any of the classes, but I recall vividly the natural beauty and the experience of attending the Cherokee play, *Unto these Hills*, which told the story of the forced westward movement of the Cherokee Nation from North Carolina to Oklahoma. It was held in an open air arena, and the atmosphere of the evening's clean air, bright stars, and crisp acting entranced me. I knew that I wanted travel and events such as attending a play to be a part of my world.

Feeling the pressure of an evangelistic minister, I responded to an altar call when I felt pity for the poor starving children in China or Africa or some other place ridiculously far away. With absolutely no aptitude for science and a dismally inadequate math background that produced more tears than mathematical solutions, I dedicated my life to being a medical missionary to that place—China, I think. Where were the adults who should have counseled such childishly tender feelings that had no merit? More importantly, why would a supposedly educated minister prey upon the feelings of immature minds and hearts to cause such a response that likely would only yield false feelings of guilt once reality set in? Perhaps I was more vulnerable than usual because of having seen the play about the Cherokee's plight and already had a mindset of feeling sorry for the disadvantaged people of the world. This, coupled with the guilt produced by the evangelist combined to momentarily offset my usual bent of skepticism and resistance to such pressure.

I knew by the time I got home that I shouldn't have responded to such a specific altar call and regretted that I had written Mother about it. I also knew, though, that it was the one sure way to gain her unconditional approval. Since the minister and his wife had sponsored the trip and had driven one of the cars, I couldn't have hidden the fact from Mother or anyone else for very long, though.

I was fortunate to have a close friend, Becky, who had not gone on the trip. When I told her about what had happened, she said, "Are you crazy? My dad would never let me go to China. You don't have to do that. Just tell Brother Wentz that you've changed your mind."

To his credit, Brother Wentz didn't lay a guilt trip on me. I told him that I knew a doctor had to be good in math and science and that I was only good at music and hated math and science. He let me off the hook, gave me an emotional pat on the psyche, and encouraged me to continue developing my interest and talent in music. The most striking thing about the entire experience was Becky's statement about her father not letting her go so far away from him. I felt a pang of jealousy because I believed that nobody in my family would think of trying to keep me home either out of concern for me or because they didn't want to have to miss me. I wanted someone to care enough to want me to want to stay home. Instead, the family in general, and Mother in particular, would have glorified my dedicating my life to full-time Christian service.

Once that short-lived problem was solved, my thoughts and energy turned to Mother's project of tearing down the old house. In the ten days or so that I had been gone, they had made quite a bit of progress. Daddy had organized the placement of like-sized boards according to interior or exterior usage. He showed us how to straighten nails with a hammer, but cautioned us not to spend too much time on that job. The old house was now just a shell of studs with a roof. Once the interior stairs leading to the attic were dismantled, the next target was the roof. I dreaded having that taken down because it would mark the point at which we could no longer occupy the house. There was an underlying feeling of uneasiness about where I would sleep. As long as there was a roof, we could sleep on the floor and think of it as a form of camping. But once the roof was gone, it would be a short time until the floorboards were pulled up and stacked with the studs and girders ready to be recycled in the new house. I never feared the possibility of a rattlesnake in the house, but I did fear that the pump house would not be off-limits for rattlesnakes. And even if the panthers wouldn't come out of the woods into our yard, their screams and cries would reach our ears in greater volume in the pump house. I wanted no part of sleeping there.

When we had dismantled the walls, I heard the cries of baby mice being disrupted from their birth place. The sounds were weak, at first muffled, then in full baby mice volume. I allowed myself a moment's worth of shriek when I saw the clump of clawing rodents fall to the floor. I ran to the back porch and told Mother that I didn't want to work on the walls any more. Daniel came up behind me and goosed me on my back near my arm pits. When I shrieked again, he laughed in derision at my discomfort and at his success in upsetting me even more. He said, "I thought you were more grown up than to let a few little mice scare you."

Mother gave him a mild scold, "Now, now. You don't need to antagonize her. She'll be okay in a couple of minutes."

The pump house was small and sat in the back yard between the clothes lines and the outhouse. In it, there was a shower with cold water supplied by a cistern set up on a mini tower behind it. The rain-catcher cistern balanced in the crotch formed by four stilts that served as scaffolding. Of course, there was no hot water—just the luck of the sun's warmth on any given day. A small generator reserved for the well pump sat beside a supply of typical garden tools along one side wall. On the other side, there was enough floor space for bags of chicken feed for the flock that roamed our yard by day and roosted in the coop by night. I enjoyed taking out hands full of chicken feed to fill a small bucket as I prepared to complete my task of feeding the chickens. I also took delight in finding and gathering eggs.

The hens and pullets and I got along fine, but the Rock Island Red rooster apparently thought he was *King of Mockingbird Hill*. He and I were not on cordial terms. In fact, we weren't even on speaking terms. He tolerated me with a cock-sure wattle and wary eye as long as I held the bucket of feed, but once it was empty, I was the one with the wary eye.

Three years before we started tearing down the house, on a Sunday afternoon, there was a house full of company—relatives who had come out to have some music and dessert. I stayed inside for a while, then went outside to play. Richard was also outside. I knew that the rooster sometimes acted like he was going to chase me, but I thought, *No, that's silly. Roosters don't act like dogs.* I didn't know at that time that he had already chased Mother and Mary, both of whom had a shade of red hair. The fear of him I had tried to ignore proved warranted that day.

There was a pipe sticking up out of the ground near the pump house. When I saw the rooster start running toward me, I took off running while keeping my head turned back toward the feathered beast. In just a matter of a minute or two, I tripped over the pipe and fell flat on my back. I had on shorts, and the rooster with his long spurs jumped onto my ankles and started hopping up toward the top of my legs. He fluffed his feathers and flapped his wings so hard that I hoped he would fly away. I tried to yell as loud as the panthers cried. The rooster was too heavy to kick off, and he had the advantage with all the bluster and scratchy feet. The pipe didn't break my skin, but pressed on the middle of my back, my legs trapped and useless. And the screams that I managed to get out fell silent as the piano and voices inside the house overpowered them. Richard was back behind the pump house, heard me, and came running. I yelled, "Quick! Get something from the pump house and shoo this rooster off of me."

Already heading into the front door where the garden tools stood, he grabbed the pitch fork and came running like a javelin thrower. He had the presence of mind not to throw the pitch fork, though, and simply ran it into the breast of the rooster two or three times. A lesser aim or resolve could have hit me instead of the rooster, but my baby brother, my *Little Vichie Booce*, was too smart and strong for that tough old bird. We both went into the house and told our story. Daddy declared that if the rooster chased me one more time, we would have a big pot of chicken 'n dumplings. Mother checked my back and rubbed it.

The rooster learned his lesson and remembered it for about three weeks. With his wounds healed and his courage rejuvenated, he dared to chase me again. That time, though, I was able to run up onto the back porch and get inside before he could attack me. I couldn't wait to tell Daddy when he got home from work. I knew that we had to have a rooster to keep the hens happy, but I also knew that we could get a new one and that we could get a different *brand* of rooster—one that wouldn't have it in for redheads.

True to his word, Daddy twisted that tough neck with a quick snap, set up the pot of boiling water on the back porch to loosen the feathers, and butchered the hens' stud. I helped pluck the feathers, but had no desire to keep any as souvenirs for a scrapbook. Before he dressed the bird, Daddy called me over to his side and called Richard to join us. He balanced the plucked, headless rooster in his hands as though it were a Norman Rockwell Thanksgiving turkey so that we could see the breast.

There in three different places were the marks of the pitch fork tines where Richard had jabbed him. For the first time, I knew that Richard really loved me even though I was not always patient with him. It was such a memorable event for all of us that the story was frequently repeated around the dinner table or when friends or relatives came out for a visit.

Three years after the butchering of the mean rooster, we were dismantling the house and getting ready to live in the shed we called the pump house. Mr. Norman came out and helped us remove everything we possibly could from the pump house. Anything that would not be ruined if it got wet was simply placed in the back yard. We had a few plastic chairs and a small table that served as our outdoor dining area. Long before grills and grilling were popular, we were figuring out what we would eat and how we could prepare it during the time it would take Mr. Norman to raise the new house.

As I recall, the construction phase took a matter of weeks. When Mr. Norman helped us empty the pump house, he explained that we would be receiving a delivery of sheetrock that would be used in the new house. As he talked, he paced and blocked off the area for the sheetrock. It included the floor of the shower, which was really just an area of bare dirt. The pallet that he installed gave uniform support to the sheetrock. He noticed that the narrow tongue 'n groove boards and the wide-planked flooring were in neat piles ready for him to use or reclaim as needed. The skeletal shell of the old house was ready to lose its top. And we were as ready as we could be to take up residence in the pump house.

There was no sheetrock or plaster in the old house, but beautiful virgin timber from the rafters to the girders, which were huge. I knew them well because one of my favorite outside activities when I was a little younger was to crawl under the house from the front yard to the back yard by stomach-crawling through the space where the lattice work was missing. When cousins visited us, we sometimes had races to see who could navigate the sandy space the fastest. So far as I know, none of the cousins became Navy Seals, but we would have been prepared for stomach-crawling demands if we had. There was not much debris under the house, but we did have to watch out for the cow ants that preferred the cooler area under the house. We called them cow ants because of their size—big as a cow—about an inch long.

We had a close call when the chimney was felled. Daddy was the only one working on that job. His method to fell the chimney was to dig the dirt out from under one side of the cement anchor. He had planned for the chimney to fall toward the back yard, which it did. What he hadn't planned on was how quickly the mooring would release its hold on the bricks. Mother screamed, "Bruce!" when she saw the top begin to wobble and the angle begin to arc. He waited until the last second before he jumped out of the way of the bricks raining down as the mortar crumbled and freed each brick.

It all happened within a split second, but when I replay the scene in my memory, I see it in excruciatingly slow motion as I gasped and held my hands to my mouth, frozen in silence as Daddy jumped and ran.

We had no intention of salvaging the bricks because a fireplace was not on the plans for the new house. Instead, we would have a circulating heater in the small hallway between the three bedrooms. That would relieve Daddy of the wood-chopping and stacking chore. After the bricks had all hit the ground, we declared a break time for our pulse and emotions to quiet down before we started gathering the bricks into a trash pile so that Mr. Norman could haul them away. Someone probably was happy to find a supply of used bricks at the dump or in a pile wherever he disposed of them.

At that point, Mary and her husband and their first daughter were living in a small house that had belonged to his paternal grandmother. She had given him the house, and he had moved it to some property not far from where it had been built. His sister and brother-in-law owned the property and also were building a house toward the back property line. The location was on Reynolds Road near the Oxhole, less than a ten-minute drive from Mockingbird Hill.

The community lore was that oxen had discovered the water-filled sinkhole and had watered there, giving that sinkhole its name. As was typical of most of the sinkholes I had seen up close, there was no gradual beachside entry into the water. Rather, the ground gave way to an immediately deep area. The only type of diving platform that could have been used would have been a floating dock. But the Oxhole only had large tractor innertubes to play on. They sufficed, though, to provide fun, exercise, and a means to cool off on those typically hot summer days.

As a child and pre-teen, I wondered how oxen could have wandered close enough to the water to drink without falling in. I also wondered why I had never seen any oxen or heard of anyone owning oxen. Whether toward community lore, religious dogma, or societal mores, my skepticism had set in even before I started school. So it was not unusual for me to wonder about the authenticity of the Oxhole's legendary history.

Periodically, we still heard the cries of the panthers when they roamed the woods behind our house. When I first studied pictures of panthers, I marveled at the essence of strength in their physique, their unique facial markings in the tawny-colored ones, and the sheer beauty of strength and power that filled the images of the ones with sleek black coats and green eyes. But more than anything else, I remembered the sound of their cries and wished I could have felt free to cry out when I had lain on the sofa in the living room and felt tears as dry as desert dust while I agonized over whether or not to cry out loud and risk Mother's reminder that I shouldn't be crying.

In time, as I began to think more about how unusual it was to grow up where cries of the panthers were not unusual, my thoughts gravitated toward a strong identification with the black panther's characteristics. Its coloring within its species is the exception. The typical coloring of Florida panthers ranges from dull gray to the most common coppery shade of fur. My coloring is the least common in my family. Mother's rich auburn was darker than mine, and Mary's strawberry blond was lighter.

My most productive time is at night. I never wanted to take naps, which inspired Grandmother Orrell to call me her little wildcat—a somewhat smaller version of a panther—long before I ever heard of the panthers or witnessed their cries.

# CHAPTER 12
# DISTANT NEIGHBORS, FIRST DATE

*Through our own recovered innocence we*
*discern the innocence of our neighbors.*
Henry David Thoreau
(1850-1862)

Nathan, Frankie, and Charlie were school and church friends who occasionally came out to Mockingbird Hill to visit and play. Summertime was the most likely time for them to show up. They trekked from the Lake Johnson area past the tung oil tree groves, the fernery, and past the sprawling Spring Garden Ranch. Long before jogging and running became the physical fitness craze, they strengthened their aerobic capacities on the gentle hills of Spring Garden Ranch Road. They were a year or two older than I, but we enjoyed playing together because I was such a tomboy.

Beginning in the fourth grade, punting skill earned me a spot on the recess football team roster. Being the only girl and the only fourth-grader who played football with the slightly older boys made me walk taller and smile wider. With only one small class per grade level in grades one through six, claiming to be the best punter in the school was not much of a distinction, but more of an accomplishment than best monkey bar climber.

The size and shape of the football were a perfect fit for my foot. The rhythm of the four beats leading up to the actual kick—left, right, left, drop-kick—caught my ear and propelled me toward each exciting punt. It was the same footwork as approaching a dive off the diving board in Lake Johnson—left, right, left, spring-dive.

I guess, in truth, I didn't really play football with the boys by just being the designated punter. At the time, though, it felt like I was playing football and was part of the team. It gave me something to do during recess besides play on the playground equipment where I had to dodge the sixth-grade red-haired bully who resented my monkey bar skills. He was large for his age and had the fiery shade of red hair that brought even more taunts than my shade. There seemed to be an undercurrent of assumption that it was even worse for a boy to be a redhead than for a girl. His attempt at playground dominance reminded me of my first day at school in the first grade. Just as I gave up playing with dolls when Mary did the same, I declared to myself that playground equipment was for little kids.

Nathan lived the farthest away and had to go right past Lake Johnson, turning right at the Hardshell Baptist Church to get to Frankie's house. From there, they struck out to Charlie's. After about a two-mile hike, they ended up at Mockingbird Hill, thirsty and ready for a snack. Enthusiasm for fishing and for playing in our back yard gave them stamina on the hills and rough oyster shell road.

Spring Garden Ranch Road came to a right angle where our property line began. The first twenty-acre tract that was part of the sixty-five acre total extended beyond the sharp turn in the opposite direction from the continuation of the road. A narrow sandy lane passed the planted pines and led to a small wanna-be subdivision made up of two or three small cement block houses. A man from up north, Mr. McClure, had speculated that a major real estate expansion would lead him to real estate wealth. But his dreams were about two decades ahead of their time.

Those twenty acres were reforested with pine trees that measured between five and seven inches in diameter and served as an anchor for that side of the property line. The other forty-five acres stretched from that right angle corner toward an opposite right angle corner where Spring Garden Ranch Road became Reynolds Road. Our property did not reach all the way to the second sharp turn, but it continued for about three-quarters of the way before someone else's woods marked the end of our land. From that first right angle curve, the boys had to walk at least another quarter of a mile before they reached the semi-circular driveway that led to our front yard.

My visitors and I usually could get fresh water from our well to go with our snack of Saltine crackers and peanut butter. Sometimes, though, we would have the same grape Koolaid as we had at Vacation Bible School.

One of our favorite activities was to jump hurdles. We had no store-bought equipment—just home-grown bamboo poles with nails protruding from the vertical to support the horizontal. Two of us had to hold the vertical support poles steady because we couldn't get them deep enough into the ground to find stable footing in the large-grained sandy soil. The bamboo grew alongside the sinkhole. When I told Daddy that I needed some poles for hurdles, he found time to go down to the sinkhole and select the poles, cut them, and hammer the nails into them. He placed several levels of nails so that we could compete with each other. Once again, I focused on the rhythm of my feet as I ran toward the bamboo hurdles—left, right, left, right, left, right, JUMP!

The former owners of the house had left a lot of things in the attic, the yard, and the pump house. Some of it was useful, but most was junk. My friends and I tried to use the two or three wagon wheel rims that had been left and were propped up against the trunk of an orange tree Taking a rolling spin seemed like an obvious way to enjoy the outdated equipment, but the rims were too narrow for us to balance on the inside surface. We also had no way to hold on without having our fingers run over if we managed to make even one full rotation. We had to settle for one of us sitting in the wheel while two others rocked the wheel back and forth. This limited success held our attention for only a short while.

The re-purposed equipment that gave us much more delight and fostered our good-natured competition was the large oil drums that Daddy brought home from the service station. They were usually orange, about the same shade as Home Depot plastic buckets are today. But they were metal and rusted if we left them in the yard. We took turns walking on the barrels and used the alarm clock from Mother and Daddy's bedroom to time our turns. I never told the boys that the oil drums would eventually become our chamber pots. They probably knew and may even have had similar items at their own house. They were sturdy with strong handles and a lid to contain some of the odor As long as we remembered to store them in the pump house after we finished playing with them, Daddy didn't care if we used them. If he ever found them left out in the yard, though, the oil drums were grounded in the pump house for several weeks before he would let us use them again.

After morphing from circus barrels to chamber pots, the rims of the oil drums eventually became so rusted that they left a circle of rust with residual particles of metal on our buttocks. It's a wonder we never developed some sort of skin infection from the unsanitary chamber pots. Once they were too rusty for use, Daddy would bury them along with the rest of the unburnable trash. Although they were intended to be used as chamber pots only during the night and the outhouse was to be used during the day, we always had at least one in the house for those times when intestinal rumbles declared a case of the *backyard trots* or when a heavy rain was pouring down. Sometimes one was in the house because whoever was supposed to empty it that morning chose not to.

It was a toss-up as to which was more embarrassing—the chamber pots inside or the outhouse outside. With reflection, I would have to say that the outhouse was the worse of those two evils because all of my female friends had indoor plumbing. They also had the luxury of real toilet paper instead of old magazines and the outdated Sears catalog. As chamber pots, the oil drums were functional for quite a while, but as circus barrels, they gave me an innocent escape into the fantasy of being at or in the circus enjoying tricks of nimble dexterity.

Richard was a fan of cowboys he had learned about through radio shows, comic books, and perhaps from western movies. Often, in the evenings when we were waiting for Daddy to get home from work after closing the service station at 9:00, Mother would gather us out on the sleeping porch so that we could listen to radio shows. If we couldn't find a show we wanted to hear, she would tell us stories of the old days when she and Daddy were young. Although most of the shows I remember were detective shows, there must have been times when we heard cowboy shows, especially the *Lone Ranger*.

One day, while we were alone in the house, Richard was pretending to be Hopalong Cassidy and proceeded to demonstrate how he would toss a knife if he were Hopalong. Mother must have been on the back porch tending to the wash or outback using the outhouse. I was sitting on the floor; Richard stood up on the arm of the sofa and said, "If I was Hopalong Cassidy, I'd throw my knife like this." When he made the motion with the intent of pretending to throw it, the large hunting knife slipped out of his hand and hit the inside of my left ankle. For a split second, it teetered in an upright position before falling over onto the unfinished hardwood floor. With a heart as tender as Daddy's, Richard started crying and said, "I didn't mean to let it go. Please don't get me in trouble."

The puncture was not very deep, but it produced quite a bit of blood. I called out for Mother. Because of the amount of blood and the newness of the knife, she thought it was a large cut. Once she got the bleeding stopped, she saw that the puncture only needed a small bandage.

The hunting knife incident made me start thinking about how I could use it in place of darts, which we did not have. How I was even aware of darts is somewhat unclear, but I probably had seen them in some of the western movies that Margaret and Bill took us to see. I was certain, though, that I wanted to learn to throw something and consistently hit a target. The hunting knife had been put away where neither Richard nor I could find it. I felt no anger or aggression while I practiced throwing a small knife that either Mother or Daddy let me use.

I made a target out of cardboard, attached it beside the front door to the pump house, and practiced until I could hit the target consistently. As I walked barefoot from the back porch to where I threw the knife, I played *dodge the chicken shit*—a sort of rural *step on a crack, break you mother's back* game—because I hated to feel the chicken droppings ooze up between my toes. It appeared that the chickens had chronic cases of diarrhea. Feeling the greenish goo was bad enough, but even worse was knowing how difficult it would be to set up an aluminum wash tub and haul buckets of water from the well to the tub to wash my feet. Wearing shoes outside never crossed my mind, though, unless I was away from home or the yard had been turned into rain-soaked mud.

Sometimes, I let Nathan, Frankie, and Charlie try their hand at my game of hitting the target with the knife. Their major mission, though, was to catch fish and to take them home in time for their family to have fried fish for supper. They knew about the sinkhole on our property, but they never tried to fish there. A common assumption was that fish didn't live in sinkholes. That may or may not have been accurate, but we believed it.

There was a small lake a little beyond our property line back behind our woods. We heard that it was called Lake Crowbar or Crowbar Lake. Larger than the sinkhole and smaller than Lake Johnson, it was the closest lake to our house, but I never saw it. I expect that my friends fished there because the larger lake between Mockingbird Hill and the town of DeLeon Springs by way of Reynolds Road, was too great a distance for them to cover on foot. Lake Hires was one of the lakes where Daddy and his brothers liked to fish because it was large enough for them to have the satisfaction of hunting just the right fishing hole for the catch of the day. It also was deep enough to accommodate an outboard motor if the boat they were using had one, but small enough for them to row if necessary.

Richard and I were never allowed to explore Lake Crowbar. It was too far from the house, meaning Mother could not hear us if we called out to her, nor could we hear her if she called to us. The distance from the little lake to our house was not far enough to drown out the cries of the panthers, though. There was no access to it other than the path through the woods; it was deep enough into the woods for the Florida panthers that roamed through the back of our property to use it as a watering hole and possibly be startled into an attack if we ventured into the grasses at its edge.

When Richard and I shared our memories of our years on Mockingbird Hill, he mentioned that he saw Lake Crowbar once when Bill took him along as he traipsed through the woods all the way to the lake. Neither of us recalls why Bill was going to the lake on that particular day. We both remember Bill as being somewhat headstrong about going through woods in a rather haphazard way—much less careful than Daddy was, especially when it came to being alert for rattlesnakes. Richard remembered that the grass was taller than he was. Since his full adult height is 6 feet, 2 inches, he may have been about four feet tall at that time. Bill took no precautions about entering the thick, tall grass, and Rich was terrified. The taller the grass became as they walked through, the more Richard heard the internalized voice of Daddy. "Don't *never* go barreling through unknown territory without proper precaution. You're in rattlesnake country, and you have to respect them."

Richard said that Daddy went on to tell him that if you hear their rattles, it may be too late to get away without being bitten because they usually don't sound the warning until they are coiled, ready to strike. We never went into the woods with him without hearing his warning: "If there's one, there's two." I wonder who taught him that maxim or if he figured it out from his own experience.

Daddy further reminded Richard that our nearest neighbor had killed a pair of rattlesnakes just a week or two earlier. They were both over six feet long. Margaret had taken a picture of them after the neighbor had cut off their heads. Driving his point home, Daddy said, "You always have to assume that there are rattlesnakes nearby. Don't *never* put your hand down a hole, especially a small hole that looks like it is deep. It's okay to go barefoot near the house, but always wear shoes and socks if you go into the woods. If you see a rattlesnake up around the house, go inside the house right away and tell your mother or me."

He reminded Richard that Mother was a very good shot with his .410 shotgun and that she wasn't afraid to use it. "And, Rich, that little .22 rifle that Uncle Ben and Aunt Marian gave you for Christmas will kill a rattlesnake just as dead as the .410 shotgun."

Daddy would take us along the path that led to the little lake every December when we hunted our Christmas tree, but we never went far enough into the woods to see the lake, even at a distance. Knowing of the Florida panther threat and the likelihood of rattlesnakes in the woods was enough to discourage us from trying to find the lake without an adult.

The memory of the sound of the panther's cries in the night remained with me for decades. Even when I first moved to Houston in 1980, where there are no panthers to invade aural privacy, the sound of neighborhood cats mating or fighting at night was enough to jangle my nerves and ruin my rest. But their siren-pitched yells were like kittens mewing compared to the cries of the panther.

Bill made at least one solo trek to Lake Crowbar when he found a small alligator that had shown up near the sinkhole. He told us that he thought it must have lost its way and needed to get back to the lake. He also didn't want an alligator to live in the sinkhole. It must have been between fifteen and eighteen inches long—small enough to fit into a burlap bag, but big enough to not invite my curiosity to touch it. With the 'gator in the sack, he took a brisk walk through the woods and turned it loose into Lake Crowbar. I was glad that he did not insist on cooking it. He was good at cooking anything he got his hands on. That meant that alligator, rattlesnake, and even possum were not beyond his culinary expertise. I had tasted and enjoyed the turtle soup he made when a large land tortoise showed up in our back yard. That was my limit, though—no more wild creatures turned into soup or stew for me.

Although Daddy loved to fish, Lake Crowbar held no more attraction for him than it did for Richard and me. I believe that his finely-honed sense of personal integrity constrained him from going onto someone else's property to fish without permission, and he did not know who owned that property. He had his favorite lakes all over Volusia County, as well as the St. John's River, where he had fished since he was a young boy. Mother often said that fishing was his only form of play. He could justify it as a means to put food on the table, but it really was his only respite from a life of grueling work with little time off, low pay, and heavy responsibilities to both the immediate and extended families. The little bit of hunting he did was not the respite that fishing was for him. When one of his brothers asked him why he didn't hunt larger game such as deer, he said, "I can't stand the thought of looking into the eyes of a deer and then pulling the trigger."

We noticed, though, that when someone else bagged a deer, Daddy didn't hesitate to cook the venison or deer sausage and serve it for dinner. Wasting the meat or refusing to accept it would have been outside the scope of his sense of proper manners and would have negated an opportunity to ensure his family had meat for a while. But when it came to hunting, he was content to take his .410 shotgun out to kill rabbits or squirrels for supper. Using the shotgun was never thought of as a sport or form of recreation. The only time we did any target practice was when he showed all of us how to use the .410 shotgun in case we had to use it. After listening to his rules for safety, I pulled the trigger once. I had no desire ever to feel the kick again, even though it was considered a mild kick compared to larger shotguns.

Many children our age would have dared to try to swim in the sinkhole and to strike out through the woods to find the lake as they searched for their independence. While none of us fit the mold of a goody-two-shoes or a scaredy-cat, we accepted the adult warnings away from those two small bodies of water. The underlying communal certainty of impending danger was far stronger than even a childhood desire to explore and to enjoy all sorts of water activities.

Things were compartmentalized in our minds according to parental and community boundaries. Lake Johnson was for swimming and Baptist baptisms; the sinkhole was for skimming rocks and playing Tarzan games in the vines near the bamboo; Lake Crowbar was for adults or pre-teens older than I.

In keeping with the "act mature" script, I developed expectations of certain privileges earlier than my peers. Approaching my thirteenth birthday, I began to lobby for being allowed to go on dates. Since most of my friends' parents had set the time frame for wearing makeup and going on dates at age sixteen, I felt that my long-standing compliance with pseudo maturity had earned me the right to those two milestones at age thirteen. Mother reluctantly agreed to let me go on my first date the fall of my eighth grade right about the time of my thirteenth birthday. She may have viewed it as merely a matter of my going to a game with him and his father, but to me, it was a date.

The strongest determining factor in Mother's acquiescence was that the boy was a member of our little church, and his father was providing the transportation. He was a year older than I, so he was in high school, but still too young to have a driver's license.

I had never been to a football game, and it was homecoming. My date brought a small homecoming mum for my shoulder. I had bought my first pair of stockings and a garter belt for the special occasion. We called stockings *nylons*, a term left over from the change of material from silk to nylon during World War II. They had a visible dark seam up the back of the leg. My older sisters taught me to always ask myself three questions when standing after sitting for a long time:

1) Are my seams straight? [Crooked seams were considered sloppy.]
2) Is my slip showing? [The code for this was, *Is it snowing down south*? All slips back then were white.]
3. Is there a stain (menstrual) on my dress? [If I couldn't tell about the seams or possible stain, I was to elicit the help of a female, even if she was a stranger.]

My first period came when I was ten years old. I had been embarrassed by a menstrual stain on the back of my skirt in the sixth grade. My friend's solution to the problem was to follow me to the restroom so that no one else could see the stain. She dampened several sheets of paper towel and sponged the stained area enough so that it would not be too noticeable. The stain had lessened to a pink tinge, but the area was obviously wet. She proceeded to unwrap a long length of paper towel and wrapped it around my skirt tearing it at the right place so that I could hold the end in front.

I shuffled back to the classroom trying to keep the paper towel wrap in place. My friend got a case of the giggles when she saw the paper towel unravelling, sliding closer and closer to my ankles with only the front end held in my hand. It wasn't the first time she had made fun of me, and it reminded me of the time when I was visiting her at her house and she declared we were going to act out a beauty pageant. She let me put on a pair of her shorts, which fit me a little more snugly than they did her. As I started to take my walk down the make-believe aisle, she announced in her loudest voice, "Here comes Miss Thick Thighs of the Year." Neither the pageant enactment scene nor the sponged menstrual stain seemed humorous to me.

The teacher, Mr. Leggett, came over as soon as he saw us at the classroom door and asked what was going on. I told him I had fallen down in a puddle on the playground and that the classmate had sponged the mud off my dress. He told us to get rid of the paper towel wrap and to go outside and walk around the school building two or three times so that the breeze could dry the wet area. Since I was the only girl in the class who had already started having periods, the principal, Mrs. McInnis, had given me permission to use the faculty restroom stall so that I could have access to the Kotex vending machine if I needed it. While the classmate and I were in the restroom, a teacher came in. When she saw what had happened, she offered to buy me a Kotex.

On my first date, I focused on the band, cheerleaders, and half-time show and followed my date's lead for cheering. The stadium benches were really rough. I'm not sure how it happened, since skirts and dresses were about mid-calf length, but when I stood up to go to the restroom during half-time, one of my stockings sprang a huge run. I felt the parting of fibers trickle all the way around my leg and down to my heel. The next thing I knew, the stocking fell to my ankle. Perhaps the grippers on the cheap garter belt did more harm than the rough bleacher seat, but at that point, the cause of the wardrobe malfunction was irrelevant. The dilemma was the issue of what to do with the fallen hosiery—walk away as quickly as possible and let it drag all the way to the restroom, or reach down, take off my shoe, crumple the stocking in my hand, and throw it away when I reached the restroom. I had no purse, just a small wallet, which I had left home.

I didn't think my date had noticed it yet, so I opted to excuse myself to the restroom. When I reached the bottom of the steps, I melted into the crowd until I thought my date couldn't see me. As quickly as possible, I bent down, took off my shoe, removed the stocking, and crushed it into my hand. Once I reached the restroom, the next part of the dilemma set in—what to do with the garter belt's two dangling straps after removing the top of the stocking from the clasps. I wondered if the metal clasps would make noise if they hit the bleacher seat. The summary solution was to take off the garter belt and the other stocking and throw the entire mess away.

While standing in the long line for the restroom, I spotted my date walking toward the other end of the small building. Feeling foolish and embarrassed, I averted my eyes and hoped he didn't spot me. He went past the short line for the men's restroom and continued on to the concession stand. He must have noticed the long line and figured that the game would resume before I could make it back to the seats. He bought a small Coke for each of us and one cone of French fries for us to share. The second half of the game dragged on while I was more absorbed by the embarrassment of the ruined and trashed stockings and garter belt than by the game I knew nothing about.

We sat in the back seat as his dad drove. On the way home after the game, he rested his hand on my leg, giving me my first other-generated physical stirrings of arousal. So far as I recall, there was not even a platonic goodnight kiss—just that one act of cozy affection. We had a pretty good time for a first-ever date, despite the mishap with the stockings. But there was no second date with him, even though we remained cordial on the school bus and at church. I never knew if he was aware of the stocking disaster and often wondered if anyone had noticed the discarded garter belt and stockings and what they may have thought about them.

Later that night, I told Mother about the stocking incident. Laughing, she reminded me of a story from her youth about an old maid whose pantaloons dropped to her ankles as she shook the minister's hand. I said, "It's not funny when it happens to you."

"No, but if you see the humor as others do, it might lessen your own embarrassment. We'll get you another garter belt and some stockings."

All of those firsts stay in my memory with no indication of intent to leave. Each aspect of such milestone memories can be seen as purposeful, regardless of the particular history. The same memory or fragment might be seen in a more negative light, but I choose to see the trajectory from disappointment to solution as a turning point from pseudo maturity to authentic self-reliance.

# CHAPTER 13

# LAKE JOHNSON

*If there is but little water in the stream, it is the fault, not of the channel, but of the source.*

Saint Jerome
(c. 342-420)

We had plenty of options for enjoying Central Florida's many bodies of water. Lake Johnson, also called Hardshell Lake because of its proximity to the little Hardshell Baptist Church and cemetery, was just the right size for frequent swims. One of the boy's fathers, or perhaps several dads, had built a barge that sat on the bottom of the lake. It had a low level diving board with a fairly good spring to it. Each season when we went for the first swim after the brief winter, we had to take our time and try to wipe away the black goop that had accumulated on the bottom of the lake. As more and more feet waded out toward the barge, more and more of the goop floated away from our path and exposed the sandy bottom. Although the water was far from crystal clear, we could see if the black scum was on the bottom or not.

Seeing the bottom of the lake turned black made me wonder how we could tell if a water moccasin was on the bottom or not, since the skin of water moccasins is also black. We saw a couple of water moccasins on the surface of the water only once when we were the first ones to the lake that spring. Mother drew the line at swimming with moccasins, so we went home without a swim that day. It seems odd now to think that water moccasins (also called *cotton mouths*) invaded our space only once. They must have been young without an established territory at that time.

When it came to activity within a sanctioned area, I usually had much more courage than when faced with something having the potential to become an off-limits choice. Knowing that Mother spent most of her time at the lake counting heads or noses, I would swim under water as long as possible, not surfacing until I was desperate for air. I can still hear Mother's voice calling from where she sat near the edge of the water, "Martha Sue, come up right now or I will have to come in after you and have you sit by me!"

I would come up, laugh and say, "I only wanted to see how long I could stay under water."

"You know I have to know where you are at all times when you are swimming, especially when there are so many in the water at the same time. Now, let me see if you can swim as far as the utility lines, and I don't mean for you to swim under water."

She trusted me not to go beyond that overhead limit. For my part, I had no desire to go beyond that point because we could hear the bark of at least one alligator on the other side of the lake. In all the times we swam at Lake Johnson, we never saw an alligator on the swimmers' side of the lake. One of Mother's relatives from Connecticut visited us once and heard us talking about how much we enjoyed swimming at Lake Johnson. The relative asked, "Don't you have alligators all over Florida?"

Mother's vacillation from utter nonchalance to over-supervision never ceased to surprise, confuse, and amaze me. She replied, "Oh, yes. But we make so much noise and splash around so much that they stay on their side of the lake."

My immature mind tried to grapple with the lack of logic between her being overly cautious about my swimming under water and her disregard for the alligators in the lake.

On one occasion, I dove off the diving board and didn't surface until I had come full circle back to the steps leading up to the top of the diving platform. Swimming as fast as I could, I was trying to be the first one back on the steps so that I could dive again. As I swam under water near the bottom of the platform, my left knee tangled with a protruding rusty nail. It apparently cut or dulled at least one nerve because I was not aware of the gash. When I stepped onto the diving board to dive again, my sister, Mary, looked up and said, "What in the world did you do to your knee? Go let Mama look at it. You may need to go to the doctor."

When I glanced down, I saw an ugly gash about two inches wide, at least half an inch across, and deep enough so that I thought I was looking at my *insides*. By then, I was already in my diving stance, so I dove back into the water. While I completed the dive and swam back, Mary alerted Mother. Knowing I was not going to dive again, I took a wider turn away from the barge and stood up when I knew I could touch bottom. In what must have been less than a two-minute interval from the time Mary saw the gash to when I stood up and started walking toward the small beach area, Mother was already herding everyone into the car, "Everyone riding with us, come to the car at once. We have to leave right now!"

She had what she called the air of authority in her voice from her years in the classroom. There was no question raised and no reluctance expressed by anyone in the group. There was no doubt that there was something of an emergency, yet not even a hint of hysteria or panic erupted.

As was often the case, there were more swimmers than could fit into Ole Betsey. That was part of the fun. Mother would let some of us ride on the running boards and hang onto the door jamb or window frame. If the running boards were crowded, one person could sit on each of the front fenders. We didn't mind that she crept along the washboard surface of the unpaved road because it was still fast enough to send a breeze over our bodies wet with sweat or lake water and to make us feel like we were sailing or flying. We hated to sit in the car with wet bathing suits because the wool upholstery, which was the same color as an Army blanket, also had the same texture. It may not have been as thick as an Army blanket, but the wool felt like nettles were stinging our skin, just as they stung our ankles when we walked through the fields.

Mother continued giving instructions, "Martha Sue, you will have to sit up front with me because we are going straight to town as soon as I drop off everyone else at the house. Mary, you will need to stand beside Richard on the running board. Make sure he does not fall off. We'll take the cousins home and they'll wait there until Aunt Miriam comes out to get them. Mary, you'll be in charge of seeing that they rinse out their ears with rubbing alcohol, change into dry clothes, and have a bite of lunch. You know, with her weak eyesight, Aunt Miriam doesn't like to drive after the sun starts going down."

With those instructions clearly in place, we pulled up in front of the house, emptied the car, and took off for the eight-mile drive into town. That was the only time I was ever rushed to the doctor. I was confused because the wound still was not hurting, and I was scared because it looked so awful, even though it bled very little. I was always *Little Miss Brave* in a doctor's office, so I wasn't afraid of going to the doctor that day. Yet I was afraid there was something wrong with me because there was no pain, very little blood, and I was not crying. But since I was obviously wounded, I thought I was supposed to be crying. Acting mature was so ingrained in me that my feelings were as numb as the wound. Maintaining the mask of maturity beyond my years mattered more to me than allowing myself to give in to the inner urge to cry. I thought of the panthers and wished I could cry when I needed to like they did.

We were not able to see our regular doctor, so we went to one whose office was near Daddy's service station. His name was familiar to me, probably because Daddy serviced his car. I watched with curiosity as the doctor cleaned and dressed the gash. He informed me, "I'm going to use this needle to deaden the flesh all around the wound so that I can be sure and get all the dirty parts out before I take a few stitches. You don't mind a shot, do you?"

"No, Sir. I'm the oldest of my group of cousins, and I didn't even shed a tear when we lived in Miami and had to get shots for a bunch of diseases when a hurricane came and we had a flood. I showed my younger cousins and my brother how to be brave for shots. I just don't like doctors to look down my throat. I hate it so much that I tried to kick the doctor in Miami because he didn't warn me that he was going to look down my throat before he gave me the shots."

I rattled on to tell him that the doctor and Mother had both told me to never kick a man or boy in the crotch because it would be very painful. "I almost kicked the doctor's crotch because I was sitting on the end of that long skinny table while he was standing right in front of me trying to get that wooden thing inside my mouth. I hate it because it makes me gag just like when I choked on bacon that was half swallowed and half still in my mouth when I was four years old."

"Ok. I promise you I won't need to look down your throat today. You are being a very good patient. Most children would be squirming and crying, but you are holding perfectly still and watching as I do my work."

"This is almost like watching Daddy get a splinter out of my finger with his pocket knife, except I can't feel anything you are doing. I usually feel just a little prick when Daddy loosens the splinter before he pulls it out."

"That is why I gave you the shot right beside the gash. It made that area numb so that what I have to do won't hurt you."

"Are you going to sew it up just like when somebody has to mend a seam or a hem?"

"Yes, almost exactly like that. I will try to do a very good job with my sewing so that you won't have too much of a scar."

"Is it real thread?"

"Yes, but it's made especially for medical purposes. You will need to come back in a week or two so that I can take out the stitches. By then, your skin will have grown back together."

Mother said, "I don't know what has gotten into her. She's usually not this talkative. I guess the doctor who delivered her was right."

She went on to explain that she had noticed that my speech seemed to be delayed. At my three- or four-year old checkup, Mother had asked the doctor if something was wrong with me. He said, "Yes. I expect her older sisters are anticipating and meeting her needs without insisting that she use words to get her needs met. You must tell them to stop doing that. Don't worry. She's female. She'll talk."

I heard that story so many times that I thought it was abnormal to be on the quiet side, yet I felt a little shy, especially on the first day of school, but I had that seed planted in my brain that I would someday, somehow, start talking up a streak. Looking back, I think the younger doctor knew how to relate to children and simply treated me as he did his own daughter. It was just the encouragement I needed to feel free to ask questions and talk with him. A few years later when I went to junior high school, I became acquainted with his daughter in Glee Club.

He took only five stitches to close the wound after removing the jagged edges of flesh that were flecked, not with freckles, but with rust and dirt from the nail. If the same gash were being treated today, I believe many more stitches would be taken. I still have the scar that includes the marks of the stitches as well as the size of the gash.

Mother would not let me go swimming at Lake Johnson again until the stitches were out and there was no sign of infection. She always had a fear that the church's cemetery drained into the lake and thought that the lake water might not be clean enough for an unhealed wound. Since the water at DeLeon Springs was much colder and clear, she let me swim there a week or so before we returned to Lake Johnson. On my first post-gash swim I went straight on to the diving board. One of the dads of the boys who sometimes visited me on Mockingbird Hill had turned the barge over and replaced the nail and any others that were loose or missing.

Like so many central Florida lakes, Lake Johnson was spring-fed. In addition to testing my stamina under water and challenging Mother's preoccupation with counting noses, I enjoyed underwater swimming because I could sometimes find an underwater spring and feel the cooler water as it gurgled up from beneath the sandy lake bottom. A lake spring was nothing compared to the boil at DeLeon Springs, but in the hottest months of the year, even slightly cooler water was refreshing.

I never participated in organized sports because there were no opportunities to do so except for the football games during recess in elementary school. I usually found athletic skills fairly easy to acquire, though. I had seen a couple of the older friends flip off the diving board, which gave me a basis for attempting my first forward flip. It went well. Alternating between flipping and diving, I spent a lot of calories that day and felt exhilarated. On our next Lake Johnson outing, I flipped for my first diving board trick and hit my head on the board. It was not a serious hit, but it scared me a little—about like hitting my head on a shelf or cupboard in the house. Being stubborn and confident, I told myself that I should go right back up on the board and flip again so that I would not be afraid to try it the next time I went to the lake. I hit my head again and never tried any more flips because I was afraid of receiving a serious head injury. Mother convinced me that the home-made diving board was not springy enough for flipping—an ego-saving explanation that also carried an air of at least partial accuracy.

When Mother noticed that the azaleas around Hardshell Baptist Church were in bloom, she said, "Can't you just imagine how beautiful the sinkhole would be if we had banks of azaleas all the way around it?"

My childish logic prompted my remark, "Well, why don't we plant some?"

She said, "You know, your dad has that old Scottish frugality, and he would never agree to spend money on such unnecessary items. He could think of a dozen other things that would have a more urgent need for spending money. It's fun to think about, though."

Mother was right. The sinkhole could have been beautified with even a modest budget for landscaping. But she was wrong about Daddy not being willing to spend money on nonessentials. The money simply was not there. There was no decision to be made and no fundamental disagreement—just not enough money to meet all the needs, much less unnecessary expenditures.

As I grew into upper elementary school and on in to early junior high school, I began to understand the budget constraints in a different light, as I observed how often Mother received a call from one of the older sisters that included either an obvious request or a strong hint that money was needed to feed the grandchildren. Resentment began to build because I felt that once the sisters were married, Mother and Daddy should be able to concentrate on my and my brother's needs. How desperate and inconsiderate it seemed to me for either sister to put Mother in the position of having to choose between telling them *no* or telling Richard and me *no*. How unfair to Daddy for her to allow either one or both of the older sisters to move back home along with their husband and child(ren) without talking it over with Daddy or only telling him of the decision once it was already made. I was so convinced that my perception was correct that I lost all concern about being viewed as the selfish one. I didn't want or expect anything beyond what seemed to be reasonable expectations for a younger daughter/sister. Those expectations were limited to safety, a place to study (my girlfriends had a desk and bookshelves in their bedroom), balanced meals (I was interested in nutrition.), and a home sufficiently free of shame that I could bring home friends without apology or explanation.

*Uncle Ben and Aunt Marian*
*Apopka, FL, 1962*

## CHAPTER 14

# GREEN SHOES AND PORK CHOPS

*We shall walk in velvet shoes wherever we go.*
*Silence will fall like dews on white silence below.*
Elinor Hoyt Wylie
(1885-1928)

Aunt Marian knew the worth of a pair of green suede dress shoes that also would find their way to school on fifth-grade feet. Perhaps she sensed that proud, happy feet would enhance the educational setting by freeing up mental space for concentration on the lessons rather than on the tired saddle oxfords that needed to sprout more toe room and to grow new heels. With an ankle strap and heels slightly higher than those on the sturdy oxfords, they made me feel prettier than I had ever felt except when I had been a junior bridesmaid at Mary and Daniel's wedding the previous year. After seeing how a pretty dress could make me look and how dress shoes could make me feel, I dreamed of having special clothes and shoes for church.

Aunts on both sides of the family had always dressed nicely and apparently enjoyed looking their best. At times, though, I wondered why Mother didn't seem to share that attitude—why Daddy paid more attention to his appearance than Mother did to hers—even though I never knew him to possess more than one suit and a couple of white shirts and conservative blue ties to make up his wardrobe for church. Beyond that, his service station uniforms took up little space in the small closet. His basic supply included one on his back, one in the wash, and one in the dirty clothes. Mother had to do at least one load of wash almost every day—such an easy chore with today's equipment, but a back-breaking effort when water had to be hauled to the wash tubs and clothes had to be guided by hand through the wringer.

The agitator and the wringer on the washing machines of the day were motorized. Upgrading from manually turned wringers to washing machines with motorized wringers was a venture into luxury once we got electricity. Rollers on the arm of the wringer looked like two rolling pins spinning in opposite directions just waiting for a steady hand to feed dripping clothes between their lips as they pulled the rest of the fabric into the tub of waiting rinse water. It was a two-handed job. While one of the operator's hands fed the rollers on one side, the other hand had to receive the wrung-out items and guide them into the rinse water to assure they didn't splash out too much water when they dropped from the wringer.

If the well was running low, or if Mother was in a hurry and skipped one of the rinses, the residue of soap made the sheets look and feel as though they had been put through the starch solution. Dingy linens and underwear were occasionally treated to a bluing solution. It never made sense to me that we used blue liquid in hopes of reversing gray dinginess to pristine white.

Daddy had what I now consider healthy boundaries. His few possessions were off limits. The ones that most intrigued and tempted me were his fishing tackle and his shaving equipment. While living in Hialeah, I learned not to mess with his shaving equipment. His *Old Spice* that he dabbed on to his clean-shaven face announced he was dressing up. On ordinary work days, the aroma was only a hint of the same fragrance that permeated the old-fashioned shaving mug soap. I never detected a body odor or bad breath on either parent, but my nose sought olfactory associations that signified and symbolized personality and presence. His *Old Spice* and Grandmother's *Bluegrass*, which she combined with Yardley's Lavender soap on Sundays or Lifebuoy soap on week days, set the expectation that all adults would have a signature fragrance. But Mother didn't.

Not long after Daddy finished shaving one morning, I ventured to play with his lathering brush to see if I could imitate his skills. Not wanting to risk taking too much time, I gave up on working up a lather on my face and went on to explore his razor. It was nothing fancy—just a metal mechanical device that took a double-edged razor blade. As I unscrewed it, the blade fell out about the time he realized that I was being way too quiet. He knocked on the door and opened it immediately. I spun around and tried to hide the not-yet-dull razor blade in my hand. My immediate thought was, *I'll just trick him. He won't look for it in my other* (left) *hand.*

My adrenaline was pumping hard enough to make me squeeze my hand tighter than necessary. The sting of clean-cut skin as the blood began to seep thrust the adrenaline into overdrive. Daddy said, "Let me see your hands."

Only my right hand popped out from behind my back and opened. "Now, the other hand."

When he saw the blood, he took the blade out of my hand and squeezed the shallow cut with his calloused tender touch. The look on his face told me that he was both furious because I had meddled with his stuff and also relieved that the wound was not serious.

"Suzie, I have told you to leave my things alone. You know that when I tell you what to do, I do it for your own good. I'm glad that the cut's not deep, but it could have been. Don't *never* touch my razor again. I already have to keep it away from your sisters because they want to shave their legs. I don't want to have to keep it away from you too."

"Yes, sir. I'm sorry."

The days that marked the delivery of a new uniform for Daddy about every six months from either Sears or Montgomery Ward catalogs were special days for all of us because it usually meant a new catalog was included. Whichever sister was at home would sit with me on the couch and take turns checking off our dream list. I paid at least as much attention to how the clothing models looked as to what they were modelling. It was a mild form of risk-taking, a mental *trying on* of different looks, even down to facial expressions and body attitude. Mother would help Richard look through the toy section and later, as he added birthdays, to the boys' clothing section.

It would take many years—decades, in fact—for me to understand Mother's pervasive compensation for the difference between the comforts of her childhood and the barebones budget of her married life. In retrospect, I believe that Daddy and his siblings each possessed a healthy acceptance of their respective limited incomes, but within that limitation, they also expected to be able to present themselves nicely on special occasions. Rather than healthy acceptance of limited financial resources, Mother tended to use denial and glorification of poverty to avert her awareness of her own feelings and to avoid some of the pain of deprivation.

I wanted to have pretty clothes like my aunts and my teachers at school. Mrs. Godbee, my third grade teacher, had worn dark green high heeled leather pumps to school and kept them on all day, even when she had recess duty on the sandy playground. I thought they were the most beautiful shoes in the world. They were even my favorite color.

Aunt Marian and her husband, Uncle Ben (Aly), did not have children. They lived in Apopka, now a suburb of Orlando, but back then, a separate town on the outskirts of the city. Working as a team of two, they operated the Atlantic Coast Line railroad depot in Apopka and lived in a small house right across the street. There were never any cross words between them or any other sort of friction. Aunt Marian was the receptionist and kept the books while Uncle Ben took care of the freight. On several occasions, I helped him move crates full of citrus on its way up north by pushing the crates along the conveyer belt that deposited them into the freight cars of the train. Whenever I push carryon luggage and smaller items along conveyer belts leading to security scanners in my share of domestic and international airports, I recall helping to move the freight along.

Aunt Marian and Uncle Ben began visiting us fairly often the year we lived in the Sapp house in DeLeon Springs, the year my third-grade boyfriend sometimes walked beside my bike as I slowly rode home. Their visits usually coincided with seasonal celebrations or dinner on the grounds at church. They both wore nice suits on Sundays. He usually donned a dress hat, and she carried purses that complemented her suit and sheer silk blouse. When it was time for them to leave, Uncle

Ben would slip a half dollar coin into my hand, giving me the impression that they were rich. Aunt Marian would say, "Come see me some time."

That was the same year I began learning to play the piano. It was so nice to be able to walk to a friend's house or to the store or drug store. Even though I had been baffled when we left Mockingbird Hill and briefly lived in the Sapp house, I recognized the advantages of living in DeLeon Springs. My friend was a year ahead of me in school, but I was blazing through her piano books faster than she could need new ones. It wasn't that I was particularly smarter or more talented than she was, but I was interested and motivated, and I knew I had to make the short visits at her house count without making her think I only visited so that I could use her piano. She was much more interested in drawing faces of cartoon characters, especially Porky Pig. I let her teach me how to copy her drawing.

After we moved back to Mockingbird Hill and were keeping Aunt Vi's piano while she and Uncle Banks looked for a house large enough to accommodate it, I began making good progress as I continued to teach myself how to play. Mother helped some as time permitted, and Mrs. McIinnis also helped me. Fortunately for me, Aunt Vi was not able to reclaim her piano until I was in the sixth grade. By then, it was obvious that I was taking it seriously and that it meant a lot to me.

The year I was in sixth grade was the first and only year that Mother had a class of piano students. Since we lived so far out in the country, she taught in a church member's home in DeLeon Springs, and I was one of her students. Looking back, I am impressed with the repertoire and technical studies that she taught. By the end of the school year, she told me she had taught me everything she knew and that I would eventually have to have a different teacher.

Before I finished sixth grade, Aunt Vi and Uncle Banks found the house they wanted and came to get her piano. I hated to see it go, but understood her need for it and knew I had been lucky to have it in our home for several years.

Aunt Marian and Uncle Ben had begun inviting me to spend weekends with them from time to time. They came over and picked me up in their car the first few times. Aunt Marian was very observant and let me know that she was concerned that I was having to sleep on the couch in the living room. She was aware that Mary's husband, Daniel, had been discharged from the Army and that he and Mary had moved home. My bedroom became theirs, along with their first daughter. Margaret and her second husband, Bill, and Peggy, her daughter, were also living with us. Richard's bedroom was the dining room, the only room with green linoleum on the floor. That little room, which led to the back porch, never saw a dining table in it the entire time we lived there. Mother and Daddy used the sleeping porch for their bedroom.

On the first weekend trip to Apopka, they took me shopping in what Aunt Marian declared was the best store in Orlando, Maas Brothers Department Store. She and I walked hand-in-hand as she guided me toward the shoe department. When we walked into the store, a strong memory of the same aroma as Burdine's Department store in Miami seeped into my nostrils as I recalled the previous most memorable shopping occasion when Mother and Aunt Ruth took Margaret shopping for fabric for her wedding dress. They let me tag along. The aroma was a heady mixture of exotic perfume, fabric dye, and newness of merchandise too pricey for us to even contemplate.

Many years later, I attended a national conference in Miami and needed a light-weight sweater. With instructions from the hotel's concierge, I walked to the nearest department store, a newly renovated Macy's. That same aroma of merchandise wealth hit me as I entered the main entrance where the windows still wore an amber film coating. The film gave the interior of the store a golden glow, but was meant to repel some of Florida's notorious sunshine. An employee verified that the company that owned Macy's had bought Burdine's many years prior to my nostalgic visit. It was the same store with the escalators in the middle of the first floor where I had worked up the courage to step onto moving stairs for the first time.

In Maas Brothers, the aroma, the attention of the sales associates, and the encouragement from Aunt Marian and Uncle Ben combined to let me know that I wanted such occasions to be a part of my future world. I wanted to be able to shop in stores that sold beautiful things, especially pretty clothes like my aunts and teachers wore—maybe even green shoes like Mrs. Godbee wore. Aunt Marian said, "Ben, if you want to go ahead to the men's department, we'll join you there after we find a pair of school shoes. The alterations on your new suit were scheduled to be completed by tomorrow, but maybe they'll have it ready a day early."

Uncle Ben was wearing a good-looking suit, so I wondered why he was buying a new one. Scanning Aunt Marian's face for a hint of approval or disapproval, I asked, "Do you mean saddle oxfords?"

"We could get you a new pair of those, but wouldn't you like to have something a little more grown-up? Your folks can probably get you a new pair of saddle oxfords." She went on to explain that she thought I could wear the old saddle oxfords with my dungarees for school, but that I could wear the new shoes with a skirt or a dress. "Maybe a pair of flats would be nice. Would you like to try on those green ones you were looking at?" She suggested that the green shoes could be mostly for church and a second pair of flats would be good for school and church.

"You mean we can get two pair of shoes today?"

"Yes."

"Could I try on the navy blue flats with the thin red and white strips around the edges?"

"Sure."

Confidence, bred from her independence and shopping with Uncle Ben, fed into her strong signal to the sales clerk to come over to help. The lady pulled the metal foot bed out from under the stool she sat on and told me to place one foot on it and to stand up. She had a quizzical look on her face and commented that if it weren't for my unusually long second and third toes, my shoe size would be one and a half sizes smaller. "I know. Mother says she'll ask the doctor about shortening them after I quit growing."

With raised eyebrows, Aunt Marian said, "I'm sure your mother means well, but she needs to take you to a specialist before a decision is made about shortening your toes." She went on to remind me that she was an RN by training and experience and that it was important to consult the right doctor.

"Ok. I'll tell her."

Both new pairs of shoes fit nicely into the fancy paper carrying bag the clerk handed to me. After meeting up with Uncle Ben, we left Maas Brothers and headed to Morrison's Cafeteria, a popular eating place I had seen advertised on huge billboards. The signs showed a picture of an African-American man with a toothy grin and overly red lips carrying a heavily laden tray on the tips of his fingers, looking sharp in his white dinner jacket and black bow tie. I wondered if Uncle Ben would have to put on a white jacket like that to go to Morrison's.

As we approached the long serving line, Uncle Ben said, "You don't have one of these in DeLand, do you?'

"No; it's kind of like the school cafeteria, though. But I don't eat there because I'd rather save the lunch money Daddy gives me. I go through the line for milk sometimes."

"You're right, except there are many more choices here."

"Do they have pork chops? That's my favorite meat."

"Yes. This is Friday when a lot of folks eat fish, but I think they'll have pork chops."

"Good. I like them so much that I always get the extra one if there is one left over at home."

We worked our way through the efficient line. I declined dessert. The pork chop was big, sizzling with juice, and my mouth was watering. Aunt Marian excused herself to the restroom while the sure-fingered server unloaded our tray. When we sat down, Uncle Ben said, "You probably already know this, but when an older lady is at the table, we usually wait for her to start eating before we start. That's because so many times the lady of the house does the cooking, and if everyone started eating before she sat down, they would finish way before she would." He went on to explain that manners were a way of being thoughtful and respectful.

Aunt Marian sat down, unfolded the large napkin, and gave a subtle nod toward Uncle Ben and me. It was time to dig in. Even though we had pork chops at home occasionally, they were not a weekly item on our menu, and my cutting skills were limited to flaky fish. When I gripped my knife and fork with total lack of control or finesse, as though they were ice picks, and I started to make the first cut with a sawing motion, the knife slipped and sailed off the plate with perfect aim at Uncle Ben's water glass. In my automatic reaction, the fork and rest of the pork chop came backwards toward me and hit the floor. I was mortified. My big plan to be just like them was already ruined and my ignorance and inexperience were exposed.

With total grace and understanding, Uncle Ben and the server had the mess cleaned up almost instantly, and another pork chop appeared on a clean plate as though a magician were at work in the kitchen. I said, "That's okay. You don't have to buy me another pork chop. I know it costs a lot of money."

Aunt Marian said, "Don't worry. We don't have to pay anything extra. This replaces the first one without a charge. They know that some accidents will happen."

A few months after the first visit, Aunt Marian conferred with Mother by phone about the possibility of allowing me to ride the train by myself to spend a weekend with them. They would take me home that Sunday afternoon. Mother understood that their work schedule would not permit them to leave long enough to drive over to pick me up that Friday, so she agreed that I would be okay on the train by myself. There was no stop between DeLand and Apopka, so all I had to do was board the train, enjoy the ride of about an hour, and get off right at their front door. That first solo train ride lit my love of travel and let me associate travel with pleasure rather than mere escape from problems.

Their tiny one-bedroom house was one of the most love-filled homes I had even been in. Sleeping on the couch there made me feel included, embraced, there by invitation and desire rather than a cast-out from my own bedroom. Their respect and affection for each other filled their home and lives.

When I started spending weekends at their place more frequently, they bought a piece of sturdy luggage for me, shopping again at Maas Brothers. On those shopping trips, I learned the value of buying high quality goods. I don't recall the brand, but the first piece of luggage they bought for my weekend trips was a square piece—green, of course, with ivory saddle stitching and trim—and a little later, the second matching piece, a hat box. Hats had no place in my wardrobe then, so the hat box became an overnight case. But perhaps having that hatbox planted the seed for the love of hats I enjoy indulging even today.

Aunt Marian nonchalantly asked one of the ladies in the dress section of the store if she could tell us a little bit about what colors looked best on a redhead. I already had my own notions about color, but the advice from the *pro* served me well when, on the first class-day in Home Economics, the teacher pointed out that I was wearing the best example of fabric that complemented hair, skin, and eye coloring. The dress had an iridescent green and gold solid color bodice with plaid sleeves and a mandarin collar that matched the iridescent plaid of the full skirt. My sense of pride filled my heart and buoyed my walk for the rest of that day as I started ninth grade in a dress from Maas Brothers Department store. Gratitude for Aunt Marian and Uncle Ben's generosity and sensitivity engulfed me.

They made the biggest purchase for me toward the end of my sixth grade. When they brought me home on a Sunday afternoon, I told them I had to practice *The Lord's Prayer* for a wedding the following week. They listened to me practice a minute or so before Aunt Marian pulled Mother aside and said, "Alice, I thought Vi and Banks were going to be able to take back their piano soon. What will Martha Sue do then?"

"She practiced at school and on a friend's piano for a couple of years before we took the piano when Banks and Vi moved into a smaller house. I guess she'll have to practice at church now."

"I don't know anything about piano practice, but it seems to me that she should have a piano of her own so that she can practice every day. How much do you think a practice piano would cost?"

"Oh, I don't know, but I expect it would be close to $100.00."

"Fine. If you can find a good practice piano for no more than $100.00, we will buy it for her. We think she has real talent and we want to help her develop that talent and interest."

In less than two weeks' time, Mother had found the piano that she thought would be adequate. It was for sale for only $50.00. When she called her, Aunt Marian told her the check would be in the next day's mail and would include enough to have the piano moved and tuned. It was a little smaller than Aunt Vi's and probably not as good as hers, but it was acceptable, and it was mine. When the piano was delivered, I was ecstatic and played every piece I knew over and over again.

It seemed, though, that Aunt Vi's piano and I were destined to remain in close contact. The piano that Aunt Marian and Uncle Ben bought held up well enough, but when we moved into the house that Mother and Daddy built on Mockingbird Hill, Daniel's brother-in-law offered to fix it up for me. I thought he meant that he would do something to rejuvenate the scratched wood. He was good with his hands and made a living as an automobile mechanic, but also was interested in music. As I recall, he played the accordion.

With an exaggerated air of accomplishment showing in his wide grin, he returned the piano in a few weeks. I burst into tears when I saw it. He had upholstered it in embossed tomato red and chartreuse green vinyl, complete with puffy filling nailed to the piano's wood with brass tufting tacks. Rudimentary understanding of acoustics was not yet a part of my studies, but I knew that my piano no longer existed as I had known it. When I tried it, the sound was muffled; the volume was limited; and the appearance was better suited for a saloon rather than our small living room, even if the new couch was forest green and the lamp shades were tomato red. There was no turning back to the scratched wood.

When we left Mockingbird Hill for the last time and moved into the house at 524 North High Street in DeLand, it happened also to be time for Aunt Vi and her children to move again. Her big upright piano had no place to rest, so once again, she asked Mother if we could keep it for a while. I was happy to let my ruined piano go and to reclaim the classic black upright that stayed with me through my first two years at Stetson University. If Aunt Marian or Uncle Ben had any negative feelings about the piano they bought for me ending up somewhere other than in our home, they never let me know. They must have realized that

I had nothing to do with its demise. And I often reminded them of what having it for three years had meant to me.

Neither Aunt Marian nor Uncle Ben ever talked about ways in which not having children affected their lifestyle. Looking back, I know how modest and frugal their lifestyle was; yet, at the time, I saw it as the height of luxury. They often ate out, wore fine clothes, went on trips, and filled their daily life with joy. They, like Daddy's brothers and at least one other of his sisters, enjoyed alcoholic drinks, and even went to the dog track to place small bets. I couldn't help but think, *How could something so much fun be viewed by so many as wrong?* At the same time, when I saw a small bookshelf in their living room filled with literary classics, I thought, *How could I not also keep up with reading and studying?*

It was obvious to me that Aunt Marian was both independent and part of a couple, but her intelligence and independence did not threaten Uncle Ben. In many ways, they were ahead of their time in outlook and attitude—not quite early feminists, but certainly mutually supportive of females in educational and career pursuits. Her assumption that I would go beyond high school, even though my two older sisters had dropped out in favor of marriage and children, filled me with prideful ambition. She and Uncle Ben made me think that I might be special in ways more meaningful than simply being the only child in my family who had Mother's coloring. It wasn't that nobody else tapped into my developing self-awareness and began to light torches to lead me. But Aunt Marian's torch was white-hot with a thousand times more candle power and clarity than any other light I could see. Her admonitions lived rather than spoken were stronger and louder than the pseudo pious inanities so pervasive in my community's environment.

I rebelled against the dribble of religiosity that was almost pre-destined to become a tsunami of internal conflict. But I was a quiet rebel and knew to bide my time and to bind my tongue. It was so refreshing to be with Aunt Marian and be able to ask questions or express opinions that were received with respect and empathy. Never once did she or Uncle Ben imply that I had no business thinking or feeling as I did. Their support of my musical interests and their understanding of my wanting my older sisters to move out and to quit bringing their expanding families to live at home whenever they hit a rough financial spot were the most important aspects of my relationship with Aunt Marian and Uncle Ben.

She was not my only role model during those late elementary and junior high school years, but Aunt Marian was, by far, the most significant one, not just because she and Uncle Ben didn't have children and had emotionally *adopted* me, but because I felt a strong bond to her ideals, beliefs, and work ethic. She valued her close relationship with Daddy just as much as he did. Uncle Ben's formal education ended when he finished the third grade; yet, he was one of the most well-read persons I have ever known. Aunt Marian had left home when she was 16 and completed training to become a registered nurse in Jacksonville, about 85 miles from their childhood home in Seville. I think one reason Daddy felt especially close to her was because he was so proud of her accomplishment and her life-long commitment to increasing her knowledge and understanding by working crossword puzzles and playing Scrabble with Uncle Ben.

Not long before I graduated from Stetson, Uncle Ben died. I attended his funeral, but I was running late and did not sit with the family. He knew of my commitment to higher education and had coached me when I balked at the reading requirements in freshman English by telling classic stories in entertaining ways, letting me know that the classics were relevant both in and beyond formal classes. His love of learning was infectious, and his thirst for knowledge was never fully quenched. Aunt Marian attended the graduation ceremonies when I completed the Bachelor of Music degree and never lost contact with me as she lived into advanced age with a keen mind that remained vibrant through all of her 95 birthdays. The twinkle in her loving brown eyes never dulled, and her influence on me will never die. Her balance between practical realism and lofty idealism continues to guide my journey.

# CHAPTER 15

# BABYSITTING AT THE FAIRGROUNDS & WATERSKIING

*Truth is the most valuable thing we have.*
*Let's economize (preserve) it.*

Mark Twain
(1835-1910)

The inappropriate behavior from Daniel that made me realize something was not right became apparent at a family get-together to celebrate my 12th birthday and Daddy's 51st. It was a covered dish Sunday dinner at our house following the morning church service. Most of Daddy's brothers and sisters had attended our church that morning.

At first, I welcomed Daniel's brotherly attention. He encouraged my interest in cooking and baking. But when he brought a pie he had made to the birthday celebration and told me he had made it just for me, his tone and facial expressions made my skin begin to crawl. It felt like he was flirting with me instead of just talking. From that point on, he consistently sought me out no matter who else was around. The flirtation would stop, though, when an adult came within earshot. If either Mother or Mary were nearby, he not only would stop, but also would leave the area, only to return after they had moved on. From that day forward, the best feeling I could hope for around him was an unsettled undercurrent of uneasiness.

Margaret and Bill were good about taking Richard and me to the drive-in movies every now and then. Once Mary and Daniel were home following his discharge from the Army, it was almost like they were trying to make up for the time they had been away. It seemed that they wanted to offer as many good times as Margaret and Bill had so that neither Richard nor I would prefer to be with Margaret and Bill. There had always been more than a tinge of sibling rivalry between Margaret and Mary. The rivalry extended beyond them to at least insinuate conflicted motivations for their offers to include Richard and me in various activities. The distance and antagonism between them grieved Mother.

Prior to my twelfth birthday, Mary and Daniel had a place of their own for a while before they moved back in with us, and I would occasionally spend the night with them. Those times spent with them were usually fun. As their family expanded, though, Daniel's demeanor and gruff mode of verbal communication became more and more pronounced. Others in the family frequently made comments regarding how they felt sorry for Mary and didn't understand how or why she put up with his hurtful tone and refusal to help with childrearing or household responsibilities.

When I was with Mary in her home during the day and Daniel was at work, she taught me to play *Rummy*. I loved playing with their daughter and didn't mind helping out with some of the housework. Mary was nurturing in a way that Mother wasn't. There was a part of me that wanted and needed that type of nurturing, but a bigger part that questioned why things such as attention to dental care and personal grooming came from Mary instead of Mother.

I understand now that the gaps in Mother's mothering were based primarily on her own lack of experience. In what I believe was her arrested development due to her parents' deaths and the pampering she had received from her mother and older sisters, she had not matured to the point of being able to reciprocate emotional warmth when she was orphaned.

I never once doubted that she loved me and wanted for us to have a close relationship, but she needed more from me than I was able to give once I became aware of her needs. And at the same time, she was not able to even contemplate possible causes for my distance. I did think, however, that she showed more concern for Margaret and Mary and was so caught up in their problems that she let Richard and me fend for ourselves too much of the time. I say this not to excuse or even explain her behavior toward me, but to finally clarify and understand the fundamental cause for our difficult relationship. The crack between us became a chasm that threatened to become a permanent break between us when I hit adolescence.

Mother's primary focus was in her career and in her church activities and responsibilities. She was affectionate both physically and verbally, but not in the same way as Mary. I needed a little of Mary's outpouring of affection, but I also needed Mother to take more of an interest in my personal needs and development. I do not recall Mother ever mentioning brushing my teeth or saying anything about how to take care of my hair. Even if she had been able to intuit what it was that I needed, she would not have been able to put herself in the role of the giver. It appeared to me that she had been on the receiving end of parental nurturance at such an extreme level that the death of her parents arrested her own emotional growth, stunting her ability to give more of what she had so abundantly received. This characteristic was not an absolute, but the part it played in her personality and in our relationship was significant.

Margaret also nurtured me, but in a different way because she had a job from the time she was 14 years old. She was more likely to encourage me in school projects and to be helpful in a more concrete way, less prone to gush verbal affection and much more comfortable when showing she cared by serving as a buffer between Mary's extreme fundamentalism and Mother's preoccupation with church and my focus on school and music. So far as I know, she never echoed Mother's opinion that I was too self-centered, and she certainly did not jump to foolishly false conclusions about my high school activities like Mary was prone to do.

When Mary and Daniel found out that I was hoping to be invited to join the Keyettes service club in high school, Mary pulled me aside and asked me if I knew what happened at initiations for clubs such as the Keyettes. I told her that I was aware there was an initiation, but I didn't know exactly what went on. She told me that new members would be taken out into the woods where boys would be waiting, and it would turn into a wild orgy. I don't know where she got that idea. There were certainly no such rumors among any of my friends; nor was there any such activity when I was initiated into the Keyettes.

What happened, in fact, at the informal initiation was so innocent as to be laughable. After being *kidnapped* from our respective homes, the initiates were taken to two places and told to use our ingenuity to accomplish the tasks we were given. One of the tasks was to find our way back to the Boulevard after being put out of the car at the African-American cemetery. The underlying racially-charged assumption was that the cemetery at that location was much scarier than the cemetery we were already familiar with. After we made a good faith effort to walk back to the assigned location, the same cars that took us to the cemetery appeared and let us get in. It was a very cold night, and I had on Bermuda shorts, not knowing what was going to happen.

From the cemetery road, we were driven to the Country Club, where we were directed to retrieve notes from the golf course holes and to follow the instructions. I remember thinking that I might be getting frost bite on my knees and not being able to feel my toes. Despite being elated to be invited to be a member of the Keyettes, I did not enjoy the informal initiation and was glad when some of the upper classmen called to us and motioned for us to come on in out of the cold. Even though I was miserably uncomfortable, I was furious at the thought that Mary and Daniel tried to intervene in my interest in being a part of that club. It simply proved to me how ill-informed and prejudiced they were. In hindsight, it seems like a classic case of sour grapes.

Margaret let me know that it was acceptable for me to want to be involved in teenage activities by providing transportation when needed. She acknowledged my friends at church or when they visited me; and she let me know it was acceptable to want nice clothes by helping me learn to sew.

In the spring of 1954, when Mary asked Mother if she and Daniel could take me to the fairgrounds, I let her and Mother know that I really wanted to go. It may have been a visiting circus, or could have been the Volusia County Fair. There was a modest-sized midway, freak shows, and ample opportunities to try to win prizes. I felt no sense of pending danger—only the chance to have a little fun and to go to the fair or circus for the first time. Mary was in the first trimester of the pregnancy that would result in the birth of their second daughter in mid-January.

Feeling no hesitation, it seemed like a perfectly innocent request at the time. But I learned that evening that there would be no innocent activities if Daniel was around. My very being was in harm's way with no way out of the quicksand.

When we got to the fairgrounds, one of the first rides we came to was the *Tunnel of Love.*

Mary asked, "How 'bout that ride? Would you like to see if you like it? I don't think it's too scary."

"No; you told Mother that you needed help. You and Daniel go ahead; I'll sit with Marlene."

"I really don't feel like going on the ride because it probably will go in a circle. I'm feeling a little dizzy and nauseous. Why don't you go ahead with Daniel and I'll watch Marlene."

Mary found a bench to sit on while I followed Daniel to the ticket booth and onto the ride. Once we sat down in one of the cars, he told me that the ride was kind of like playing one of the kissing games at church social events.

He had taught the Sunday School group a game that involved guessing the makes of cars. So far as I know, he did not mess around with any of the girls during that party, but he encouraged us to enjoy the kissing game—a chance for him to be a voyeuristic cheerleader of sorts. As I recall, the game involved guessing what make of car someone was thinking about. If the guess was correct, the two got to take a walk—sort of an extension of playing *Spin the Bottle.* It was expected that some kissing would take place on the walk. When Mary saw that some of the couples were taking too long on their walk, she intervened and stopped the game with a bribe of refreshments in the house.

As soon as the *Tunnel of Love* ride left the lighted area and was in total darkness, he started fondling and kissing me. The ride was not in complete darkness for the entire time, but kept going in and out of the dark. Every time we reached a stretch of darkness, he started up again. I felt invaded, disloyal to Mary, and totally alone—trapped by the *Tunnel of Love* in a scene on a two-bit carnival ride that had nothing to do with love. It seemed to me that it should have been part of the horror show. I wished I had stayed home. In one of the lighted areas, I said, "Somebody's going to see you. I hope they tell Mary."

"Don't you see that we're the only ones in this part of the ride? You will not say a word to your sister or anyone else if you know what's good for you. Nobody would believe you anyway."

Practicing the art of spontaneous deception, when we got off the ride, I sat down beside Mary and said, "Now, I feel dizzy too. I'm not going on any more rides because I think it would make me throw up."

She said, "Okay. We'll just do a few more things and head on home. Marlene is getting pretty tired. Would you like to try to win a prize?"

"I guess so."

During the year leading up to my 13th birthday, being around him rapidly escalated my feelings from discomfort to fear. Not long after the trip to the fairgrounds, he managed to have access to a boat with a motor large enough to pull skis. He organized an outing for the youth of the church to be held at the St. John's River. I had never water skied, but I had done my share of roller skating. Several others took a spin on the skis before he called for me to have my turn. Acting like he wanted to show off to everyone else how fast the boat could go, he told me to get into the boat for a fast ride.

We were right in front of about twenty people, so I saw no harm in riding in the boat with him. Sure enough, he gave the boat its full power. As we approached the area where I assumed we would turn around, he slowed down just enough to make the bend in the river and slowed more as he headed closer to the bank, which was not visible from where the others were waiting. It was as though we were back in the *Tunnel of Love*. After a few kisses and some groping, he turned the boat around and again accelerated. I kept turning away and tried to move to the back of the boat, but he grabbed my arm every time and pulled me back close to him.

He pulled into the ski launch area and told someone to bring the skis out to me. Figuring out how to get the skis on and how to get up when the boat tugged on the ski rope were welcome distractions from the sick feeling in the pit of my stomach and the scrambled brain activity that was trying to process what had just happened.

I got up on the first try and was happy to feel the wind against my skin and in my hair. He turned around before the bend and passed the group before he turned around again, completing an elongated oval course for my turn on the skis. When we were close to the group waiting on the banks, I yelled, "Get me off of these skis! My knees are shaking. What do I do?"

Someone in the group yelled back, "Just turn loose and aim toward the bank. Swim the rest of the way if you have to." I didn't want to touch the bottom because I knew it was squishy.

"How'd you like that speedy ride?"

"I'd rather ski than ride in the boat."

The experience on the *Tunnel of Love* ride was preamble to a series of events that grew in seriousness, pain, and consequences throughout the rest of my adolescence. It started a realization that anything appearing to be a fun-filled activity had the potential of being turned into part of his horror show as he tried so desperately to prove something to himself, something that would compensate for both real and perceived weaknesses, something that would fill the emptiness that could be triggered into a vacuum trained on the one unlucky enough to be in his path, something that would convince himself that he was a big man with such a huge sex drive that he had to act on the mislabeled drive.

# CHAPTER 16

# DRIVING LESSON— NOT IN OLE BETSEY

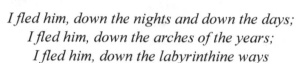

*I fled him, down the nights and down the days;*
*I fled him, down the arches of the years;*
*I fled him, down the labyrinthine ways*
*Of my own mind; and in the mist of tears*
*I hid from him; and under running laughter.*

Thomas Cole
(1801-1848)

One of my older cousins on Daddy's side of the family and her mother (my aunt) liked to read what Mother considered trashy magazines such as *True Confessions*. Aunt Bessie or Vivian would pass on as many as six or so at a time. I read some of the stories and through them had learned something of sexuality as it was presented in that type of publication. Mother readily answered all questions having to do with anatomy and physiology to the best of her ability, but she never mentioned any emotional aspect of sex.

Recalling the magazines that they passed on to me reminds me of the fancy taffeta dress that Vivian also gave me the summer before I entered high school. Stories in those magazines taught me that not all sex was merely about reproduction.

After reading a story about how someone had accidentally had sex with her brother because each sibling had been adopted by different families, I demanded that Mother show me my birth certificate to prove I was not adopted. I had long wondered how and why I was the only one of four children who had Mother's coloring. More than that, I realized I was so different from my older sisters that I believed I could have been adopted. It felt as though I had come from and occupied an entirely different world. It wasn't long, though, until I accepted physical resemblances between me and both of my parents, along with the facts on the certificate.

In late summer of that year, Vivian passed on a cocktail dress to me. At thirteen, I had no need for a cocktail dress, but I was the only one in the family who was close enough to her size to be able to get it on and zipped up. I thought it was the most beautiful dress I had ever seen. The iridescent purple pleated skirt was made of taffeta and whispered when I walked. Pink and purple plaid off-the-shoulder sleeves set off the solid pink bodice, which allowed my limited cleavage to show. Daddy had not paid much attention to the dress when he saw it hanging over the top of the door to my bedroom.

That Sunday afternoon, as usual, a car load of relatives came out to Mockingbird Hill for music and dessert. After the dishes were cleared from the table, Mother told me to hurry and get dressed for the evening church service. I was to sing a solo. She said, "Make sure you make yourself presentable for your solo." The *new* dress from Vivian seemed to be the perfect attire as I anticipated what the four-years-older body-building boy I had a crush on would think of my appearance.

I went to my room and took the dress off the wire hanger. It was a perfect fit—snug in the waist, low in the neck, and with narrow half-sleeves barely touching my shoulders. Feeling proud of the way I looked, I pranced out of the bedroom. Daddy took one short look and said, "Where in the world do you think you're going in that get-up? Did your mother give you permission to wear it?" The tiny muscles around his mouth flexed in rhythm with the increasing tempo of his breath.

"No. She just said to get ready for church. Vivian and Aunt Bessie brought this and some other dresses to me yesterday. Vivian paid a lot of money for it."

"It looks okay for her, but she is a lot older than you and probably didn't wear it to church. Get it off and put on one of your own dresses right now. We have to leave soon."

Daddy's youngest brother and his family were still there, but their presence did not spare me from Daddy's disapproval. Feeling the awkwardness of tempers flaring, Uncle Bob and everyone with him rushed out to his car. Mother followed to wave them off, leaving me alone with Daddy. I said, "This is the prettiest dress I've ever had, and I am going to wear it. You can't make me take it off."

"You'll do as I say, or you'll stay home. Someone else can sing the solo. I won't have a daughter of mine looking like a two-bit street-walker, especially at church."

I burst into tears and ran outside to let Mother know what was going on. Uncle Bob's oldest daughter was a year younger. When she saw the dress, she said, "Martha Sue, where'd you get that fancy dress?"

"Our cousin, Vivian, gave it to me, and now Daddy says I can't wear it to church."

"It looks pretty, but it does look like a party dress." Her cool response to the notion of wearing the dress to church made me wonder if she was jealous.

Mother waved as Uncle Bob's car backed out of the driveway, then gently turned me around and pointed me toward the front door. On the way inside, she reminded me that I had to mind my father. "He doesn't understand why you want to wear such a fancy dress to church, especially to an evening service."

"I know; can't you make him understand?"

"We'll see."

Inside the house, he threatened to take his belt to me. That rarely happened and hadn't happened for a long time, but I could still hear the siren of the belt ripping through its loops, and the slap of leather on my rear end. I feared he would follow through on his threat if I pushed him much further. I went to my bedroom and found a ¾ sleeved shrug and slung it around my shoulders. "Will this do?"

"No. If it falls off, your shoulders will be almost bare and it will show too much of your chest."

I thrust my arms into the sleeves of the shrug as though I was at war with it and looked at Daddy with a question mark in my eyes. "That'll do, but I'd better not hear of you taking off that sweater and showing too much skin."

Six years later, when he walked me down the aisle at my first wedding, he disliked the white dinner jacket *monkey suit* I demanded he wear even more than he disliked my taffeta hand-me-down.

From one of the *trashy* magazines, I read that females who were raped often became frigid. Mary and Daniel had informed me that Mother was frigid—a pseudo diagnosis based on the prized book they had bought soon after they were married. It was a book on sexology. My sympathies for Daddy developed when we still lived in Miami, but I had no reason to believe that Mother was an emotional or sexual cold fish. While I didn't yet know or understand the terms, *introvert* and *extrovert*, I recognized that Mother was more outgoing and that the most rewarding part of her life centered in her teaching and leadership at church. Although warm and cordial, Daddy was less outgoing and centered his emotional life in the family and his one form of recreation—fishing.

It seemed to me that she was not fair when it came to decision-making, but I certainly did not see her as cold or domineering. In my mind at the time, frigid meant that a woman would not even share the same bedroom with a man. I had a lot to learn about sexuality and relationships.

The sort of boundary-less talk that Mary and Daniel engaged in around me made me as uncomfortable as if we were desecrating parental privacy. It felt inappropriate and smacked of a form of disloyalty that I could not identify. At the same time, I thought that Mary was trying to be the cool sister. She seemed to want to fill in the gaps left by Mother's somewhat sterile birds and bees talks.

The ripple of competition between Mary and Margaret also played its own part in affecting how they related to me and to each other. Part of Mary's motivation to overshare with me appeared to be based on an attempt to create a close bond between herself and me. Now, I believe that the deeper and strongest aspect of her colluding with Daniel's inappropriate conversations with me was prompted by her own denial of her husband's underlying reasons for including me in conversations where I had no business as either a spectator or participant. It was all part of Daniel's cunning manipulation to ensnare her as the enabler whose role could extend as far as he wanted to cast his net.

Under the guise of educating me beyond the basic textbook facts of life, they probed with a joint effort to determine the pattern of my menstrual cycle.

After explaining the basic cycle of periods, Mary asked, "Are your periods regular?"

"Yes. I don't keep track of them, though."

"You need to so that you will know if you are ever late. Sometimes, an infection or an ovarian cyst can cause your period to be late. If you don't keep a record, you won't know if there is a problem."

Daniel asked, "When was your last period? I can figure out when the next one will start if you can remember when the last one started."

"I don't know, but I think it was about two weeks ago."

"Okay. Write down the date of the next one, and Mary and I will calculate when the next one will be due. Then, you can start keeping track of the expected date each month."

Without giving a firm commitment to keep a record of my menstrual cycles, I gave enough implied compliance to get them to stop the questions.

At that point, I felt violated right in front of my sister and her husband, the abuser. Having a right to speak up was something completely foreign to me, so I, too, went along to get along. But simultaneously, I looked for opportunities to put physical and emotional distance between us. Playing with their daughters and with Margaret's daughter and son served as a safe place for me when there was no physical escape. The joy with the children was genuine, but playing with them also served a darker purpose as it lent a thin shield from Daniel's overt attention and attacks. His threat of molestation and ability to corner me undermined my love of playing with the children.

With hindsight, it is clear to me that there was no justification to their claim that I needed to know when my period was due. More pertinently, he needed to know my cycle's pattern so that he could make some attempt to not get me pregnant. That is perhaps the nicest thing I can say about his behavior throughout the six years of overt attacks.

Even that bit of superficial decency was based on his selfish core and cocky attitude.

During one of the sex education talks, he announced that men didn't like to use condoms because it was like taking a shower with a raincoat on. His face showed the smirk that reliably appeared when he was feeling a moment of gleeful triumph. Right in front of Mary, he was warning me that he would not wear a condom. Rather than furthering my knowledge and understanding of sex, it was a clear threat and warning—a declaration of his bully power and intent to use it if I refused to cooperate with him. For a teenager already cowed by his behavior, the threat of pregnancy in the 1950's was the promise of total ruination.

My sympathies toward Daddy had to do with Mother's insistence that he attend church when he was exhausted or when bad weather on top of hurricane-related flooding made him anxious over whether Ole Betsey could hold up to the street flooding between our home and the church.

For a necessity such as inoculations, he didn't hesitate to encourage Mother to take Richard and me and our cousins to the doctor. His attitude and opinion smacked of cautious safety; Mother's felt like irrational risk-taking and danger. I wondered why such a good man had to go to church at all, much less when other concerns seemed to make more sense to me. The fact that Mother rarely gave in to his preferences and that she seemed to always stand firm in her belief that she was in the right made me feel sorry for him and view him as a type of underdog, even though I was too young to verbalize my thoughts, even to myself.

She proudly told the story of Margaret's realizing how stubborn our mother could be when Margaret was one of her students in the third grade class at DeLeon Springs Elementary School. The story went that Mother had recess duty while one of her colleagues had a planning period. So Mother was supervising her third grade class and at least one other class out on the playground. When Mother's class returned to their classroom, Margaret hung back and stayed outside the door, crying. Mother's colleague came by on her way to the ladies room. Thinking that perhaps there had been a small accident on the playground, the teacher said, "What's wrong, Margaret? Did you get hurt?"

"No."

"Then why are you crying?"

"I'm crying because my mother never changes her mind."

When Mother told the story, she always gave me the impression that she believed sticking to her word, including to one of her children, was an honorable thing. To Margaret on that day, it meant an unreasonable stubbornness against which she was powerless.

Having high hopes of someday having a boyfriend who would show me what it was like to be kissed tenderly without slobber or disloyalty, I knew that frigid was not a word I wanted to be used to describe.me. If Mother was sexually cold, I didn't want to be like her, but I didn't want my brother-in-law to take it upon himself to be my tutor with his twisted notion of what sexuality was all about. In reality, his abhorrent behavior toward me had nothing to do with sexuality and even less to do with love. It was simply and completely a means of manipulative control that sustained his compulsion to defend himself against the psychological and emotional demons that controlled him. What a profoundly pathetic vicious cycle.

It would be nice to believe that Mary and Daniel were aware of my attempt to distance myself from Mother in some ways, and that they had at least a modicum of honorable intent regarding providing some fun that neither Daddy nor Mother could or would provide. But it is almost impossible to venture that thought beyond an intellectual nod. Daddy would never have gone to the fair or circus, and Mother would never have attempted to talk him into agreeing for her to take Richard and me. That was just too large an extravagance for him to agree to spend money on

Despite the creepy feeling I had around Daniel, I welcomed the chance to take part in fun-filled activities. I wondered how Mary could have been so blind and place such utter trust in someone who was so completely unworthy of trust. Admitting that she was not capable of confronting him was a reality I didn't want to see, so I chose to tell myself that it was just a matter of time until she would tell him what she really thought about him.

The molestations in the *Tunnel of Love* ride at the fairgrounds and on the boat ride at the water skiing event were limited to fondling and kissing, but the implications for the future were limitless.

Sensing that Daniel was dramatically different from Daddy, I assumed that the differences reflected the gap between their ages. It didn't take long, though, for it to become clear that the age difference was not what accounted for the opposites in character and characteristics.

Daddy spoke kindly to everyone because he was kind. Daniel barked orders to Mary and anyone else he addressed because he was a bully and a dictator at heart. Daddy respected men, women, and children alike. Daniel showed only disdain for females of all ages and grinned his lop-sided grin when he knew he had hit a verbal or emotional home run. He accepted no consistent role of childcare toward their three (eventually four) daughters. If one needed a diaper to be changed and Mary was already busy with one of the other children, he would yell at her to get up and take care of the daughter who happened to be near him as though Mary were just lying around. He had to have known where she was and what she was doing because they were living with us, and the house was tiny.

Not only did he accept the fifties' traditional gender separation of labor and go into a growling temper outburst if anyone hinted at questioning that mindset, but he also credited the outlook to God. He seemed to believe that there was men's work and women's work and was determined to keep it that way. Such menial chores as housework or child care were far below his inflated opinion of himself. Ridicule, intimidation, and utmost control were his means of relating, especially to females.

When Daniel's cousin who had been our pastor resigned and moved, a man from North Carolina came in as the new pastor. He and his wife had four children and encouraged the younger adults in the church to provide more activities for the youth. Daniel seemed happy to rally behind that request.

Mrs. Wentz, the pastor's wife, once asked Mother what she thought about the possibility of Daniel becoming the director of the youth activities. The conversation took place not long after my twelfth birthday dinner. Out in the front yard of the church after the evening service, Mother looked Mrs. Wentz straight in the eye and said, "Mildred, I am going to be perfectly frank with you. He seems to be a good starter, but he's not very good about finishing what he starts."

Mother let Mrs. Wentz know that she had taught Daniel in one of the lower elementary grades, and that she had seen that tendency to leave things unfinished carry over into his adult life. She went on, "If you and Brother Wentz can keep him motivated, he might do a pretty good job."

That was the first time I ever heard Mother say anything less than glowing about anyone. It made me start paying more attention to Daniel's behavior at church. On the surface, I felt like I should defend him because of the fun activities he had provided the family. In some ways, he readily filled the gap left by the much older brother who had been stillborn fourteen years before my birth.

I would come to understand the depth of Mother's grief and would pity her apparent lack of adults in her life with whom she might have shared her pain; yet, I feel that she should have spared Richard and me from her sorrow, particularly during our childhood years. The portion of her grief that she transferred onto me went from second-hand to first-hand when I, too, lost children at birth. By then, though, she and Daddy had moved to the Springfield area in Missouri, and a trip home to be with me when identical twin girls lived only a few hours was a financial impossibility. Twelve years later, she was able to visit me when my son was stillborn. I let her know that I fully understood the disappointment and grief that she and Daddy had experienced.

My feeling about Daddy's age was two-sided: embarrassed that he was older than the dads of my friends and cousins and, at the same time, guilt for feeling that way. It was more apology than shame, with no clear borderline between shame and guilt or between guilt and apology. The onslaught of negative feelings swirled into a constant stew brewing with occasional outbursts when I reached a point of intolerance of their effects.

We had never had fireworks for the Fourth of July or New Year's Eve. Daniel changed that by taking Richard and me with him and Mary (Margaret and Bill may also have gone with us) over to Lake Johnson to shoot fireworks a few times. He was building trust and what we now would call bonding.

One of the most interesting things he did was to introduce the family to star-gazing. He didn't have a telescope, but he could point out some of the constellations. Being out in the country, the dark nights invited such free activities and brought a certain amount of fun to the family as we followed his lead and instructions regarding the night sky.

In addition to the opportunistic proximity, flirting, and too-frequent touching, he used conversation to promote his puffed-up opinion of himself and to appear to be an authority on whatever subject he chose to pontificate about. On one occasion, he was spouting off about his belief that the Bible instructed men to marry their sister-in-law if their wife died. We were standing beside his car while Mary was sitting in the car, not feeling up to standing because of morning sickness.

His remarks made me think that he had some idea that Mary would not survive the pregnancy or some future pregnancy, and that I would have to become his new wife. I found that idea utterly repulsive. The notion that I would ever consider such an arrangement was insulting in its assumption that I had nothing better to do with my life. But how could he have encouraged me to follow my aspirations without at least inferring that my sisters should not have dropped out of high school and that he should have pursued additional education himself? In the milieu of that rural Baptist Church, though, education was scorned. His cousin had actively preached against it while he was the pastor. It was just too threatening to such a narrow view of the world and of religion in general and fundamentalism in particular. The threat, from that perspective, was that an education would destroy your faith. My view was in strong shades of opposite.

I didn't buy others' fears regarding education and faith. For me, education was a necessity in order to be able to grow into an honestly mature person and to provide a means of financial support. Since neither of my sisters had completed high school, I feared that some people might think that completing high school would be a sufficient goal for me. But it was just the beginning.

Not long after he talked about his (mis)understanding of the Bible's teaching regarding marrying a sister-in-law if a wife died and before we got very far along with the tear-down project, Daniel offered to teach me to drive. At thirteen, I knew I would be able to get my driving permit in the fall when I turned fourteen. I also would be able to get my first job at McCrory's Five & Dime. Margaret had already started letting me drive her car occasionally on county roads. Mother also had let me sit close to her in Ole Betsey, to steer the car. When Daniel asked Mother if he could give me a driving lesson, she readily agreed. I said, "I don't need a driving lesson, Mother. You and Margaret are teaching me."

"Oh, Honey, Daniel can let you sit behind the wheel and really drive the car. He will be able to see how well you already can use the steering wheel and also help you get the hang of using the clutch, brake, and accelerator. "

She had no clue that I was desperate to not be allowed to be in the car with him. The driver's seat might as well have been made of molten lava for all the attraction it held for me. When I couldn't convince her to let me skip the driving lesson, I got in on the passenger side.

As soon as we left the driveway and turned onto the road, he said, "Get over here like you do when your mother or Margaret lets you steer. They're goin' to think somethin's wrong if you stay over there." His pointed middle finger jabbed the seat close to his thigh.

I moved close enough to hold the steering wheel with my left hand and tried not to let any part of my body touch his. We headed toward the right angle turn going toward DeLeon Springs on Reynolds Road. Once we passed our property line and approached the right angle turn, he unzipped his pants and reminded me that a real woman would do anything a man wanted her to do. He tried to push my head down for a blow job, but I resisted. He then grabbed my hand and put it on his penis and said, "Now do what you know I want you to do."

He was right in assuming that I knew what he expected. I knew because my sister, his wife, had told me that she knew he would never leave her because she did anything in bed that he wanted her to do, even in the middle of the night when he woke up. When I asked her what she meant, she said, "You know—you can have sex with your hand or mouth. You don't always have to go all the way. But not all women will do those things."

I knew that I couldn't get out of the car, and that even if I could, there was no one to help me. Because of his forceful ways and language, I thought that if I did manage to get out of the car, he would try to run me down or chase me with the car and force me to get back in. I did what he demanded and moved back over to my side of the seat. As he flung the ejaculate-filled Kleenex out the window, I said, "Just think. There was life in that."

"Only if it gets to the right place." Jabbing the seat with his extended middle finger again, he went on, "Now, get back over here and stay close so they'll see you're steerin' when we pull up."

His despicable smirk twisted on his face as he apparently felt triumphant not only for his success in coercing me into his car, but also for beating the system by not depositing his semen in the right place. When I told him I didn't want to steer the car, I stayed on my side with my arms across my chest, needing the comfort of someone else's arms. If I could have been prone, I would have curled into a fetal position. With eyesight dulled by sadness, confusion, and despair, I gazed out the window and wondered if my face would tell Mary or Mother that something had happened that had nothing to do with learning to drive. Avoiding eye contact, I gritted my mental teeth until I could jump out of the car and climb to safety and relative comfort up in the top of the hickory nut tree.

There was no joy in that driving lesson. I had accomplished nothing, but he accomplished exactly what he had set out to do. It wasn't just a matter of coercing me into providing a sexual favor. Much more importantly, he planted seeds of fear, intimidation, self-doubt, and false guilt in my mind. He tended that invasive garden with utter devotion. While realizing the success of his intention, he proved just how untrustworthy he was. He had painted a full-color banner emblazoned with a skull and crossbones in my mind. I knew that if I ever had to be alone with him, he would not stop until he had achieved his goal. The certainty that there was no safety when he was around was cemented in my mind.

There was never any apparent sense of care for me from him other than not wanting to get me pregnant. Yet, his need to control me outweighed that pittance of concern and gave way to the threat to use pregnancy as a means of punishment if I refused to accommodate his demands. There was no sign of regret or any indication of second thoughts beyond his utter delight in doing and getting away with each act of sexual aggression and assault. And he never once in all the time since 1953 offered even a perfunctory apology. The depth of his blatant disrespect for Mary braised my heart and bruised my soul with disgust.

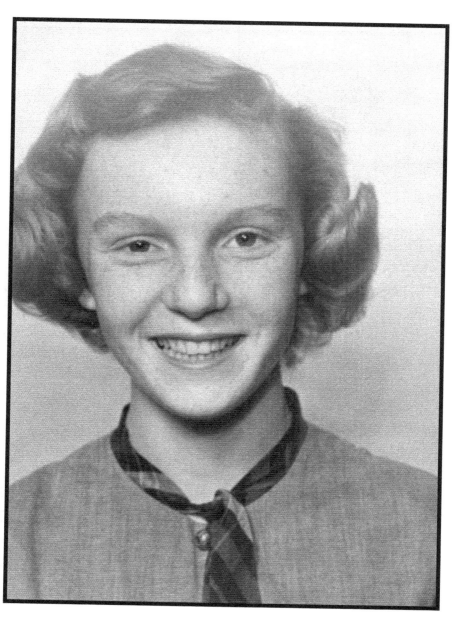

*Sue in 8th grade—same dress worn at birthday party
the year before and on first day in 9th grade*

*Sue in 9th grade*

# CHAPTER 17

# MUMPS AND CAMPBELL'S CHICKEN NOODLE SOUP

*Never be bullied into silence.*
*Never allow yourself to be made a victim.*
*Accept no one's definition of your life, but define yourself.*
Harvey S. Firestone
(1868-1938)

The threat of ongoing sexual molestation hung thick in the air like the aroma of a fish too long left flopping in a sink full of tepid water. And all the while, the threat masqueraded as the fun-loving brother-in-law who happened to be the youth sponsor at church. Being alone with him without an attack of one degree or another was a fantasy I knew would not be realized. Not a moment's opportunity for him would go untested. Any sense of security I may have felt when he was not around fled my presence as quickly as I wanted to flee when he appeared.

Not only did I have to dodge him at home and at church, but I took it upon myself to make sure he did not have access to my friends at church. If one of them went to the restroom, I went with her. If one had nursery duty, I volunteered to stay with her. It seemed reasonable to assume that since he wanted to break me in right, he would want to do the same to anyone who, through no fault of her own, became his target. He was a grand master at calculating opportunities and manipulating people and circumstances to comply with his sick needs. The threat was pervasive while Daniel waited for the perfect opportunity to escalate the threat to attack. Its presence was as palpable as the warning odor of a skunk or the maracas-like chatter of a coiled rattlesnake with fangs sensing their target.

One of the ironies of that time was that Mary did not have a driver's license. Daniel's lack of help or encouragement for her to get her license served as a means to keep her contact with others limited. And she played right into his control by honoring her commitment to be a submissive wife. What a travesty of integrity that they had the nerve to credit God with their respective outlooks, attitudes, and emotional dysfunction.

How could Mary not have thought that it was odd that he would offer to teach me to drive, yet he did nothing to help her get her license? Much later, when I was an upperclassman at Stetson University, I helped her practice parallel parking and to study for her driving exams before taking the tests. She passed and seemed to be happy to have the ticket to a little independence. There was so little I could do to help her; yet, I felt a burden of responsibility for her happiness. As an older sister, she had helped me many times in numerous ways, but all I could do for her was babysit and help her clean her house when she was too weak or too pregnant to do it by herself.

Child molesters and rapists are highly skilled with practical acts of stalking, manipulating, and bluffing their way through potential pitfalls. Daniel kept insisting that Mary keep trying to produce a son. Girls were certainly not on the top of his wish list. In fact, when he came to church after the birth of their third daughter, he strutted up as the service was letting out and announced, "Just what I need; another stinkin' little girl."

Mother intervened before he could say anything more. "Daniel McDonald, I'm sure you must be kidding. You know that she'll be beautiful, and she deserves to be loved."

Because of his twisted views and strong feelings about the issue, Mary was almost constantly either pregnant or recovering from a miscarriage or a birth. That summer, their oldest daughter was a little over two years old, and Mary was pregnant with their second daughter due to be born in January.

The undercurrents and riptides that would threaten to rob me of my potential were all in place. Sometimes they appeared as a tight mental or emotional vise, squeezing out my energy and hope. Sometimes they appeared as a powerful push or pull, ever at-the-ready to affect my feelings, upset plans, and off-rail ambitious intentions. In time, the power of positive influences and experiences would tilt the scales closer to a healthy balance that eventually outweighed the negatives. But that took decades. Before achieving personal and professional success and fulfillment, I paid the bitter dues of suffering that any type of abuse wreaks on every survivor.

It seemed that no matter what apparently good thing happened to me, Daniel would turn it into something perverse with a bitter aftertaste and ugly consequences. Even at church, he demanded that I sit on the front pew near the piano on the left side. He insisted that I cross my arms across my chest just as he did so that he could hold my hand in a hidden way while simultaneously holding Mary's hand on the other side. It felt like a dog must feel chained to a tree or post. But my chains were hidden. He seemed to bask in the thrill of not getting caught, especially when his actions could have been detected by anyone who might have been suspicious.

When he took the young people of the church for a swim and campfire outing to Lake Winona, he made sure he stood or sat beside me as we gathered around the campfire, first to roast hot dogs and marshmallows, and later to sing songs and tell ghost stories. I knew that if I defied him and stood or sat away from him, I would pay the price of a tongue-lashing or worse as soon as he could corner me.

When we started the ghost stories, he had the entire group hold hands around the campfire. The fun was ruined by wondering why he kept squeezing my hand. I later asked Mary why someone would do that. She said, "Oh, when a boy wants to let you know he likes you, he squeezes your hand three times to mean 'I love (or like) you.' It can also mean that he wants to do it if he is older and thinks he can get away with it."

Could she not put two and two together and know that I was asking about her husband's behavior? She went on to say that the girl didn't have to squeeze back. It was optional. Typical of so many other sexual predators, he was an expert at putting himself in places and situations where young girls would be in attendance. His personality was charismatic, and he was a natural at assuming the sale, no matter how criminal, immoral, or illegal the product. His cunningness was as calculated as a mathematician's formula, and his courage to deceive was as clever as a hungry hyena's.

When he heard that my physical education class at school was doing a unit on tumbling, he got hold of a couple of old mattresses and hauled them to church for outdoor tumbling practice. Fortunately, rain soaked the mattresses before he got the chance to ogle as friends from the church and I practiced tumbling in our leg-revealing gym uniforms or shorts.

Mumps was making the rounds within the family. Margaret and Bill's son, Jim, had just recovered. Daniel was nearing the point of recovery. My turn would come in a couple of weeks. Mary had her hands full with taking care of their daughter, caring for her sick husband, and trying to maintain the current pregnancy. She would eventually lose at least half a dozen fetuses to miscarriage and two sons in late-term stillbirths in addition to birthing four daughters.

When Mother told me that Mary had asked her to take her for a short outing, I begged her to let me go with them. Mother said, "You know, your sister's handling a lot right now. I think she just needs a little break from childcare and taking care of Daniel. He's probably not the most pleasant patient in the world. You'll be doing her a big favor by taking care of Marlene while she gets out for a little while. I don't think Daniel's still contagious. He's almost well."

Mary's idea was that they could drive to the south side of DeLand, near Lake Beresford, where two new houses were for sale. Ostensibly, she wanted to look for paint combination ideas because she hoped to be able to paint their new house. Dread set in as soon as I heard about the proposed outing, but no amount of pleading would change Mother's mind. Since we were in the process of tearing down the old house and building the new one, Mother was enthusiastic about going to see the new houses. And she was adamant that I would stay behind and take care of my niece. They knew how I loved to play with the children in the family, yet neither of them questioned why I didn't want to be assigned that duty on that day. It was so much easier to blame my attitude on their belief that I was becoming more and more self-centered and demanding.

One of the painful burdens about the tear-down project was that my need to dodge Daniel curtailed almost all of the sharing I might have done with Mother concerning furniture, paint, furniture arrangement, and other typical matters of concern when making a move. Daniel's behavior robbed me of those times with Mother I wish I could have had.

When Mother and Richard and I arrived at Mary and Daniel's place, Mary explained that Marlene was napping, and that Daniel would just need some soup warmed up if he woke up and was hungry. There was no doubt in my mind that he would wake up and have an appetite that I wanted no part of satiating. She went on to say that I could also eat some of the soup.

Richard was not expected to do any of the babysitting. He took his fishing pole and went down to the Oxhole to try his hand at fishing there. Looking back on that day, it's a wonder that Mother let him try that because she was always so cautious about water safety. There may have been an adult with him, perhaps Daniel's sister or brother-in-law, but I do not recall with certainty whether Richard was allowed to fish alone or not. I am certain, though, that he went to the Oxhole.

We had been there just a few minutes when Mother and Mary gathered up their purses and started out for the car. Shivers ran up my spine as I heard Mary tell her husband goodbye.

"Try to get some good rest, Honey. Sue is here to take care of you if you need anything. She'll be checking on Marlene too."

She checked on her daughter and kissed my cheek when she headed for the front door. Thinking her husband was almost asleep, she crooked her finger at Mother. They closed the door quietly before stepping down the wobbly temporary front steps. The walls of the house wrapped around me like a dank pall, stifling the very air I breathed.

I settled onto the couch in the living room and tried to read something—a book or magazine—anything that might help me to calm myself. My throat was too tense to swallow the lump of fear threatening to choke me. There was no way to dissolve such a lump.

Marlene's bed was in a small room just off the only bedroom. It was really only a large closet, but the small bed fit against the outer wall. The toilet was on the far side of the bedroom where he lay in wait. As the clock hands approached the one-hour mark since Mary and Mother had left, I began to think my fears would be in vain—at least for that day. At the same time, I heard Marlene cry out. I tiptoed in to comfort her. With just a few rhythmic pats on her back, she soon went back to sleep. That was a trick I had learned when they lived in our house and I took care of her then.

Seeing that her father appeared to be asleep, I eased into the bathroom and used the toilet. Afraid of waking him, I didn't flush the toilet. As I tiptoed back around the foot of the bed, he called out in his typically gruff tone of voice, "Didn't you forget to flush the toilet?"

"No, I just didn't want to wake you up."

"You ought to know I wouldn't still be asleep. I'm hungry. Go warm up that soup for me."

Glad to get out of the room, I went to the tiny kitchen and poured the Campbell's Chicken Noodle soup into a pan, diluted it with water, and put it on the stove to heat on *low*, hoping it would take a long time to heat. I stirred it constantly and stepped to the bedroom entryway to tell him when it was ready. "You're supposed to be helpin' me. Bring it in here. I don't feel like walkin' in there."

Hoping he really was weak, I took the soup into the bedroom. He was standing beside the bed as I entered. Still taking off a white t-shirt, he was nude from the waist down. I had never seen a grown man completely naked.

The room was so small and so inadequately furnished that I could not find a place to set down the soup. He took it and placed it on the floor near the window at the head of the bed.

Standing just an arm's length from me, he moved toward me and pulled me to him. "Don't you want to see what I have for you?" he said, careful to speak quietly, eyebrows raised as though he had an enticing secret to share.

Some of the details are faded, but I vividly recall the pain I felt as my hymen ripped from his forceful thrusts with no vaginal lubrication.

When I cried out in pain, Marlene woke up and whimpered. She climbed off her bed and started coming toward the bedroom. When he heard her, he withdrew and took two or three steps into the bathroom. In one synchronized motion, my legs sprang off the bed, my feet hit the floor, and I smoothed down my skirt.

By then, Marlene was close enough to see me. She looked surprised and confused, as though she expected to see her mother in the bedroom. I glanced out the window and saw Richard walking slowly from the Oxhole to the house, still too far away to hear me if I yelled. Marlene stood in the doorway holding her blanket. Since my panties were the only item of clothing removed, I didn't have to waste time re-dressing.

When I passed her on my retreat from the bedroom, I asked her to go back to bed. I was trapped by the perpetrator between his own daughter and my brother; yet neither of them could do anything to help me. The best I could hope for was a quick trip by Mother and Mary.

The fear that he would attempt to repeat his attack was worse than fearing the initial attack. Mary had told me that once a female aroused a man's sexual appetite, he would not stop until he was satisfied. I didn't know whether multiple attacks could occur within a short time span, but I had no doubt that I would have to dodge him as long as I lived at home. Later, I wished so many times that I could have lost my virginity to lust or love rather than to evil masked as an older brother figure.

Not yet back in her bed, as I passed the doorway where Marlene was standing, she looked up at me and said, "Love Daddy?"

I ignored the question and asked her again to go back to bed. It was time for her nap to be over, but I had to take care of myself before I could take care of her. I have wondered so many times if she has any memory of that awful event since my own first conscious memory dates from about the same age as she was at that time.

When I got into the living room, I heard Mother's car coming up the driveway. He also heard the car, rushed in from the bathroom, threw a washcloth to me, and said, "Hurry up! Wash up at the kitchen sink and get this washcloth into the dirty clothes pile right away. You have about one minute to get back to the living room before your sister and mother get to the front door. I have to get back in bed. Don't forget—you left something in the bedroom."

At the kitchen sink, I wet the washcloth, pulled up my skirt, and quickly wiped my genital area. I don't remember exactly what I was wearing, but it had to have been a skirt or a dress. I was surprised and concerned when I saw blood on the cloth when I started to rinse it under the faucet. There was also mucous, which I assume was his ejaculate, even though I was in so much pain by his forceful attack that I do not recall being aware of him climaxing. With all that was happening to me and all that was whirling in my mind, what happened to him or didn't happen to him was the farthest thing from my thoughts.

After rinsing the washcloth, I stepped to the bedroom door and tossed it onto the pile of dirty clothes. From that spot, I had only to turn around and take two or three steps to get to the couch and proceed to act out the role of being a perfectly normal thirteen-year-old teenager by the time Mary and Mother came in. I sat back down where I had been reading when he called out to me about wanting the soup. The screen door squeaked when they opened it and stepped inside. Mary looked happy and asked, "How'd everything go?"

I reported that Marlene had awakened a couple of times, but was resting quietly.

"Did Daniel wake up and eat? He really needs some nourishment because he has not been able to eat much since he came down with the mumps."

"I heated the soup like you told me to, but he didn't eat very much."

"Okay. I'll try to get him to eat a little later. Mother and I saw two really cute houses. We'll take you to see them some time."

"I need to check on Marlene," I lied, and went to get my panties.

"Lookin' for these?" he taunted in a whisper as he held them up like a prize, shaking them as someone might shake a set of keys to entertain a baby. I snatched them, stepped into the closet to put them on, and checked Marlene's diaper as I headed back to the living room to the conversation I didn't want to hear.

My thoughts raged with the bitter knowledge that taking me to look at houses some other time would never make up for what had happened that day when I had begged to go along with them. They chose to label me as demanding, self-centered, and materialistic rather than spend the time it would have taken for either or both of them to get the truth out of me.

My insides roared and screamed, but I did not shed a tear or reveal a shred of truth. The trap of un-me-ness had clamped down on my psyche and spirit, and all I could think of was how fast we could get home and how quickly I could climb to the top of the hickory nut tree. There was no way I could change their minds about my outlook and attitude without taking on the burden of telling the truth and facing the consequences of the confrontation. My focus had to be on avoiding him no matter where I encountered him.

By the time my next period was due, we had moved into the new house and school had started. Keeping an exact record of menstrual cycle dates was not a habit of mine, but I began to feel uneasy when it seemed that it was past time for it. There was a girl in my class who also attended our church. She confided in me that she thought she was in trouble when her period didn't start on time. She told her mother. The remedy was to go to the local potion-maker for advice. She was told to drink strong black coffee with lots of black pepper in it to bring the period down. She was relieved when the potion appeared to work.

It was rare for Daddy to ever miss a day of work, but at the same time as I was worrying about my period, he was home with flu. Mother slept with me to minimize her exposure to the virus. I was concerned enough to tell her about the friend's experience and to also say that I thought my period might be a little late.

"Do you think maybe I should do that treatment and see if it will work on me?"

Turning onto her side to face me, she said, "Martha Sue, if you've done something you shouldn't do, you need to let me know. Personally, I can't imagine how a female could lose control enough to let a man have his way with her, but it does happen."

Feeling like she had thrown cold water in my face, I turned over and pretended to go to sleep. Her response sounded as though she needed to know if I had caused a situation that would make me be concerned about my period so that she would know it was time to punish me. In physical education at school, I participated in every activity aggressively, hoping that the exercise would make my period start. It took only a few days for relief to appear.

Mother and I never referred to that incident when we did discuss my history many years later. I've wondered numerous times if she recalled it after she knew what had happened. When we did talk about it decades later, she took her wallet out from her purse and showed me a picture that had been taken the first Christmas after my first marriage. In the picture, I was standing between Daniel and my then-husband. Mother said, "Well, look at this. There you are standing right beside him. Why did you get that close to him?"

"Look at my feet, Mother. You see how the toe of my right shoe is curled up? That was a sign of the tension and anxiety I felt. The persona of the loving sister was the requirement for silence." She put the wallet away, but I think she must have sensed that her remark was deeply hurtful. It represented the generalized view by the culture of the time without even a hint of support or understanding. I think she saw it as a mean thing that he had done, but showed no sign of indignation similar to what I had seen when Mary told her that Margaret's first husband had tried to rape her. Mother became one more of Daniel's victims as she, too, colluded in the code of silence. Her lack of empathy or comfort for me was the in-home microcosm of society at large.

After that brief conversation, we turned on the news and heard about the Jim Jones tragedy. Mother said that she sometimes worried that Daniel might turn into a Jim Jones type of character. Never blind to his faults and never able to be around him without breaking out in red blotches on her face, she also told me about witnessing a scene in Mary's home when she had been there not long before she was at my house. Because of those remarks, I knew that she believed me, but I longed for and needed something more than an objective assessment of his personality.

To be fair, I will say that her lack of emotional honesty was at least in part because of the emotional distance I had consciously put between us. She knew I didn't want her to be gushy sweet toward me, but she had no clue as to what caused that attitude. Not long after the mumps-sitting rape, she and I were walking on the boulevard in DeLand. I gave her a sassy lecture on what I had learned about budgeting in Home Economics. My point was that if she and Daddy made a budget and stuck to it and quit doling out money to the older sisters, we could have a better life. Her response was, "Honey, I feel that you were born with your palm open and all you want is for us to fill it with whatever you want."

That remark stung with the realization of its superficial accuracy. But the depth of true meaning was beyond Mother's ability to see or confront. The best she could do at the time was to give an accusatory judgment with neither interest nor concern as to what was causing my resentment of what we didn't have and my envy of what I thought we could have and deserved.

As soon as I turned fourteen, I went to work at McCrory's Five & Dime. I made thirty-five cents an hour and used almost every penny to put clothes on lay-away. When I turned sixteen, I moved up in pay at Winn-Dixie, where I made fifty cents an hour and where I worked every hour I could until my first marriage at the end of my sophomore year at Stetson. My mental jaw was set on financial independence as part of my future's foundation.

The icy wedge of detached isolation burrowed further and further between Mother and me. My necessary preoccupation was with avoidance of Daniel and survival in all its variations. Hers was the completion of her degree, her church responsibilities, and her mission to do what she could to help/save both Margaret and Mary, but especially Mary.

# CHAPTER 18

# NINTH GRADE DANCE

*True ease in writing comes from art, not chance,*
*As those move easiest who have learn'd to dance.*
*'Tis not enough no harshness gives offense;*
*The sound must seem an echo to the sense*

Alexander Pope.
(1812-1990)

To my delight, the ninth grade dance was a square dance. I had already developed a very narrow view of what styles of music were worthwhile, based on what I was learning and the values I was being exposed to under the leadership of my choral director, Robert L. Auman. It wouldn't be much of a stretch to describe my attitude as a bit of snobbish disdain for the country music I sometimes heard on the radio in our home and the Gospel music I heard at church. In fact, the more distance I put between me and pop culture, the more (false) security I felt. But I could go beyond tolerance and truly enjoy the folk music used for square dancing. Margaret stepped in as my advocate when it was time to get permission to attend the dance.

Although I didn't sense extreme opposition to dancing from either parent, Mary had set the precedent of not going to dances. She consistently adhered to extreme views that could be characterized as fanatic fundamentalism based on ignorance, a closed mind, and a misguided belief that she had been told to be submissive when she survived what she believed was a near death experience when she was 12 years old. Mother told me with pride that Mary had been strong enough to stand up for her beliefs and took a failing grade in physical education because she refused to wear shorts. I thought, *That's stupid. Why would you not want to wear shorts when you're taking PE? I don't see anything wrong with wearing shorts. I'll never take an F for not dressing out.*

Years later, when I was in high school, I was wearing a pair of striped shorts of a modest length. They were cut more like bloomers and had buckles on the side where the band of the leg could be tightened, but they were flouncy around the thigh except for the belted band. Someone knocked on the screen door, and I could see that it was the Sunday School Superintendent from our church. We had moved to town by then, but were still attending church in DeLeon Springs. Knowing that he would want to talk with Mother, I called to her, "Mother—Mr. Wilkes is here."

"Oh, yes, I was expecting him. I'll get the door."

She stepped into the living room from the kitchen and said quietly, "Do you really want him to see you dressed like that?"

With no hesitation, I stepped in front of her, opened the front door, and greeted him. He was cordial and chatted about mundane things as he walked across the small porch and went into the living room. Mother was ready to offer him coffee. There was a part of me that wanted to prove to Mother that wearing shorts was not something I had to be ashamed of or hide. Her super-sensitivity to what others might think or say determined many of her attitudes and opinions.

While still in elementary school, I had noticed that our minister, who was one of Daniel's cousins, preached against wearing shorts and any other preference or habit that might be associated with pleasure or practicality. Typically called *preacher,* he used an extremely loud voice that reminded me of airplane engines revving when they flew over DeLand on bombing practice runs from Jacksonville Naval Air Station during World War II. I disliked loud noises and wondered why he thought he had to yell in such a small room. His beliefs and opinions fed right into Mary's extreme views. In one sermon of multiple *againsts,* he said, "Men, if you can dance with a woman on Saturday night and think about your Sunday School lesson at the same time, you are not much of a man."

Again I thought, *That's stupid. You're not supposed to think about Sunday School when you dance. You're supposed to have fun and get some exercise.*

At eight or nine years of age, I knew the difference between appropriate fun and inappropriate fun, or at least I thought I did. And I certainly had strong opinions as to what would be right for me. Appropriate meant that Mother would allow it; inappropriate meant that she probably wouldn't. As I thought about each *against*, I kept adding to my mental list of social issues that I would allow myself to enjoy when I was old enough to make my own decisions based upon my own opinions and beliefs rather than upon what my environment was attempting to ingrain in me.

Both then and in retrospect, I appreciated the fact that Daddy's family gave me an equally strong and opposite example of social mores. His brothers were all outdoorsmen who enjoyed fishing as much as he did. I noticed that his brothers managed to drink a beer or two at a picnic, and his sisters enjoyed wine with dinner or with their card-playing friends. Yet, somehow, they did not turn a family event into a drunken brawl or reduce full and wholesome participation with children and adults to an out-of-control bash.

In addition to giving me a realistic example of social drinking, their views served the unintended purpose of giving Mother a reason to feel superior. In particular, when referring to the issue of smoking, Mother would pucker her lips into a disdainful droop and say, "I've never allowed any tobacco products in any shape, form, or fashion to touch my lips."

Or, in reference to social drinking, with the same disapproving lip posture, she would say, "I've never even tasted any of that John Barleycorn stuff. You know, when I was just a girl, I even served as president of the state youth group of the Women's' Christian Temperance Union. Your grandfather, Grampa Skilton, wrote and had published a song that served as the anthem for our group. It is called 'Mother's Bow of Ribbon White.'"

She went on to remind me that she wished I could have heard him sing it with his clear tenor voice. Whoever was within earshot would then get the mini-sermon about our bodies being a temple of the Holy Spirit. The only choice was either to passively pretend to absorb the words and messages or to hope she didn't catch me when I turned off my receptors and felt an internal roll of my eyes. There was to be no difference of opinion, questions, or argument.

Slide shows in science class and observing the choral director, Mr. Auman's, negative example of having a chronic cough because of smoking cigarettes served to steer me away from even the temptation to smoke. It just didn't appeal to me. But I knew that I would never be a teetotaler. Nothing about that view made sense to me except when Mother told me that Daddy's father had been a heavy drinker and that one of Daddy's brothers was an alcoholic. Knowing the reasons for his stance against alcoholic drinks made more sense to me than Mother's puffed up piety. Long before I had heard the common statement, *pick your battles,* I intuited that some things were better left unsaid and that every disagreement could not be treated as critically important. I was confident that, in time, I would simply make my own decisions regarding how I would live my life based upon my own beliefs, preferences, and commitments.

Whether intended or not, Mother was forcing me to learn to exercise patience, which she often reminded me I needed to learn. Biding my time came to be a default setting for coping—endure; bide; find a constructive escape; restart—a vicious cycle so charged with negatives and positives that it seemed I might explode.

I never saw or heard Margaret express the same extreme viewpoints as Mary, so I knew she would speak up for me to be allowed to attend the dance. Surprisingly, it didn't take much convincing for Mother to agree to allow me to go. As usual, Daddy went along with Mother's decision. Margaret assured her that she would provide transportation to and from the dance and, if possible, would buy me a new dress for the occasion. I was ecstatic. Margaret always lived on a meager income, yet was so generous to everyone she knew and loved.

With lightness of step and fun as our goal, oldest and youngest daughters went shopping the next day. The stores that carried girls' and women's clothing were Vogue, Betty Dreka's, Virginia Dare for those who Care, Gibbs, and J.C. Penney's. Vogue and Betty Dreka's marketed to upscale income households; Gibbs carried upscale merchandise for both men and women; Virginia Dare marketed to a younger demographic and carried less expensive merchandise than the more upscale shops; and J.C. Penney's was the go-to store for work clothes and school clothes.

A memorable highlight of fun during my junior year was the only time I ever was a model for a fashion show. Keyettes was a strong motivating force for me in high school. It had the highest academic requirements of any service club and included members who were strong leaders in both academic and social areas. For me, it was a high honor to be invited to join the club, and validation that I was not setting my sights too high.

One of the Keyettes' annual fund raisers was a fashion show in which the members served as models. The fashions were provided by Betty Dreka's. The excitement and fairytale elegance of that experience will never leave me. Modelling was not one of my desires or fantasies, as it was for some of my peers. What I cared about was being able to walk into a beautiful store, smell the unique aroma of newness in high quality merchandise mixed with exotic perfumes, and know I belonged there, if only for a short while.

Knowing I would not be able to purchase the outfits I modelled, even at a deep discount, I enjoyed having a sales associate take a personal interest in helping me select several outfits that would set off my red hair and brown eyes. Seeing how the outfits I chose would fit into the rest of the fashion show was a bonus. I remember the dark olive green knit dress with white angora trim that I was wearing when the *DeLand Sun News* photographer snapped our picture. I have no idea who the sales associate was, but she let me experience what it would be like to really shop at a high quality store by myself. Although I had not experienced it at the time, I now can say it was like going to an elegant restaurant and ordering from a menu without printed prices.

Walking past the upscale stores, Margaret and I went straight to Penney's. I was hopeful that we would get to ride the only elevator in town. Penny's had a basement and a second story. Once there, we found the dress right away. It cost $2.98 and was made out of black and white gingham check fabric with tastefully small bright red flowers embroidered around the hems of the skirt and puffed sleeves. The waistline was shirred with elastic that hugged my waist. To me, everything about the dress shouted carefree happiness. We agreed that it would be appropriate and would accommodate my two crinoline petticoats under the full skirt. Crinolines were becoming popular and would reach the peak of their status before I finished high school. Teenaged girls in that day subscribed to the notion that *more is more*. The number of crinolines and the amount of space they required became an unspoken measure of a girl's popularity and fashion with-it-ness. I bought my first couple of crinolines with my own baby-sitting money and could hardly wait to get home and try them on with my new dress for the dance.

When we were back in the car, Margaret said, "Don't let Mom see you with that neckline stretched off your shoulders. Leave it up where the elastic is tight and holds it in place. The round neckline is just right for you. The elastic in the neck is just to go with the elastic in the hem of the sleeves. It isn't really meant for an off-the-shoulders style in such a casual dress. You know our mother would have a hissy if she saw you wearing it off your shoulders."

"I know. I hadn't even thought about wearing it that way. It looks good the way it is." My mind drifted back to the previous year when I asked Mother to make a skating skirt for me. "Did you know that I got in trouble last year when I rolled the waistband of my skating skirt several times so that it would be shorter?"

"Yes. That's why I mentioned that you shouldn't wear your square dance dress off the shoulders."

When we had picked out the fabric for the skating skirt, I showed Mother the length I wanted, but she ignored my request and made it long enough to come to my knees, about three or four inches longer than I wanted. I was so proud of it, but at the same time felt embarrassed that it would make me look like such an old fuddy-duddy. "I wouldn't have rolled the waistband if Mother had made it the length I wanted. I only wanted it to be a few inches above my knees, which was quite a bit longer than most of the others I saw at the rink."

I remember how the silky satin felt against my skin and how flirty the reversible red and ivory colors looked as I crossed one leg ahead of the other and my feet followed the curves that turned the rectangular floor into a grand oval. Mother even made a pair of reversible bloomers to wear under the skating skirt. That made me even more disappointed that the skirt was so long since the bloomers would have kept my panties hidden if I fell and the skirt flew up. I couldn't see the harm in a shorter length for the skating skirt, but the strong undertone was clear: comply or stay home.

"You just have to remember that Mom never got to do things like this because the rink was not even built when she was a girl. It may seem like she is being overprotective or too old-fashioned, but she really does want you to have a good time."

"I know. She really worked hard on the skating outfit even though I know she needs to get glasses. The sewing machine was broken, so she had to sew it all by hand. She also had to pay a lot of money for that fancy fabric." I reminded Margaret that Penney's didn't allow lay-away on fabric, so Mother had to pay for it all at once.

"That's right. The sewing machine broke right after she finished making my wedding gown. The fabric was the same as your skating skirt fabric, just a different color. Mom is a very good seamstress; she just doesn't enjoy it like I do."

We both knew and understood that Mother would rather be with people and teaching at school or church than to be at home cooking or sewing. It was obvious that Margaret enjoyed her work as head cashier at the same grocery store where I would later work, but she also enjoyed sewing and cooking.

"I think you are going to like making your own clothes just like I do. You can have so many more outfits if you make them yourself. They will also be higher quality than what you or I can afford to buy ready-made. By the way, how's your Home Ec class coming along? Let me know if you ever need help with any sewing projects."

Meanwhile, at school, word was getting around as to who planned to attend the ninth grade square dance. With about 170 classmates who would eventually make up the graduating class, it didn't take long for news to spread. I had no social interest in any male classmates then or later because I had a huge crush on someone who was four years older.

There was a boy who rode the school bus that Mother drove from the time I entered eighth grade until the year I graduated high school and she graduated Stetson University, 1959. Since the beginning of the previous school year, she had been acquainted with this fellow redhead who was tall, on the quiet side, and polite. She had even suggested that it might be a good idea for me to get to know him. I had not paid attention to her suggestion, but was pleased when he asked me if I would like to go to the dance with him. I didn't really think of it as a girlfriend/boyfriend invitation. It was simply two ninth grade friends, really just acquaintances, who would share transportation to and from the dance and would be dance partners most of the evening.

The physical education teachers split one grading period equally between a unit on square dance and a unit on ballroom dance. It was a good way to make use of the time when high temperatures, high humidity, and full sun squelched enthusiasm for outside activities. The classes were gender-segregated until the last week of the unit, when the teachers would juggle the schedule so that we could dance with opposite-gender partners like at a real dance. The fact that some may have preferred to dance with someone of the same gender was not ever raised, at least not in the open.

When I told Margaret that a boy who rode Mother's school bus had asked me to go to the dance with him, she was delighted, and said, "I guess that means that you won't need me to take you and pick you up."

I said, "I'll check with him because he didn't mention it when he asked me to go to the dance with him." Two days later, he assured me that his dad would provide the transportation and they would be at my house 15 minutes before the dance was scheduled to begin.

When the day for the dance rolled around at the end of that week, I washed my hair as soon as I got home from school, made sure the new dress was not wrinkled from hanging in the small crowded closet, and took my time primping. Shampooing was a major grooming chore because there was no shower, and the sink that was set at an angle in the corner was very small. Looking back, I don't know how I could have spent so much time primping because I didn't wear makeup yet—just a little lipstick and loose face powder.

The only time-consuming grooming activity for me was playing with my hair. For as long as I could remember, Mother had indoctrinated me with the notion that redheads are special just because of their hair color. I claimed my red hair as something I could latch on to and feel good about because I didn't feel pretty. But I also understood that rightful pride did not require simultaneous feelings of superiority. Mary had shown me how to set my hair with bobby pins to get gentle waves that fell almost to my shoulders, but I had to keep brushing it until it was almost dry before I could set it. Mother often stroked my hair and would say, "Suzie, Dear, your hair is like spun gold. Some day a man is going to love running his fingers through it."

One time when I was setting my hair with a gel, Mary came into my room and noticed what I was using. When she had taught me how to set my hair, we had used water, but styling gel was the trend once I reached junior high school. In a conspiratorial sisterly tone, she whispered, "If you want to know what a man's *come* feels like, just rub that gel between your fingers."

With a dismissive look, I simply said, "Oh." It took some determined pretense to squelch my need and urge to let her know that her husband had already tutored me in that matter. In her attempt to be the knowledgeable older sister, she lacked basic boundaries for what was appropriate or inappropriate to share with me. It put me in a position of having the added burden of worry that I might accidentally reveal the terrible secret that had driven a wall between her sweetness and my chaos.

The ninth grade dance was such a simple event, especially compared with the extravaganzas that are put on in current school settings. With the luxury of a new dress, an invitation to attend with a friend, and easily getting permission to go, it felt like an extravaganza of a party just for me. Having unhurried time in the bathroom and my bedroom to myself were rare strokes of good luck. Even though I wasn't enthusiastic about spending time with the particular boy, I felt like I was getting ready for a very special evening. I could pretend that I was in the middle of a perfectly normal adolescence. My stubbornness helped me to practice ignoring the mind full of questions and confusion, the heart full of pain, and to focus on some of the thoughts I had claimed as points of light within the darkness threatening to suffocate me. I thought to myself, *I will not be bitter. I will not be frigid. I will stay sweet. I will not hate all men.* With those reminders serving as soothing ointment to my anxious nerves, I relished getting ready for my first dance.

About 20 minutes prior to the time I expected the boy to pick me up, the phone rang. When I answered it, his dad introduced himself and asked to speak to my mother. He apologized and explained to Mother that he had just discovered his car had a dead battery, and he wondered if someone from my family could pick up his son and take him with me to the dance. Mother said, "Sure. I'll get her older sister to take them." We had to drive about halfway out to De Leon Springs to pick him up, but Margaret didn't complain. My friend and his dad came out to the car as soon as we pulled up in front of their house. They both thanked my sister for providing transportation.

When we got to the dance, it didn't take long to discover that my dancing skills were far ahead of his. I had just assumed that if a boy wanted to go to a dance, he would be able to dance, especially when I knew that his physical education classes had just completed the square dance unit. I tried to help him and even asked the D.J. caller if he could slow the tempo a little so that it might be easier for some, but he was at the mercy of the recorded music. Technology had not yet figured out how to adjust the tempo of recordings without changing the pitch and distorting the tone quality.

Part of the decorations were outlines of shoes attached to the walls. I happened to be facing the wall on which the footprints pointed to the main exit. My friend apparently deduced that if he couldn't keep up with the tempo and the calls, he shouldn't be at the dance. At some point after leaving our group, he followed the direction of those decorative footprints out of the fieldhouse into the parking lot. I don't think I was rude to him in any way. It was just obvious to the entire set that he was embarrassing and frustrating himself. Since he leaned toward being a quiet introvert anyway, it was not a comfortable situation for him.

My friend left the set after two or three dances, presumably to get some water or use the restroom, and in his absence, I started dancing with someone else. The caller encouraged us to dance with different people to get used to adjusting to a variety of partners. I was having such a good time that I never gave another thought as to where my date was or who he might be dancing with. If I had bothered to wonder about his whereabouts, I probably would have assumed that he had found someone whose skills were at about the same level as his.

After I had been dancing with different partners for most of the rather short evening, the caller announced the final dance. I thought that he would show up then because the teachers had talked to us about etiquette and the expectation that dancers would dance with their date for the first and last dances. When I still didn't see him in the small fieldhouse, I went ahead and partnered in the set where I had been dancing. I looked for him as the crowd began to disperse, but I still couldn't find him.

I waited until almost everyone had left the field house, then walked outside to see if he was waiting out there. It seems so odd now to think about, but he was obviously no longer at the dance location, and I didn't hesitate to go straight to Margaret's car without a worry or concern at all about where he was. The sense of safety was so inherent within the community that the possibility that he may have needed some sort of help did not cross my mind. I told Margaret about the mismatch in dancing skills and enthusiasm, and she said, "I'll bet his dad got a new battery installed or the old one charged and he called his dad to come get him. He should have let you know he was leaving, but you were probably so busy dancing that he couldn't find you standing still long enough to talk to you. Did you have fun?"

"Yes! It was the most fun I've ever had at school." I was really glad that it had worked out for Margaret to provide my transportation. Otherwise, those sisterly moments would have been missed. That night of carefree musical exercise in a social setting was such a respite for me, and the emotional bond that Margaret and I shared topped it off.

It was my good fortune to be able to walk to school and to not face the awkwardness of seeing my would-be date on the bus. I felt certain that seeing my dance companion at school would be at least a little uncomfortable, but seeing him in the confined space of Mother's school bus would have been even worse.

When I saw him at school the following Monday, we both gave an awkward half-wave when we passed each other in the hall. I said, "Did your dad come and get you from the dance?"

He explained that when he discovered that he couldn't keep up with the steps and calls, he decided to call his dad. His dad borrowed a car and came to pick him up.

"Why didn't you let me know that you were leaving?

"I didn't want to interrupt. You were having such a good time. Thanks again for picking me up."

Although Margaret undoubtedly would have gone out of her way to make sure I was ready for the evening and would have stood by to provide transportation, even at the last minute, I feel certain that she had an even deeper level of motivation. Not long after the ninth grade dance, she and I were in the kitchen in the house at 524 N. High St. She and her family lived on the other side of town, but she often stopped by the house to drop off or pick up one or both of her children. I dearly loved all of my nieces and nephew and enjoyed playing with them. Since she had dated Daniel before he started dating Mary, she knew him quite well. After getting a glass of ice water from the refrigerator, she turned to face me directly and called my name. I tossed the damp dish towel over my shoulder as I turned to face her. There was an uncharacteristic note of seriousness in her voice. "I'm going to ask you something, and I want an honest answer. Has Daniel ever tried something *funny* with you? And I don't mean *ha-ha* funny."

I lied. "No. When we go swimming, he likes to squat down in the water so that I can stand on his shoulders and jump or dive into the water. He lets other girls from church do that too."

"I know him very well, and I just want to warn you. Don't be surprised if he does try something *funny*. I've noticed how he looks at you and acts around you. Mary is too weak to notice or say anything, but my eyes are open. And he knows I'm not afraid to open my mouth."

"Okay."

I felt nothing but defeated resignation. Not even my outspoken sister could change the situation. More than any other memory of her life, this one stands out with a surge of gratitude for her caring enough to try to keep me safe. At first, I was stunned—stunned at Margaret's perceptiveness and at her caring enough to try to protect me; stunned at my own dishonesty; and stunned at the lost opportunity to talk about what I was facing. I felt utterly alone and frozen in a voiceless stupor.

Already convinced that Daniel's prediction that nobody would believe me was accurate and that the best I could do was stay away from home as much as possible and to try to keep my head on straight by myself, I settled into the typical syndrome of fear, self-recrimination, anxiety, and hopelessness. All those feelings were coupled with the ongoing stalking from him, the attempts by Mary for us to be close, my own social development, and torrents of pushes and pulls in every direction. At the same time, though, I was directionless and floundering academically as well as emotionally. My silence for over sixty years was the classic and prevailing response to sexual abuse.

Margaret turned to usher her two children to the car, and I turned to finish the dishes. That was the only time I had a perfect opening to talk to anyone about what was going on. But Daniel's brain-washing and threats had been too effective for me to be able to take that leap out of silence. Margaret's warning was too late for the first attack and a timely forewarning of the second one.

Remembering this island of verbalized concern has been comforting as I reflect on the history and use this episode as a strong validation that to at least one person who loved me, it was apparent that I needed help. I have to wonder if she recalled this shared moment when she received the copy of Curtis Winfrey's book and read his accusation against me. One of my deepest regrets is that I never initiated an open conversation with her regarding the entire history, but such openness was not a part of our background or routine. In my misunderstood view of my responsibility to guard Mary from the pain of reality, my commitment to make sure she was not hurt by what was happening to me far over-shadowed what should have been healthy self-concern.

The ninth grade square dance was a moment when I could act my age, engage in a social activity with my classmates, and, if even for a short while, focus on the moment at hand without wrapping my behavior in the trappings of stiff pseudo-maturity that was far more effective at suffocating than nurturing. I wondered what the high school proms would be like. All I knew for certain was that they would not be square dances.

# CHAPTER 19
# TONSILLITIS AND GRAPEFRUIT

*It's an adult myth that childhood is idyllic.*
Malcolm Forbes
(1919-1990)

Soon after entering ninth grade, I started trying to convince Mother and Daddy to move to town. If they had not been worried about finances, my requests that bordered on demands would have been dismissed as inappropriate sass, and I would have been informed that it was not my place to tell them where we should live. Perhaps I sensed that they were uneasy when they found that the old well would not sustain the needs of the new house. Contracting for a new well was out of the question. But the underlying reason for my request was to live farther away from Mary and Daniel. I realized that I had some sound arguments on my side and knew to appeal to Daddy's frugality.

In junior high school, I had already become active in the Glee Club. As I started high school that year, I aspired to join a service club and knew that those two activities alone would require that I stay at school late or arrive early. With only one old car for the household, I knew Daddy would be concerned about the logistics as well as the expense. In my mind, the benefits of living in a new house did not outweigh the need to be closer to the high school and farther away from the person who showed no signs of stopping his torment.

Initially, we had the new house to ourselves, but Mary was already talking to Mother about their financial woes and had started hinting that they needed to move back in with us. I pitched a fit.

"Why can't you or Daddy tell them they have to live in their own house? If you keep letting them move back home, they'll never learn how to manage their money, and Richard and I will never have our own rooms. I don't even know why they're my sisters because they are so different from me. The only thing we have in common is our blood. I don't want to ever be like them! If they were strangers I just happened to meet, I wouldn't even want to know them. I hate this mess!"

While I sobbed too uncontrollably to say anything further, Mother did just as she documented in the diary of her pregnancy with me and the first couple of weeks of my life. At that time, she ignored my cries and let me cry it out, writing that she believed that responding to my cries would spoil me.

"If you can't control yourself, you will have to go to your room until you are ready to come out and talk."

With no other recourse, I went into my room, threw myself across the bed, and sobbed alone until it felt like I had no more tears. Defeat pressed my anger farther into every cell. There was nothing I could do to change the situation. The physical isolation drove the internal isolation even deeper and forged its strength beyond her ability or willingness to dissolve or even soften it. No matter how upset I got, I could not make her understand my point of view and fears, much less tell her the real reason for my attitude.

When I came out of the bedroom, she said, "You mustn't be so critical of your sisters. How would you feel if you had children and no money for food?"

"If I ever have children, I'll have a good job, and enough money for food. I'm going to go to college so that I won't have to mooch like they do. I will never move back home like they keep doing."

"I hope your dreams come true, Darling."

"Don't worry. They will."

Trying to connect, she reached over and stroked my hair as I continued to struggle with more emotional turmoil than I knew how to control or contain. Shifting the focus of the moment, she said, "Are you ready to talk about the possibility of moving to town?"

Jolted because I thought that my pleas had not been heard, I asked, "What do you mean?"

"Do you think you would be happier if we lived in town?"

"Yes; that's what I've been trying to say. I don't see any of my friends from DeLeon Springs at school because they're in different home rooms and classes and I don't really know the kids from DeLand."

I reminded Mother that the home room assignments were made according to the alphabetical listing of our last name, but I had heard that the academic classes were grouped by IQ. That helped me understand why I was having such a hard time in math. "I may be smart enough to learn math, but the kids in the class who went to elementary school in DeLand already know so much more than I do. I hate math because I feel so dumb in that class. Maybe if I could stay after school for extra help I could do better in math."

Mother already knew that my biggest dream was to take piano lessons at Stetson. I had noticed that acquaintances who took lessons at Stetson were asked to play accompaniments in Glee Club much more frequently than I. She explained that she and Daddy could not afford to send me to Stetson for piano lessons yet, but that she had looked into another teacher for me—the same teacher who had taught her when she was a young girl. I was thrilled to finally have my first official piano lessons my freshman year in high school. Until that time, Mother had been my only teacher.

Ever the benign dreamer and schemer, Mother had investigated the possibility of completing her degree so that she could return to teaching. She told me about her hopes and explained that she planned for the four of us—she, Daddy, Richard, and me—to discuss the idea that night after supper. She needed emotional support from Richard and me, and she needed Daddy's approval of the financial arrangements. He listened patiently, then said, "How do you think we can afford this? I've heard that Stetson is pretty expensive."

"It is if you live on campus, but it wouldn't be too bad for me, and I've already figured out what I can do to earn the money to pay for the courses."

Without missing a beat, she went on to say that she had talked with someone at the school district's transportation department and found out that they needed bus drivers. The income would be just enough to pay for the classes at Stetson, and the schedule was flexible enough to give her time to drive the route, park the bus at the edge of campus, take her classes, and be ready for the afternoon route.

Daddy agreed, pointing out that we would have to sell the new house before we could buy one in town. It wasn't long before we knew that Mother had located a couple who had a place about a mile from the high school and less than three miles from the service station and who wanted to move to the country. The most unusual thing was that they were willing to do an exact swap of properties. They certainly got the better end of the real estate deal, but we got what we wanted too.

After living in the new house just a few months, we were moving to a very small house (less than 900 square feet) that had been built in 1928. The house was modest, but reasonably nice, and the lot was large enough to have at least half a dozen citrus trees, a grape arbor, and a detached garage. For me, the proximity to the high school was its best feature. It seemed ideal. A bonus was the sheer white Pricilla curtains left in what became my bedroom—a wish come true. They were even prettier and frillier than the ones I had seen in Aunt Jessamine's apartment in Miami.

It wasn't long, though, before Mary talked Mother into letting them move in with us. The rationalization was that Mary could be in charge of the household chores while Mother took care of her studies and drove the school bus. Their second daughter was due that January, and their third daughter would be born less than two years later. Daniel had some rather menial job, one of quite a few he had before God miraculously told him he should never dirty his hands with work again. It struck me as funny that he had a direct link to God telling him what he wanted to hear, but apparently God never told him to be kind, to respect others, to be a faithful help mate for his wife, or to leave his youngest sister-in-law alone. One rape down, one to go, and *lesser* assaults as he continued to paint a target on my body and soul.

In addition to the financial issues that prompted Mary's request, with hindsight, I wonder if she also may have been trying to keep her own mind and self together. She easily could have hoped that being around other family members, particularly Mother and Daddy, would force Daniel to adjust his disposition. Mother was obviously aware of his personality unpleasantness and labeled the symptoms as the short man syndrome. So far as I know, there is no such official diagnosis, but the wisdom of the ages correlated certain personality traits with a man's short stature. In this instance, the wisdom of the ages prevailed.

Once again, my bedroom became theirs. I slept on a pallet beside the bed with their first daughter beside me. When the second daughter was born in January of the next semester, she slept in the bed with her parents. Mother worried that one of them might accidentally suffocate the new baby. Richard slept on the sleeping porch, and Mother and Daddy had the larger of the two bedrooms.

With my sister and their newborn daughter lying in my bed and their older daughter sharing my pallet, the sound of the toilet flushing would often awaken me. Through eyelids almost shut, I could see his silhouette tip-toe from the bathroom and stand still at the foot of the pallet, staring at me before he made his way back to the bed. Light streaming in from the street lights was just enough for me to see the lopsided smirk on his face. Burrowing further under the covers did nothing to remove the image from my mind. Turning onto my stomach and putting my arm over his daughter to shield her from his gaze gave a momentary shift of focus from needing protection myself to providing what little protection I could for her. But I longed for restful nights and sweet dreams; for the freedom of choice to sleep under the covers or not. I longed for peace and security. He was talented and well-practiced in the fine arts of intimidation, verbal abuse, and taking whatever he wanted by any means necessary. If the same degree of determination had been put to honorable pursuits, perhaps he could have achieved something worthwhile.

After their second daughter's birth that mid-January, they stayed at our house until Mary's six-week postpartum checkup, then found a rental place. Not long after they had moved out, Mother gave me permission to stay home on a Monday because I was exhausted and had tonsillitis. Even though my throat was sore, I could have gone to school if I had been rested.

Mother usually was pretty understanding when I was too exhausted to get out of bed and get ready to go to school. Or perhaps she was so exhausted herself that she simply chose not to take on the battle of getting me up in time to get to school. She would typically tell me to gargle with hot salty water if my throat was sore. If I ran a fever, she would splurge on a bottle of ginger ale. But she never asked about what was bothering me, why my attitude toward Mary and Daniel continued to worsen, or why I stayed away from our home as much as possible. Chalking up everything to my adolescence, it was easier to address my faults with her *shoulds* than to face conflict openly. When she saw that moving to town did not restore my happiness, she blamed it on my selfishness and pre-occupation with acquiring pretty clothes. But I was working at McCrory's Five and Dime as many hours as possible in addition to babysitting for several couples, earning money to support my lay-away purchases rather than expecting them to be provided by my parents.

When I looked back over my report cards many years ago, I saw that I averaged missing school about one day per week. The absenteeism, emotional strain, and exhaustion finally compromised my academic standing my senior year.

I think Mother may have felt a little guilty about insisting that I spend so much time and energy at church in rehearsals and services. Our unspoken agreement seemed to be that she would let me stay home when I felt bad if I would participate in the music program at church. I knew intuitively that the agreement also applied to school music activities. In effect, I could *earn* the chance to participate in school music activities as long as I also participated in the music program at church. That was a strong point of resentment for me because I felt that adults should be in charge of the church music program and that students should be allowed to participate in the school music program with no church-strings attached.

Much of the time, I felt exhausted. The constant internal battle between acting mature and yearning for normalcy within the family sapped my energy. Even though we no longer lived on Mockingbird Hill, the panther's cries within me still shouted silently: *I want my childhood! I want my adolescence! I want to be a normal teenager without having to dodge, run, or hide from my own brother-in-law! I want him to leave me alone! And I want someone to hear me and understand.* But silent cries are seldom heard.

Not long after they moved out of our house to a rental place, Daniel stopped by the service station to ask Daddy if he could pick some grapefruit from our tree. I was able to reconstruct the unfolding of that afternoon's events when I overheard the confrontation that took place between Daddy and Daniel a little later that afternoon. When asked about the grapefruit, Daddy said, "Sure. Get whatever you need, but you should wait a while so that Alice will be home when you go over to the house. Sue is home from school, sick with tonsillitis. It wouldn't look right to the neighbors if you went over there when she's home alone."

"Ok. Meemaw gets home about 5:00, right?"

"Yes."

With that understanding and agreement, he pulled out of the station on to Woodland Boulevard. Daddy noticed that he made an immediate left turn toward our house rather than turning right toward his house. Not being able to dismiss his nagging concern, Daddy called to his boss and said, "Lou, I've got to run home for a little while; I'll be back as soon as I can."

"Sure. Go ahead."

Daddy, too, pulled out on to the Boulevard, made the same left turn, and headed home. His temperament was unusually even, but on the rare occasions when he did become angry, he expressed himself in no uncertain terms and quickly got over the anger. He was furious that afternoon.

Defying Daddy's instructions, Daniel went straight to our house and did not even stop to pick any grapefruit before he entered the back door, routinely left unlocked. As I lay in bed more asleep than awake, I heard the back porch door open and close. I had not heard the car pull up along the side-street and park in the edge of the yard near the kitchen window. As soon as he was inside the house, he called out to me with a malicious, sing-songy taunt. "Oh, Sue, you have a visitor." I froze, pretending to be sound asleep. "You might as well answer me. I know you're here."

When he entered the kitchen, he called out again, speaking as though we had planned a consensual clandestine tryst.

"I know you're not asleep this time of day. We're finally alone again."

I scrambled out of bed and went to the bathroom, thinking I could lock myself in that tiny room and wait until I heard Mother come in the front door. He must have anticipated that action and changed his direction. Rather than coming to the living room to enter my bedroom, he chose a sneakier route through my parents' bedroom and entered the Jack-and Jill bathroom from that side. It was perfect planning on his part because we both entered the bathroom from opposite directions at the same time. My hands were on the doorknob, fumbling to make the lock work. He grabbed my shoulders and turned me around in one fast motion.

With his right hand on my upper chest, his left hand was free to twist the door knob and, with singleness of purpose, push me the few feet toward the bed. He moved his hand from my chest to my other shoulder as he pushed so hard that I fell onto the bed. Lying at an angle across the mattress with my feet dangling off the edge over the space where the pallet had lain not long ago, it felt like I had been tossed onto the garbage heap. I recall how foolish I felt to be regretting my preference of night gowns to pajamas, thinking pajamas would have given me some slight protection. I thought I heard the sound of Mother's school bus near the house just as he mounted me and demanded, "Now move! Don't just *lay* there!"

The only movement I wanted to make was to throw him off of me and to run beyond his reach. I prayed that Mother would come in and catch him. But the panther within me was voiceless, paralyzed with fear, pain, and shock.

The tires of the school bus crunched gravel as Mother drove onto the strip of ground between the edge of our front yard and the edge of the street. If she had come straight into the house, she would have interrupted him. Maintaining her routine, though, she stayed in the bus long enough to log whatever data she was required to document each day in her driving journal. Daniel was so brazen that he wouldn't interrupt himself despite the fact that he had to know she was parking the bus. The Venetian blinds were closed, but not completely, and the curtains were held open with tie-backs. He could have glanced up and seen the bus and watched for her to head up the sidewalk to the front door. Proximity to the danger of getting caught seemed to heighten his pleasure and sense of accomplishment.

Daddy knew that Daniel would beat Mother home if he went straight to the house from the station. He was absolutely correct—correct in his lack of trust of Daniel and correct in his fatherly instinct that someone needed to be there for me, if only to guard my reputation from curious neighbors. While the *Reverend Rapist* pumped his hips, Mother filled out the bus report. I tolerated and endured with eyes squeezed shut and fists of fury held down by arms much stronger than mine—too numb to feel anything physical; too traumatized to have a voice; too much in shock even to worry about being exposed to another possibility of an unwanted pregnancy. Too completely robbed of authenticity of self to do anything except survive.

After an excruciating few minutes, I heard Daddy's car drive up into the back driveway. That instant of hope re-voiced my spirit. Finally able to speak, I said, "You're finally going to be caught this time, and I'm so glad."

He said, "You'll see. I'll never be caught, and if you're ever stupid enough to say anything, nobody will believe you. People, especially men, can tell by the way you walk now that you've been 'had.' No decent man will want anyone (who's) not a virgin. If you know what's good for you, you'll stick with me. Remember, if you say anything, I'll make you sorry you ever thought of sayin' a word to anyone about me. You know you like this just as much as I do." He went on to remind me that everybody knew he would never look at anyone else besides Mary unless someone flaunted herself at him.

"You'll thank me one day for breakin' you in right."

His sick, sickening venom molested my mind even more severely than his stocky body molested my body. His unholy spirit came close to making me renounce all church association and affiliation. After gyrating off of me and away from the bed while trying to get his pants up and zipped, he said, "Hurry up! Get yourself cleaned up and back under the covers."

He sounded as though he were speaking to the most vile, dirty, ugly creature he could imagine. He spat out his words in utter contempt as though I were at fault, forcing him to put up with my lack of appreciation for his efforts. His premeditated mission was accomplished without even a whiff of the acidic scent of a grapefruit.

I still had tonsillitis. He had no grapefruit.

He made it to the sleeping porch before Daddy confronted him. "Why in the world did you come over here right away when I told you to wait until Alice would be home? She's out front right now, but you just came out of the house. Don't you know how it looks to the neighbors for you to be here in the house when Sue is home alone?"

Improvising an excuse, Daniel said, "Oh, it's okay. I just went inside to get a sack to put the grapefruit in. Sue's feelin' better now."

I was still in the bathroom trying to make myself feel clean as the all-encompassing trap of resignation tightened. There was no acceptable escape. I was in a daze as I overheard Daddy's confrontation with his son-in-law. With the back bedroom windows open and the bathroom door slightly ajar, the air carried the sound straight to my ears—one of the few times I ever heard Daddy raise his voice to anyone.

I believe my parents would not have allowed Mary and Daniel and their children to live with us again if they had known the truth. If only I could have let them know. There would still be times, though, when Mary and he and the children would occupy part of our home. My days and years of dodging, running, and searching for escapes were far from over.

The attack that day was the second time he manipulated circumstances to fulfill his criminal intention. Those two events, though, were just that—horribly demeaning attacks I wished a million times to forget, but they were acute points in time that caused less emotional and psychological trauma and turmoil than the chronic infusion of vitriolic verbiage he used against me.

Since one of my goals that began to tug at my mind as early as age five was to get an education, I especially resented his undermining my seeking financial help for college from my parents. I was aware that Mother probably would have a full-time teaching job by the time I finished high school, making it possible for them to pitch in toward college expenses. When he overheard me mentioning my hopes to Daddy, Daniel said, "Sue's never goin' to amount to *nothin'*. All she wants to do is go to college and have a good time with the boys so she can get herself a husband and have babies. Any money you give her will be a waste. You ought to be savin' for Richard."

Daddy's raised hackles were accurate. He saw through Daniel's malicious words and never failed to let me know how proud he was of my academic pursuits and success. When I would stop by the service station to get a ride home after rehearsals at school, he invariably introduced me to customers by saying, "This is my daughter, Sue. She's going to go to college."

Later, after I had become a student at Stetson University, he would say to customers, "This is my daughter, Sue. She's a student in the School of Music at Stetson."

Daddy's pride in my educational status beamed from his bright blue eyes, speaking before he could get the words out.

While I was still in high school, Oscar Olson, one of Daddy's regular customers at the station, reminded me of what he had told me when I was in the sixth grade: "Just keep going to school." I would guess that he probably had an undergraduate degree since he was in a managerial position with Florida Power & Light, but I doubt if he had a graduate degree. Yet, he encouraged my ambition, and when we happened to be at the service station at the same time, he always smiled with kind eyes and nudged my goal a little closer to possibility in my mind.

Negative seeds of false guilt, doubt, fear, and shame vied for mental and emotional space in my mind every time I was around Daniel. He continued to make attempts at physical connections with me, even if a full-body mount was out of the question. For instance, when the house was overflowing with both Mary's and Margaret's families for a get-together, as the adults headed from the living room toward the dining room for supper, and the children came in from outside through the back door, he used the guise of waiting gentlemanly for me to pass before he followed me to the dining room. When I started to pass him, he motioned for me to step aside. I took another step. He grabbed my arm and pulled me toward him as he stood in the doorway to my bedroom. It looked and felt like he was declaring that he possessed or owned that physical space and, by inference, that he owned me.

With urgency, he hissed into my ear, "Get your stinkin' panties off while you have a chance to right now. When we come back in here after supper, sit across from me and keep your legs spread apart. Nobody else will pay any attention, but I'll get a good look. If you know what's good for you, you'll do what I tell you."

I was terrified of what he might do or say if I crossed him. I initially obeyed him, went through the bathroom, and removed my underwear. With every minute, though, I felt more and more unwilling to cooperate. After eating just a few bites, I left the table to be with the children on the back porch. In the joy of their innocence, I found solace and temporary safety. On that occasion, though, I had to remember to keep my skirt under control so that the ugly secret would not be revealed. When the children begged me to lie down and flip them over my head as they balanced on my feet, I worked up the courage to return to my bedroom and put on clean panties.

When the adults gathered in the living room after the meal, I sat at an angle where he had no chance to be a voyeur and where I had the best chance to avoid eye contact with him. That hint of a display of grit triggered a demeaning tongue-lashing at his first opportunity, but it also gave me enough capital in Self to think that maybe the worst of his pernicious prey on me was over. That fleeting hope was soon gone when the reality of the sense of shame marbled with fear once more took over my ego. Hemmed in between a dead-end wall of his narcissistic power and my gelatinous ego, the trap door thrust its dead bolt into the spinning darkness of my soul.

All through high school and until my sophomore year of college, I was on call to babysit, especially when Mary suffered miscarriages. On one such occasion, Mother went to the office of the Dean of the School of Music at Stetson and asked him to have me leave my class and come home to take care of my nieces because Mary had had a miscarriage.

I felt mortified because Mother had crossed a line that, to me, marked me as a townie who was not quite a real student. Classmates who were from other towns would never have been called home for such a relatively minor family emergency. I feared that Mary's emotional and physical weakness would put me in a position for a third attack. I told all of the adults that I could only stay with the nieces for an hour or two and had to get back to my classes, rehearsals, and practice hours.

Mother tried to solve the problem by letting the nieces spend a couple of nights with her and Daddy. She compromised by leaving me with the nieces while she drove the bus route, then took me back to campus. When she asked if I could go to Daytona to the larger Sears store the next day (Saturday), I agreed to go with her to help with the three nieces.

When we parked in the Sears parking lot and started to get out of the car, one of the nieces started crying. Neither Mother nor I had any idea what had prompted the crying. I put my arm around my niece's shoulders and assured her that we were going into Sears and would have a good time. "I know. I want to go, but I can't, and I'm scared to stay in the car by myself."

"You don't have to stay in the car."

She explained that the top she was wearing was sleeveless and that if her dad (Daniel) found out that she went out in public in a sleeveless top, he would whip her when they got home. My heart broke for her— just an innocent little girl in the first or second grade already caught up in the fear of her father's behavior with his twisted views. Mother and I promised her that we would not let him or anyone know what she wore on our shopping trip to Sears and swore her sisters to secrecy.

When we got inside the store, Mother splurged on some chocolate covered peanuts at the concession counter. The treat helped to quiet my niece's immediate concerns.

# CHAPTER 20

# DADDY'S DEATH

—◦⌒⌒◦◦—

*Remember me when I am gone away,*
*Gone far away into the silent land.*
Christina Georgina Rossetti
(1830-1894)

Once I completed the Master of Music degree, I began to believe that my dream of becoming a professor was more than a mere pipe dream. Ever since Oscar Olsen had told me that getting a doctorate was mostly a matter of perseverance, I entertained the dream that grew from wishful fantasy to firm commitment. But Daniel's invectives against my abilities and worth, the strain of a tight budget, and the emotional burden following sexual abuse encouraged normal self-doubt. It escalated into an underlying assumption that it would take some luck along the way for me to earn a doctorate. The realization that what passed as luck often came, in reality, by way of friends and mentors slowly became real to me. Those friends typically knew much more about friendship than I knew. Mentors gave me a chance to respond to their outstanding pedagogy and exemplary role model. They never made me feel as though they were not betting on my success.

Buried even deeper than my ambition and aspirations were the internal messages that I was not able to squelch for a very long time. I truly believed that if my professors realized how poor my preparation for academic success was, they would not want to teach me. They were going out of their way to help me make up the gaps in my music background, but I felt undeserving of their care. How could I deserve such outstanding friends and mentors when I was such an emotional wreck? How could I ever overcome the inadequate background and the emotional stew that nearly consumed me with a constant simmer threatening to scorch or boil over? The friendships and mentoring offered by those whom I respected the most served as the balancing force that enabled me to focus on what I had to do in order to be successful academically and musically. That focus was exactly what I needed in order to get through the emotional turmoil in order to complete my academic training.

While a senior in high school, I knew that I wanted to graduate from Stetson University, but I also knew that I wanted to get away from home for the first two years of college. With virtually no guidance from anyone, I stumbled into a small Baptist college in Tennessee after a member of the church told Mother that it was a good school for "good Christian girls." I knew enough to make sure the college was accredited, but I did not know to research the standing of the department of music. As it turned out, it was not accredited by the National Association of Schools of Music, but was attempting to meet standards to receive that designation.

I was torn between majoring in music, home economics, or physical education. As I made my way through the freshmen registration line, when asked about what I expected to major in, I gave the three possibilities as my answer. The person helping me sent me over to the chairman of the music department with instruction to tell him I was thinking about becoming a music major.

The person who then talked with me was an excellent professor of music theory and also a skillful recruiter. I declared music as my major. In those days, the academic calendar was much different from today's. I spent Thanksgiving on campus and went with the Florida club to visit Gatlinburg. I took the Greyhound bus home for the Christmas break and worked as many hours as possible at Winn-Dixie. "Prof" Giffin from Stetson came through my lane and talked with me. I knew him because he had visited the choral room at DeLand High School and I had seen him conduct choral concerts in Stetson's Elizabeth Hall. He said, "How's everything going up in Tennessee?"

"It's going very well. I've had lots of dates. I've seen fall leaves and snow, and I got to go to Gatlinburg the week of Thanksgiving."

"That's all well and good, but I mean how are you doing academically? What music theory text are you using?"

"McHose—the Eastman text."

"That's good. We use that too. What chapter are you on?"

"Chapter five, I think."

"Our students are several chapters ahead of you."

"What about your music history text?"

"Oh, we don't have music history."

With a nod and raised eyebrows, "Prof" said, "If you ever expect to graduate from Stetson, you go up there, take your semester exams, and get yourself home as soon as you can so that you can start the second semester at Stetson."

"I'll think about it. I know you get a lot more outstanding visiting artists than we do."

With those words of wisdom and encouragement, I did exactly what he told me to do. I went back just long enough to take the exams and came home on the train. I was afraid that the large trunk I had taken when I went up to Tennessee on the train would not fit on the bus.

It was an academic and musical struggle for me once I was enrolled at Stetson. On top of those two issues, Mary and Daniel once again moved back into our house. Mother and Daddy had sold the place at 524 North High Street and were renting a house right down the street from it. I spent as much time as possible on campus. My avoidance skills were well-honed by then, but I still had to be on guard if I was ever home at the same time as Daniel, and often walked to Daddy's station to ride home with him. There was still only one car for the family, and it was too far to walk from campus to the house.

Carrying the burden of sexual abuse affected every aspect of my life, particularly my academic pursuits, my marital history, and my attempts to have children. Although the marital history and attempts to have children are beyond the scope of this book, a brief chronology is necessary in order to put major life events into the context of the struggles with sexual abuse.

At the end of my sophomore year at Stetson, I married Dan W. Crum, whom I had known for a couple of years when he attended our church while he was finishing his studies at Stetson. We married in June, 1961, and I was out of school for two years. After his discharge from the Army, we returned to DeLand so that I could finish my degree and he could take some additional courses in the School of Business.

I graduated from Stetson in 1966 and filed for divorce in late 1967. During the last two years of the marriage, I suffered two miscarriages and lost premature identical twin girls (July, 1967).

I returned to Stetson to take education courses and also to take additional organ lessons. Not certain whether I would end up having to support myself immediately or if I would go to graduate school, I had to prepare for either option.

In the late spring or early summer of 1968, I loaded my small car and drove to Boston to begin the Master of Music degree at Boston University. About two weeks after arriving and starting summer school, I literally ran into someone in a practice room and struck up a conversation with him. Two weeks later, Allyn Hoverland and I married and had a fantastic honeymoon in New England and Canada. He was an organist and had been hired to teach at Limestone College in Gaffney, South Carolina. I left my graduate school dreams in Boston and began hoping for another pregnancy. To his credit, Allyn would not agree to my staying home hoping for a pregnancy and insisted that I apply for a teaching job, even though I was not certified to teach in South Carolina. Because of Title I funds being available, I was hired to teach in Gaffney and taught in two schools for the two years I lived there. I received full salary (about $5,500 per year) and credit for student teaching at the same time.

After spending two years together, we realized that we had made a mistake, and agreed to divorce, but remained friends.

I then entered Winthrop University (then Winthrop College) in Rock Hill, South Carolina, to attend graduate school. I completed the Master of Music degree in two summers and one full academic year. After receiving the master's degree in August of 1971, I stayed in Rock Hill, SC, and opened a new school with a generous budget to equip my music room in an ideal way. My career and sense of self-worth blossomed. After teaching three years in Rock Hill, I sought a position in higher education and was hired to teach at Simpson College in Indianola, Iowa. By then, I had been divorced for four years and was enjoying a healthy late-term adolescence.

While teaching at Simpson, I met the chairman of the Department of Religion, Fred Holder. We became friends and married in May, 1976, about a month before Daddy's death. We moved to Houston in 1980 after having lost our stillborn son in June, 1979.

At that time, I did not want to be around pregnant women or small children. I also wanted to explore what options there were for me in the business world. For the first year in Houston, I sold life insurance annuities to teachers. Fred became a stock broker the second year we were in Houston and told me that he was required to have a life insurance license in addition to his broker's license. My response was to say that since I already had the insurance license, perhaps I could also become a stock broker and we could work together.

Soon, I too, had the required license to be a registered representative with Dean Witter, Reynolds. By the end of two years in that capacity, I was ready to re-enter the classroom, and taught elementary music in Fort Bend County until 1991 when I went to Frostburg, Maryland to teach music education and voice at Frostburg State University.

Fred and I divorced in 1989, and I started dating Christopher A. Colvert. We had been dating about two years when I moved to Frostburg. When it became clear that I needed to come back to Houston to complete the doctorate at the University of Houston, Chris and I married in July, 1993. He died suddenly in June, 2008.

I mention this history to make the reader aware of how long and how far the effects of sexual abuse affect the survivor. My first marriage was an attempt to find an acceptable way out of an unsafe home. I feared that I was not safe even in a different town in Florida. There was no hiding and no dependable escape from Daniel's continued attempts to ensnare me.

My second marriage was a desperate attempt by both parties to find some emotional warmth and support when we both needed it. We were kindred spirits within the world of organ study. We both loved to travel. But we did not have the fundamental strength of mutual interests beyond music and travel to support a marriage. Most fundamentally, he did not share my desire and need for children. But he treated me well and opened up the world of foreign travel to me.

Although Fred was twelve years older than I, we were temperamentally well-suited to each other. We had a deep understanding of each other's backgrounds and personal journeys. He had a welcoming family for me, and he had two children who were also welcoming, at least in the beginning. In retrospect, I consider this as the first "real" marriage. We were married for eleven years before I filed for divorce. It was a painful breakup for both of us.

Chris and I were married for fifteen years and together for four years prior to the marriage. He gave me fun and brought out my sense of humor. He related to my family, and they welcomed him. His family gave me an extended family filled with good times and two children who gave me joy. They, in turn, gave me grandchildren whom I adore. I held them when they were minutes old. I doubt if any of them will ever fully know or understand how important they have been to me.

From each marriage, I grew in self-understanding and in relationship-building. I learned to accept the good that each attempt at marriage had given me and to put aside the pain that each breakup produced. With each year and decade, I grew away from the chains that had bound my spirit and squelched my freedom to be myself. But the cycle of regrowth into understanding, forgiveness, and bright outlook was not complete until I entered therapy and began writing.

Prior to re-entering Stetson after marrying at the end of the sophomore year, I had not personally known anyone who had a doctorate in Music or in Music Education. The new Dean, Paul Langston, had just completed his doctorate. He had even spent time in Paris studying with Nadia Boulanger, a famous teacher of composition. In addition to sparking immediate admiration, his outstanding credentials intimidated me. I thought that I neither could nor would ever measure up to his talent and intellectual prowess. Ironically, it was he, along with organ professor, Paul Jenkins, who in time, made me believe that I had far more potential than I had tapped as an underclassman. Eventually, after dropping out of school for a couple of years and returning to Stetson, my confidence began to grow, and my academic progress began to catch up with itself.

After establishing my teaching career in South Carolina and remaining there after completing the master's degree, I was highly motivated and eager to extend my learning and experience. One of the criteria regarding any professional development was how the activity would appear when listed on my resume. It was the early seventies. Gloria Steinem had been a featured speaker on campus. Sensitivity training groups were emerging in likely and unlikely places. It felt like the prevailing popular culture and I were in sync as we struggled to grow into what we were to become.

By the mid-seventies, I began to notice that Daddy looked thinner and seemed to have less energy every time I visited the family. When they first moved to Missouri in the mid-sixties, he reverted to his farming roots and showed great pride in fixing up the small house that sat on the first property they bought—125 acres located on what Mother named the Goat Trail. It was not uncommon for sharp rocks in the road to declare war on tires that dared to creep along the roadbed. Driving on the Goat Trail required time and patience because even if the rocks failed in their attempt to puncture a tire, if the driver had a heavy foot on the accelerator, they would fly up like a foul ball and pit the windshield or paint. Mother continued teaching until she reached the compulsory retirement age, seventy, never flinching at scraping the car's windshield in the winter or braving the adventuresome Goat Trail.

After living on the Goat Trail for several years, Mother and Daddy sold the remote acreage and bought a place with five acres—still rural and modest in size, but not so remote. The house was much nicer, and the five acres were just right for what Daddy wanted and was able to do. He developed an interest in growing angel wing begonias—the first and only time I knew him to spend time on a non-essential, impractical hobby. He also befriended several stray cats that discovered his tender heart.

On one of my first visits to the smaller acreage home, Daddy asked if I would like to see how he turned a bull into a steer. Of course, I was eager to follow him to the feed troughs where the few head of cattle had gathered. He made sure they had plenty to eat, then said, "You need to look at their private parts. One of the neighbors taught me how to do this. See that rubber band around the scrotum? That cuts off circulation to the testicles, and they will shrivel up and drop off—sort of like the umbilical cord on a newborn baby."

"How do you make the calves stand still while you do that?"

"If they're hungry enough, they'll keep eating while I do what I have to do. It only takes a few seconds."

He reminded me of the time when Richard was raising two calves for a 4-H project out on Mockingbird Hill. One of them got sick and died. Daddy wouldn't risk using it as meat, so Rich and I helped him dig a hole for burial. A few months later, Richard became discouraged with the project and agreed that it was time to butcher the surviving heifer. Mother had fallen for a traveling salesman's pitch to buy a deep freeze along with a food plan—the Lucky Lady Food Plan. The sales hook was that savings on the groceries would pay for the freezer.

Once Margaret and Mary had moved out of our home, whenever they visited us, they frequently asked if they could take something out of the freezer to have for their dinner. Neither Mother nor Daddy would deny the request. As a result, Daddy was paying for the freezer, the food plan, and still having to supplement our own supply of groceries. Once Li'l Abner died, Daisy Mae didn't stand a chance to avoid the freezer.

Since Daddy's formal education ended after he completed eighth grade, I don't know how he knew so much anatomical vocabulary. Perhaps Aunt Marian had shared some of her nursing school texts with him. I watched as he butchered Daisy Mae and listened while he identified each of the body systems and names of the organs. What intrigued me the most were the lungs. They were a beautiful shade of pink—not one of my favorite colors—but I marveled that something so important that was not normally seen could be so pretty. I picked up a stick or perhaps a tool and started trying to flatten the air sacs almost as if they were pink bubble wrap. That did not set well with Daddy. "Don't try to mutilate the lungs. Just enjoy seeing them and the other body parts. Once I finish dressing the carcass, I'll be ready to cut the beef into roasts, steaks, etc. and wrap the pieces for the freezer. Go tell your mother that we are almost ready for the freezer paper and tape. Get a pen too."

On smaller projects, such as skinning squirrels or rabbits or scaling and dressing fish, he would let me help more. But he knew that he needed to work fast so that the meat would not spoil. He also didn't want me to use a knife that was as sharp as the one he was using. I went in and told Mother about needing the freezer paper, tape, and pen. She stayed outside with us and went to work on our improvised assembly line. Daddy cut; I wrapped and taped; and Mother labeled. Richard helped me do some of the wrapping, but he wasn't as involved in the process as I was. He probably was battling a combination of sadness that one of his cows had died and feeling that he had failed in his project. The freezer got filled and so did we when we enjoyed the short-term abundance of beef.

The only nonessential expense that Daddy allowed himself was an inexpensive pipe and Prince Albert tobacco. When he worked as a butcher in Hialeah, he occasionally would receive a prank call from older children or teenagers. He said, "They act like they're the first ones to ever ask, 'Do you have Prince Albert in a can.'"

He went on to say that he would let them know that he did. The predictable response from the caller would be, "You'd better let him out. He can't breathe in there!" Laughter would erupt on the end of the line, and Daddy would simply hang up. He would go along with the prank the first time or two, but then would recognize the voice and hang up without answering the question.

Since he worked at a service station most of his life, he didn't smoke on the job. And he didn't smoke very much at home. I feel certain that budget restraints accounted for at least some of the limitation. Tobacco was budgeted with a watchful eye on the extra change, or the lack of it, in his pocket. He also knew from long experience that Mother strongly disapproved of the pipe and resented its presence in our home. I expect that the pleasure of his pipe was a considerable part of his love of fishing.

I only went fishing with Daddy a few times. The time that is most vivid in my mind is when he took Mother, Richard, and me out to Lake George. He must have rented the boat we used. Mother always said that she didn't like to fish, but she enjoyed being out on the water. I lost interest after I didn't catch any fish. Daddy and Richard were dropping their lines and fishing, but not catching many fish. The wind picked up and Daddy tapped his pipe on the side of the boat. Ashes blew back and got into my eyes. I told him that he should stop smoking so that it wouldn't happen again. He absorbed my adolescent lecture with patience and pointed the boat toward the bank. Rain joined the wind, and the temperature dropped enough to make me start shivering.

We sheltered in swampy water with branches of trees overhead taking the brunt of the rain. I asked what we would do if lightning started. He told us there was nothing we could do except be patient and wait for the sky to clear. We were better off near the shore than out on the shallow lake with the wind whipping up white caps. Despite my love for the water, I never had an urge to go out in a boat to fish after that.

When Richard and I were little, we would vie for the chance to blow out the match after Daddy lit his pipe. After one of us blew out the flame, he would give the match stick three strong shakes to make sure it was not going to re-ignite; then, he would carefully open the match box and place the burned end opposite the unused match tips. He explained that he didn't want to take a chance that the warmth of the recently lit match might be enough to set the entire box on fire. Throwing the used match stick on the ground or in a lake or river would never have occurred to him.

In addition to his pipe, Daddy always had his pocket knife with him. For many years, Margaret carried his old knife that he let her have when she was his young fishing buddy. About once a week, he would take out the whet stone and sharpen the knife. It couldn't have been an expensive knife, but he cared for it as though it were a custom-made blade of exquisite worth and value. It had to be at-the-ready to scale and gut fish or skin and dress rabbits or squirrels, just as his dress shoes were always polished and ready for church. And when one of us came to him with a splinter in our skin, he used the pocket knife to finagle the splinter out. If he ever broke the skin enough to draw blood, I don't recall it happening. As he worked with the splinter, he kept up a gentle tone of conversation, keeping our attention on what he was saying.

One of the few long-lasting wedding gifts Mother and Daddy treasured through five decades of marriage was a large knife they called the butcher knife. It started out in 1926 with a blade approximately one inch wide and about eight inches long. By the time they used it to cut the cake at their fiftieth anniversary reception about three weeks before Daddy's death, the hilt end of the blade was less than half an inch wide, and the rest of the blade curved to a tip of less than a quarter of an inch. The butcher knife was not part of a set, but was the one knife that could wield precise power over meats, cakes, and pies in our kitchen.

Such a small number of iconic possessions that combine to make up Daddy's image—pipe, knife, Old Spice with shaving mug, fishing tackle, work uniforms, one suit, a pair of dress shoes and a pair of work shoes, white boxer shorts and sleeveless undershirts like Marlon Brando made famous in *A Streetcar Named Desire*; a ready smile, and bright stars in his deep blue eyes—are all treasures cherished beyond measure, remnants of a simple man who did his best to love, protect, and encourage. These embers are a permanent flame of warmth and comfort yesterday, today, and tomorrow.

My first two years of teaching in Gaffney, South Carolina taught me at least as much as I taught my students. The experience was enough to earn an offer for a teaching assistantship at Winthrop. After completing the degree, I stayed in Rock Hill and taught elementary school music for three more years. During the third year of teaching there, I began to search for openings in higher education and applied to Simpson College in Indianola, Iowa. When I talked to Mother and Daddy about the possibility of living within four hours of them, they were enthusiastic, but with caution. Mother immediately thought of our being able to see each other more often than only during major holidays. With no less excitement about the possibility, Daddy, as was typical for him, also thought of the practical issues.

244 CRIES OF THE PANTHER

"You know, the Iowa winters are even worse than they are here. You'll have to make sure that your car is winterized. And you might have to buy a snow shovel and use it."

"Oh, Honey, she'll learn to love the snow just as much as I do. I'll bet some of her students would help with shoveling the snow."

The call in which the department chairman invited me to interview came just before Spring break. He explained that I would have to go to New York to interview with him because he was on sabbatical with the Metropolitan Opera Company. If that interview went well, he would then have me go out to interview with the other faculty members and students on campus. He instructed me to take a cab from the airport to the Plaza Hotel. The room I had must have been the smallest in the entire hotel. It had odd angles that made it feel like an attic dormer bedroom, but the lobby and restaurants made up for the cramped sleeping quarters.

It was my first trip to New York City except for a few hours on a layover when I took my first trip to Europe in 1969. St. Patrick's Day fell during Spring break and gave a festive air to every part of the interview. Neither the department chair nor I cared when we got soaked while watching the St. Patrick's Day parade in the rain. When I started shivering from the cool temperature, we ran up the steps of the Metropolitan Museum of Art and had lunch there. I became so animated when I talked about the pedagogy of the leading European music educators of the time that my host responded with equal enthusiasm.

"Sue, I believe that your training and your personality are exactly what we are looking for. I will call the acting department chair this evening and tell him to expect your visit to campus. Could you plan to make the trip within the next couple of weeks?"

"Yes. It will be fun to meet other faculty members and students. Tell me about the organ department."

He gave me a detailed description of the students, the campus itself, and the teaching and practice facilities. We talked about his vision for the department of music and of how he thought I might be able to help the department achieve its purpose and goals. I felt so alive, so focused, and so fortunate to be reaching out and finding where my goals would lead me. That night, we attended a performance of *Tosca* by the Metropolitan Opera Company.

In addition to being overjoyed at the prospect of my dream job becoming a reality, I was also nurturing the thought of being close enough to see my parents and other family members more often. Driving four hours was much more affordable than flying from South Carolina to Missouri. Mary and Daniel were living in Florida, so I didn't have to worry about having to avoid him on most of those visits.

During that academic year, Daddy's unexplained weight loss was diagnosed as cancer of the kidney. He refused treatment or hospitalization. Richard was pastoring in Kansas City. One of his parishioners was an oncologist and asked if he could offer a second opinion on Daddy's condition. All agreed, but the diagnosis was the same, as was Daddy's decision to not accept treatment. He had figuratively watched one of his brothers go through treatment for lung cancer and had determined that he did not want to go through the pain and false hope of aggressive treatment, only to lengthen his life by a few months and leave a huge medical bill.

He seemed to be hanging on by sheer will power until he and Mother could celebrate their 50th wedding anniversary on May 9, 1976. With low energy, he delighted in having all the children and most of the grandchildren there to share the joy of the reception they had in their home. Partially to control swelling in his legs and ankles, and also to help keep him warm, a nurse had wrapped his legs in mummy-like white bandages. Before guests started arriving, he apologized for not having on dress socks.

One of the joys he gave to grandchildren was to give them a "horsey ride" on his knee. With a voice that sounded much like Perry Como's, he would sing and bounce his knee,

"Ride a little horsey,
Go to town.
Hold on _____.
Don't fall down."

246 CRIES OF THE PANTHER

On the last word, he would collapse his knee, hold tight to the child's hands, and delight in the giggles that followed the rider to the floor.

When the house and yard were full of family and friends celebrating the special anniversary, one of my nephews approached his grandfather, who was sitting in the rocking chair. He rubbed the bandages, tapped Daddy's knee and said, "Ride a horsey, Peepaw?"

With a depth of sadness mixed with resignation, he shook his head and said, "Ask Aunt Suzie. Her knees make better horsies than mine do now."

I could not have imagined seeing Daddy too choked up to sing along, but he simply watched and smiled as my nephew and I played the game.

At the reception, I was surprised to see how many neighbors came from all over the county and how warm they were to Daddy. Without exception, those who knew him and visited him while Mother was at school mentioned his cooking, especially the Southern gravy he made to serve over rice with every meat he cooked. It was no surprise to see many of Mother's teaching colleagues and church friends there, but I didn't know how many friends Daddy had also made. It comforted me to know that those in his rural community who knew him loved and respected him.

Later that evening, my husband (Fred), who also smoked a pipe, noticed that Daddy's pipe was not within sight. "Bruce, would you like me to find your pipe and bring it to you?"

"I sure would. I've really been missing it." With a little help, Daddy managed to sit up and prop himself against the wall long enough to take a few puffs. I think that just knowing it was available mattered more than the actual smoke did. Having the aroma of Prince Albert tobacco close at hand must have comforted him.

About three weeks after the anniversary, my husband and I arrived at their home after being told that hospice personnel had advised Mother it was time for the family to gather. Mary and Daniel were already there with a motor home. Daddy's youngest brother and his wife (Uncle Bob and Aunt Ruth) had already been there for about two weeks. They were sleeping in Mother's bed, and she was sleeping on a pallet in Daddy's room beside the hospital bed that had been loaned or rented. His sister next older than he, Aunt Marian, and Uncle Ruric's widow, Aunt Betty, and her daughter arrived soon after I did. Daddy was completely immobile, but was clear-headed and talked as much as he could before lapsing into frequent shallow naps.

Aunt Ruth had always been interested in nutrition and tried to be sure her family had a well-balanced diet. She told me she had figured that Daddy was taking in only about 200 calories per day and that she was concerned that he was becoming dehydrated. He had told Mother that he did not want to go to the hospital, but she had not told me or Aunt Ruth of his wishes. In my attempt to be a caring daughter and to help with the situation, I went to the kitchen and said to Mother, "Aunt Ruth says that Daddy is taking in only about 200 calories a day. She thinks he may be getting dehydrated. We have to get him to the hospital so that they can put in an IV for nutrition and hydration."

Before Mother could answer, Daddy mustered up his strength and called out to me,

"Come back here, Suzie." I went down the short hall to his room and sat on the edge of his bed. "I know you and Aunt Ruth think you are doing the right thing. But I've told your mother that I do not want to go to the hospital and I don't want any kind of treatment."

I held his hand, stroking it like he used to stroke my hand or forehead when I had a fever or just needed his gentle touch.

"We're concerned that you are not getting enough nutrition and can't hold down any liquids. We don't want you to suffer if we can get you some relief."

"The best help you can give me is to help your mother."

"Okay. I love you, Daddy."

"I love you too, my Darling."

Later that afternoon, I was in the guest room where I always slept when I visited them at that location. The house was small, but had three bedrooms. Daddy's room shared one wall with mine. Aunt Ruth was visiting with him, and I overheard the conversation. "I'm really enjoying getting to know Martha Sue. She seems like a very nice young woman. I used to think she was kind of aloof and unfriendly."

"If you think that, you just don't know my Suzie like I do. She is a real jewel. She wouldn't want me to tell you, but we might have lost this house if she hadn't been helping us with the payments the last couple of years."

"I can believe that. I'm glad I've found out I was wrong about her."

Now, I wish I had had the courage to walk the few steps into Daddy's room at that time and be a part of that moment. But avoiding as much of the reality of his suffering and death as possible was still my default setting. I can understand how Aunt Ruth (and probably others) had believed that I was not very friendly.

Instead of joining Aunt Ruth at Daddy's bedside, I put on work clothes and went outside to prune the rose hedge. The week before Father's Day may not have been the right time of year to do the pruning, but it was what I needed—silence except for his cows in the field and the occasional car on the rural road, physical exertion, sweat mixing with tears that wouldn't come in front of anyone else, and time to remember how strong he was when his top weight was 140 pounds before the disease whittled his body down to 80-something pounds—bones lonely in a pillowcase of loose skin.

I needed private time to recall the twinkle in his bright blue eyes before starvation faded the sparkle into clouds of dullness, time to appreciate the care he had unfailingly shown and the cures he was able to work on any ill or hurt that came my way and was apparent to him—time to regret all the time I had not spent with him, and time to wish I could give as much to him as he had given to me.

At some point in the third grade, I had told Mother that I wanted to die before she and Daddy died so that I would not have to go to their funerals. The double funeral I had been taken to by a babysitter in Miami was still fresh in my mind. Mother clasped a hand to her chest and said, "Oh no! You must never wish for that. The worst thing in the world for parents to have to do is to bury a child. Don't worry. You'll be strong when Daddy and I die."

In her attempt to comfort me, I received a message that I should squelch my emotions and certainly not talk about how I felt. That was not her intent, I am sure, but that was how I (mis)understood her message.

Years later, I told both Mother and Daddy that I didn't want to view their bodies when they died and that I didn't want for the casket to be open at their funerals. Neither of them expressed any concern, disagreement, or disappointment about my feelings. At the same time, I assured them that I wanted them to stay alive as long as they could enjoy life, but that I would accept their death when they no longer could enjoy living.

I had learned that Episcopal funerals didn't allow open caskets and that they leaned more to being a celebration of the deceased person's life rather than an evangelistic play on guilt. In fact, by then, I had become Episcopalian. One other member of the family agreed with me concerning the open casket. We were able to get the funeral director and my brother to agree to make an announcement at the end of the funeral service stating that anyone who did not want to participate in the final viewing could feel free to step outside.

My oldest nephew and I were the only two who followed that suggestion. I don't know whether or not he had gone to the funeral home and viewed Daddy's body. I had not. If anyone in the family criticized me for staying home that evening, I was not aware of it. It most likely was not a surprise to others because I had used babysitting as an excuse to avoid attending other funerals. If Mother insisted that I help with the music, I positioned myself behind the floral arrangements so that I didn't have to see the body displayed in the open casket during the entire service. More than ten years after Daddy's death, I was able to overcome my reticence when my father-in-law died. Viewing his body at the funeral home and singing at the service was not nearly so difficult as I thought it would be.

Right before receiving the call summoning me to Daddy's side, I was in the process of moving back to Iowa and had reserved a U-Haul truck to move from North Kansas City to Indianola. Knowing how practical and frugal Daddy was, I went into his room and, once again, sat down on his bed. He was groggy, but awake, and listened to me as I explained that the truck was reserved and that I would lose the deposit if I didn't pick it up the next day. He encouraged me to go ahead and make the move and come back after I unloaded the truck. I hugged him and told him I would be back in two days.

The next morning, Margaret made the call. "Suzie, we lost Dad a little while ago. Mom left his side long enough to walk some neighbors to their car. Dad called out for her, so I ran to the front door and told her to come back in. When she called his name, he looked toward her, opened his eyes, and winked before he gave up his last breath."

Margaret assured me that everyone would understand that I had to complete the move before turning around and driving back to Missouri. It felt like I was sleep-walking, going through some sort of robotic demands I had placed on myself, but my husband and I got the job done with some help from college students and friends.

Once the diagnosis had been confirmed with the second opinion, he had agreed to spend as much time as possible with Richard and Linda so that he could be near the larger medical facility in Kansas City. Since he did not want any form of treatment, I have to assume that being with his only son also played a part in that decision. Richard is a natural source of strength and comfort to his parishioners and to all who know him.

After finding out that Daddy was going to be in Kansas City so much of the time, I resigned from the college position and taught music in North Kansas City Public Schools that year. I could easily get to the hospital if necessary or spend a few minutes with him at Richard's home several times a week. Those times were precious. I never regretted resigning from that position. My career was just growing into the dream I not only nurtured but prepared to bring into reality, but I had decades ahead to enjoy the places and people my preparation would lead me to. Daddy's remaining life was numbered by months.

Before heading out for my move, I finished pruning the rose hedge, went inside, and took

a quick bath (no shower). When I went in to see Daddy before leaving, he told me that I didn't need to be working so hard. I assured him that I understood, but that I felt better if I stayed active. As he drifted off to sleep again, I went back outside to wash the headlights and clean the interior of my car. While I was sitting in the driver's seat cleaning the dashboard, Daniel came up and got in on the passenger side. Once more, I felt trapped. With a conspiratorial tone, he said, "Wouldn't you like to run away together?"

Unable to be honest, I was sarcastic and said, "Oh, I'd like to run away, all right."

With no further words spoken between us, I got out and went back inside. There was still no safe escape from him. I was thirty-four that summer, but I still felt like a helpless, mute child around him. On my own turf, though, I was competent, respected, and a leader in my professional environment.

Some of the younger children were playing on the front lawn. I joined them and lay down on the grass so that they could take turns balancing on my raised feet as I lifted them into the air and flipped them over my head, letting them land on their feet. I had done that with every one of my nieces and nephews. Daniel and Mary came out to watch. Swaggering with his air of false authority set in his bantam rooster stride, he said, "You'd better cut that out now. You're gettin' older."

More determined than ever, instead of stopping, I started turning cartwheels. When I defied him in that way, he turned around and left. Despite being voiceless around him, my *I'll show you* attitude was growing and gaining strength. Decades later, the last time I flipped nieces and nephews over my head, I was in my sixties, flipping the next two generations.

While I was still living in Iowa, one of Mary's and Daniel's granddaughters got married. I drove down to the Springfield area for the wedding, which was held in a very small church. So far as I could tell, there was no professional photographer, so I took pictures to share with the bride. Other family members and friends also were taking photos. Daniel was up on the platform for the first set of pictures. When I ran out of flashcubes, I sat down on a pew and was enjoying watching the bride and groom pose for additional pictures and was not aware of where Daniel had gone when he left the platform. The next thing I knew, he was sitting right behind me, leaning on the back of my pew, close enough that I could smell his breath. I felt the hair on my skin stand up when I caught a glimpse of him peripherally. I jumped. He laughed his derogatory laugh, apparently delighted that he had made me jump. Changing his tone to a deeper, quieter intensity, he said, "I'm right here, Sue."

Implied in that short statement was his determination that I would never get rid of him, along with his delusion that I shared his wishes. With a feeling of creepy fear spreading throughout my body, I got up and went out into the vestibule and tried to melt into the crowd of a dozen or so people. Longing for family ties, feeling sorry for my sister, and loving their children gave me the strength to take the risk to be around him at all. But the wedge he constantly drove between the rest of the family and me by demanding such a high price for my presence around them finally helped give me the strength and courage to put distance between me and him and his family. The confidence that the distance inspired strengthened my resolve to face what he had done to me and to begin to set out on a path toward healing and renewing my spirit. The less I was around him, the more I could become myself.

When I returned to the Springfield area for Daddy's funeral, I felt as though I were sleep-walking, robotically fulfilling expectations and responsibilities, wishing I could find a way to justify not attending the funeral. I had requested that Daniel not be allowed to have a part in it, but could not convince my brother and Mother to inform the local pastor and the funeral director that Daniel would not have a part in the service. I was able to align with Aunt Marian and Uncle Bob and Aunt Ruth and my nephew, Jim. Aunt Betty and Judy also sat with us. We all shared an unspoken belief that a large part of Daddy's beliefs, understandings, and attitudes matched our own. Such mental and emotional stances may not be provable, but their depth is profound—an almost palpable sense of intimate kinship wrapped in a mantle of love and respect. At the same time, though, I felt alone, apart from most of my immediate and extended family, an island of sadness in need of the calm beauty of gently rocking waves of clarity.

*Alice Skilton Orrell*
*(1905-2001)*
*Mother--Ms. Nursing Home of Missouri, 1994*

# CHAPTER 21

# MOTHER'S DEATH

*Truth is on the march and nothing can stop it.*
Emile Zola
(1840-1902)

Mother's general health remained remarkably good until a year or so before her death. When she was in her late eighties, she began to show signs of depression and wrote rather depressing poetry. She still lived alone, but was unable to drive because of failing vision. She confided in Richard that she thought it was time to think about a nursing home. She was interested in moving to Maranatha Village, the nursing home owned and operated by the Assemblies of God denomination in Springfield, Missouri.

Since Richard is an ordained minister in the Assemblies of God church, Mother was hopeful that he could get her on the list of potential new residents. It wasn't long before a room became available. There her outlook improved significantly, and her poetry returned to its more positive life-view.

The Association of Nurses in Missouri sponsors a Miss America type of beauty pageant each year for nursing home residents. The Activities Director of Maranatha approached Mother and said, "Alice, you are one of the liveliest residents here. We think it might be a good idea for you to try out to be Ms. Maranatha."

"What's that about? What would I have to do?"

"It's an opportunity for you to share your talents with others. We pattern it after the Miss America Pageant. The state winner is always invited to the governor's conference on aging to make a short speech and possibly display the talent that helped her win the title."

"Well, I guess I'd have to have a new dress, but my daughter could help with that."

"So—you'll give it a try?"

"Sure."

With those plans, Mother's energy perked up along with her anticipation of the contest. She was never prone to vanity, but did enjoy the spotlight in various ways since she had been a young girl. So far as I know, she had never experienced stage fright.

The Activities Director let her know the date for the contest was approaching. I was never told how many ladies competed, but Mother was the local winner. The Director explained that she would now be expected to represent Maranatha at the regional contest. It seemed that beauty contests were becoming her new forte in her older age.

After she won the regional contest, Richard called to let me know that Mother would be competing for the state title. He asked if I could come up for the event, which was to be held at a resort at one of the lakes. It was early in the school year, and I was in a new position, but I agreed to drive up. Five generations of us sat behind the judges' table where we could see the computer screens, but not well enough to see the numbers being tallied.

When I first saw Mother the day before the contest, I asked, "Well—have you bought your bikini yet?"

"Why, I wouldn't think of it. I didn't need one to win the local and regional contests, and I'm not about to start exposing my body now."

I laughed.

There were supposed to have been over a dozen women in the state competition, but a couple of them were not able to compete. When we first arrived at the lodge that was hosting the event, we were told that Miss America of 1968 would be the emcee. Mother was about the eighth contestant to go up on stage for the interview and to share her talent with the audience. She was the first who did not need any sort of mobility assistance.

When introduced to her official escort, Mother said, "That's very kind of you to offer to help me, young man, but my son is here. He'll walk with me."

Rich pulled her aside and told her that she was expected to use the arm of the escort because it was his job to help her. He also may have mentioned that it might have something to do with insurance coverage and that it would mean that he could enjoy the event and not have to think about when he would walk with her.

She accepted his explanation and was a good sport about taking the arm of the young hired hunk. Out of the dozen or so contestants, Mother was the only one who had a degree, had had a professional career, and displayed a talent other than needlework of some sort. Those attributes apparently got the judges' attention.

Not long before the final contestant had taken her spot on stage, my then-second grade great-great niece whispered to me, "Aunt Suzie, Meemaw's going to win."

Believing it was not a slam-dunk, I said, "We all want her to win, but what makes you so sure she will win?"

"She has more points on the computer than anybody else."

With her young eyes and keen mind, she had been watching as the computer screen showed the point tally.

With regal presence, Mother received the tiara, roses, and sash, symbolizing her status as *Ms. Nursing Home of Missouri, 1994*. It was a joyful time for all of the family members who were there. The crowd size was estimated at about 300. One of the responsibilities of the title bearer was to be a featured speaker at the governor's conference on aging. When she gave her speech and read some of her poetry there, the crowd was about 3,000. She was still in her element, even though the audience was the largest she had ever spoken to. Approaching her 90th year, she learned that she also relished being a big fish in a big pond.

Two years after she had lost her crown to the next winner, she was invited back as a special guest of the governor for the same conference. Richard and Margaret reported that the trip itself was not as easy as the previous one, but once Mother was on stage, there was no problem with her delivery of her crowd-pleasing speech and poetry reading.

I believe that being in Maranatha extended both the length and quality of her life. She was a strong extrovert and needed to be around people to renew her energies. Having staff to take care of her personal needs was a luxury that she appreciated.

She didn't have to give in to a walker or wheelchair until the final year of her life. She still played the piano in the dining hall occasionally, and she welcomed being interviewed by graduate students from several universities. Even though vanity had not played a part in her younger years, it was obvious that it pleased her to see the large portrait of herself in her state title regalia in a place of honor in the hall where the head managers had their offices.

On Tuesday morning of Holy Week, 2001, with just a couple of minutes to spare, I arrived at the early morning choir rehearsal at my school. Knowing that Mother was not doing well, I quickly answered the phone. Richard said, "Sis, I think you'd better head on up here. Mom's condition is deteriorating rapidly, and the doctor thinks she'll live only a few more days."

Since it was Holy Week, I had already planned to drive up on Thursday because Thursday and Friday would be school holidays. Rich further explained that the order to withhold medication and nutrition was being followed out of fear Mother could choke to death. The staff members at Maranatha Village were maintaining her comfort as well as they could through a morphine drip.

At age 95 years and four months old, Mother did not desire any heroic efforts to be used to maintain her vital functions. Not long after she had settled into the nursing home, she meticulously labeled every picture that hung on the wall to designate who would get the picture after her death. In many ways, she was a practical realist, but that approach to life served as a balancing factor to her far deeper and stronger bent toward idealistic romanticism. She often spoke of the quarrelling among her siblings after their parents died. In an attempt to shield us from a similar experience, she promised each of us that she would see to it that there was no disagreement over who received the few material possessions she had to share with us. With her flair for entertaining by reading her own poetry and giving readings of others' works, she could easily project a dramatic scene onto her mental stage and see it even though by then she had long lost all practical vision.

As soon as I finished talking with Richard, I notified the principal of my immediate departure and asked my friend and teaching colleague to take care of my class until the substitute arrived. Stopping by my house just long enough to grab a suitcase and to call my husband at his office with the news and plans, I headed out on the 13-hour drive from Houston to Springfield, Missouri.

The receptionist on duty at the front desk was expecting me and let me know it was alright to go on back to Mother's room. Knowing why I was there, she did not even remind me that visiting hours were almost over.

As expected, most of the family were still there. When I arrived at Mother's bedside close to 9:00 P.M., she was resting with her eyes closed. When I kissed her cheek, though, she stretched out her arms to hug me and said, "I'm so glad you're here, Honey. You didn't drive too fast, did you?"

"Not fast enough to get a ticket, but I let my foot rest on the accelerator as heavily as I dared."

In his usual demanding, domineering manner, Daniel was standing at the foot of Mother's bed, claiming what would have been the seat of honor at a dinner table. With a too-loud *I'm in charge* voice, he declared, "She may be talkin' some, but she's already gone. That's just an empty shell of a body in the bed."

I was aghast at his insensitivity. She was obviously coherent and still aware and concerned about current situations. A little confused due to the morphine, she would open her eyes from time to time and remind us that she was supposed to have her hair done on Thursday. One of us would assure her we would remember the appointment and also remind her that it was still Tuesday.

Rather than being focused on Mother's condition or needs, Daniel was determined to turn all attention to himself by presuming to be the only one who knew how the deathbed scene was supposed to be played. As usual, he thought that he was the only one with the right knowledge and understanding. The only thing that seemed to matter was that he be acknowledged, in control, and unquestioned. Margaret was not in the room with us at that time because her husband was in a hospital on the other side of the city and also was not expected to live more than a few days.

As soon as Mother returned to her restful repose after greeting me, Daniel spoke up again and said, "Now that Sue's here, we need to let Meemaw know that it's alright to die. One of the nurses reminded me that a person won't die until the children give permission."

Infuriated, but respectful of the need for civility and quiet, I stewed mentally and wondered why no one was willing to challenge him. I was most angry with myself for still being a part of the silence that gave him power over the situation and over me. Out of respect for Mother, though, and in order to keep the peace, I said, "Mother, you know I always told you and Daddy that I want you to be with us as long as you can enjoy life. I hate to see you in pain, and I know that life is very difficult for you now. Just know how much I love you."

I was not about to use his suggested verbiage and tell Mother it was okay for her to choose to die. I was willing to go along to get along, but only to a point. Mother no more needed my permission to die than she needed her despicable son-in-law's intrusion in her final days with us.

Richard and Mary spoke a little longer and specifically told Mother that they would understand her need to *go home to Jesus*. At that point, Daniel began to ask Mother if she was already seeing loved ones in heaven. He said, "How 'bout Peepaw—you see him?"

She responded in her habitual way, "Oh! Bruce, Bruce, Bruce." She had developed a habit in her older age of saying a word three times. To me, her response meant that she remembered Daddy and missed him. He had died in June, 1976, twenty-five years earlier.

Daniel continued badgering Mother with many additional questions, trying in vain to find out who was in heaven and who wasn't. A great-niece joined him, making them a tag team for one question after another. I finally had had all I could take. With clenched teeth, I said, "Please! Leave her alone. Don't you see how sick she is and how these questions are upsetting her?"

With quiet agitation, Mother picked at her fingernails as her eyes flitted back and forth underneath thin-skinned sagging eyelids. The inquisitors refrained for perhaps one or two minutes before cranking up again. Finally, as only Mother could do, she flattened her palms against the mattress, raised her head off the pillow, leveled her right index finger at Daniel, gave her infamous Skilton stare, and, with some of her last remaining strength said in her *I mean business* voice: "You will just have to live your own life in such a way that you are able to find out for yourself. I'm sick, and I'm tired."

Daniel's response was to snicker as though listening to a nonsensical statement. Addressing nobody in particular, he said, "Did you hear that? It sounded like Meemaw said I'd have to see for myself. She doesn't even know what she's saying." There was no humor in Mother's voice, and there was no reason for him to be snickering. Like a pouting toddler in a huff, he sulked out of the room.

Mother then rested her head, closed her eyes once again, and exhaled an exclamation point into the air that made me want to clap and cheer. I was never more proud of her than after she had delivered her message to the Reverend Rapist. Not even her graduation from Stetson University at age 53 nor her winning the state title of *Ms. Nursing Home of Missouri* could top her final words to him. The last bit of energy she had was spent on rebuking him and attempting to gain some distance from his thoughtless harangue.

It wasn't very long before I noticed that a young female family member was not in the room. I motioned for Richard to step into the hall with me. I said, "Do you know where Daniel and our teenaged niece are?"

"No. I haven't seen either of them for a while. I think Daniel went into the next room to rest."

Rich explained that the nursing home was letting us use the extra bed in Mother's room and the empty room beside hers for rest as we stood vigil those last few days of her life. "I'm going to see if she is in the restroom. If she isn't, we have to check on her. I'll be right back."

I walked down the hall to the restroom near the front desk. It was empty. "You've got to check on them. She's not in the restroom. Don't turn on the light, but stick your head into the next room and see if he is alone.

I waited near the door to Mother's room while Rich checked the next room. When he stepped back into the hall, he told me that both Daniel and the niece were in the extra room, one in each bed, and that they both appeared to be asleep.

"Do you have any idea how creepy this makes me feel?"

With profound sadness covering his face, he assured me that he understood my concern. I said, "When I get back to Houston, I'm going to find a therapist who can help me deal with all that Curtis Winfrey's book with its false claim against me has stirred up. I probably will pursue writing about it—either prose or poetry."

We had never talked about my history with Daniel before, but I felt sure that he was aware of it. I knew that he and his wife had made a conscious effort to guard their own daughter any time they were around Daniel.

On the following day, as we gathered again around her bedside, Mother mouthed the words as we sang hymns we thought would be meaningful to her. When I found out that she was not allowed to have anything to eat or drink, I remembered how she hated the dry mouth side effect of one of her medications. I couldn't stand the thought that she was now even more uncomfortable because of not having any liquids. I found a straw, placed it in a glass of water, and put my fingertip over the end to vacuum just a drop or two of water and dribble it over her lips. She would smile and lick her lips as though it were a taste of her favorite ice cream, raspberry ripple, from Hubert Jacobs' Dairy and Creamery in DeLand. I also kept a cool, damp wash cloth on her forehead.

When Mary said, "Now, that looks like the action of a devoted daughter," I didn't know what she meant or how to respond to the remark. It sounded as though she was surprised that I would show any loving action toward Mother. It reminded me of how little I was known by my own family.

Through many visits to the nursing home and to Mother's room while she was a resident there, I had become conditioned to tolerate the mixed odors of cleaning products, body fluids, and strong room deodorizers. I could stand seeing the back of a silver-haired lady in a wheel chair or behind a walker and thinking, *There she is!* as I walked down the hall, only to find a face I did not know. I could stand the aroma of canned peas being heated in the kitchen for yet another meal that most residents would only pick over. I could stand the sound of the wheelchairs and the shuffling slippers in the hall. But I could not abide standing by as the caregivers turned Mother in her bed. It was necessary, and even caring, but when she screamed out in pain and fear of being dropped despite their most tender efforts, I had to leave the room. She had prided herself on her robust health that had lasted until her final year or so. I had never seen her incapacitated except on the way home in the ambulance when Richard was born and when I was 10 years old and she had had a hysterectomy. But even then, she at least had been mobile, although she had not been allowed to lift anything heavier than a bed pillow for a month or two.

Maundy Thursday came and went. We had to tell Mother that the hair appointment had been changed since she was still in so much pain. We assured her, though, that her hair would be fixed just as soon as she felt better. She had always felt helpless when it came to personal grooming because of the effects of her birth order. She had told me that she had never shampooed her own hair by the time her parents died because her five older sisters and their mother had taken complete care of her.

Very early in the morning of Good Friday, the 13th of April, 2001, one of the family members called me at the motel where I was staying and told me I needed to get back up to Maranatha. Mother's breathing was becoming progressively shallower, and she had stopped rousing from sleep. I was sleeping in my clothes, so was able to jump into the car for the five- minute drive back to the nursing home. I stood on her left side and held her hand as Richard stood on her right side and held her other hand. Her breathing slowly but steadily decreased and her skin tone became progressively less pink and more grave-ashen gray as the fingernail with the polish removed became more blue than pink.

She lingered until early afternoon while we watched as her body wound down. Finally, around 1:30 or 2:00, she gave a deeper and final exhalation that sounded like a balloon losing the last of its air. Both my brother and I were crying, but neither of us was gripped by absolute anguish. All of us were relieved that she was no longer in pain. As Richard and I continued to hold and caress her hands, Daniel left Mary's side and eased into the tight space between the edge of Mother's bed and the wall, stepping sideways to reach me.

In his haste to reach me, he apparently failed to think of how it would look for him to leave his wife alone while he sought me out. Almost pinned to the corner of a small room, I felt like a panther inside a cage, but it wasn't chain link with barbs that enclosed me. It was the body that had invaded every aspect of me decades before. I immediately thought, *You will not use my mother's death as an excuse for you to touch me.*

When he draped his right arm around my shoulders, I gave a strong shoulder shrug to get my point across, letting body language replace the words that remained voiceless in the solemnity of the moment of Mother's passing. There was no struggle of indecision or quandary of action; his arm had to be moved, and I had to get away from him. Speaking with a voice loud enough for Mary to hear, I said, "I'm going over to be with Richard. You need to be with Mary. Please move."

Because of the tight space and the tightness of my voice, he had no choice but to move. It is possible that in her co-dependency disguised as concern for me, Mary may have nudged him toward me, just as she had told him to take me on the *tunnel of love* ride at the county fairgrounds so long ago. Regardless, he should have stayed with Mary and comforted her. I walked around to the other side of the bed and put my arm around Richard as we both cried and tried in our own ways to process the enormity of what we had just witnessed—both losing the mother we had loved and me announcing to myself and to Daniel that he no longer held any residual power over me.

When it was time to leave the funeral reception and head back to Houston, for the sake of civility, I gave him a curt hug while I silently celebrated the promise to myself that I would never see him again. Mary gave me her usual tight hug and sweet smile as we said our *good-byes*. I felt a profound sadness when I thought of the probability that I would only see her again if she outlived him.

The most poignant part of the entire experience was seeing a tear slide out of Mother's right eye and down her cheek when I joined Richard, even though she had, apparently, exhaled her last breath. If I let myself—either then or now—dwell on how she must have felt as she heard all the questions and pronouncements from Daniel, it would haunt my mind and heart as long as I live. She knew what he had done to me. She had grieved over the way he had talked to Mary and the children and scorned his lack of help with the many child-rearing responsibilities. I recalled Mother's statement that she sometimes wondered and feared that he might turn out to be another Jim Jones. His demand of sacrificial suicide was much more subtle, but equally as strong as Jim Jones'.

While I have tried to come to peace with what Mother had to have been aware of as her body slowly approached its final breath, I have had to tell myself to focus instead on the fact that she knew that all of her children were there and honored and valued her. Margaret had been able to spend part of each day that week with us and, along with Richard, had been a constant help to Mother, especially after she moved into the nursing home. Knowing Mother, she most likely handled her own thoughts in the same way as I handled mine. She was not quite a typical Pollyanna, but she certainly chose to seek and to see the positive rather than the negative aspects of any person or situation. Her level of denial was virtuosic. I wish her senses had been more than wishful thinking and that her emotional temperament had allowed her the freedom to confront conflict decades earlier as readily as she finally uttered her displeasure with Daniel as he badgered her on her deathbed.

Being able finally to immediately get away from Daniel's disingenuous show of so-called comfort at Mother's bedside was the outward sign of the internal breakthrough that occurred in the midst of the vigil and final farewell to Mother. By then, it had been almost 50 years since my twelfth birthday party when I had first known that his attention was not appropriate and that I didn't like being around him. And it would be about sixteen years until I would inform the entire family of my writing and intent to publish the finished memoir.

Mother's death was the beginning of my active pursuit of my own journey toward emotional healing, integration of my history of familial sexual abuse, and facing the issue of clearing Daddy's name after Curtis Winfrey's book was published. As so often happens, the beginning of facing my history was attached to the end of something else— the end of Mother's silence; in fact, the end of her very life.

Along with promising myself that I would never again see the man who did his best to destroy me, I also started shaping my internal vows into plans. The first priority was to continue teaching until I reached retirement age and to pay back funds that I had withdrawn from my retirement account.

The next part of the plan was to find a therapist. When I retired in 2009, following my husband's sudden death the previous year, I extended my new beginning into teaching piano and built my studio from one student to over thirty. As I focused on private teaching of one student at a time, I felt a surge of new energy and fulfillment.

I found the therapist I needed. I feel utmost respect for her and am deeply grateful for her expertise and personal care. A major crossroads in the therapeutic process was informing the family of the writing project and facing the reactions. That was not any type of suggestion from her, but entirely my decision when I felt ready. Only one person responded with a rant. The others who contacted me personally all offered unwavering support, understanding, and love. I thank those who chose to be supportive for their courage to express their support despite any misgivings they may have had concerning possible repercussions from Mary or Daniel or any of their family members.

The bravest and strongest person of all was Mother as she faced the diabolical badgering that Daniel and the great niece dished out to her as she felt her life slipping away. Her strength and courage transferred to me as I faced the issue of informing the family of the truth regarding Winfrey's accusation and the writing of my memoir. With that deathbed gift, Mother set me free and enabled my truth to find its way into the open, thought by thought, word by word, and chapter by chapter. And my own refusal to allow him to ensnare me in false comfort gave me the jump start I needed for the long process of healing.

Twenty-five years passed between Daddy's death and Mother's death when she finally confronted Daniel. Considering what he had done to me and that she had known about it, the rebuke was mild. Coming from her on her death bed, though, it was as if a Supreme Court Justice were speaking with all the skill, strength, and finesse of Mother's early elocution lessons that she had practiced in her childhood home. On her death bed, she overcame her frail physical condition by relying on the depth and strength of emotional resolve to finally get at least a portion of her own pain out into the open. I believe that her words to him gave her a sense of fulfillment as she faced the last few days of her life knowing how I felt around him and grieving for the pain he caused me and all of his family. Confronting him had to have given her some sense of closure as her pulse continued to weaken. I will always wonder exactly which thought prompted the tears that wet her cheeks even after her final breath whooshed out of her lungs.

It has now been over eighteen years since I made the vow to never see the abuser again and to do whatever it would take to heal the wounds he left gaping in my mind and spirit. That meant, of course, that I had to simultaneously accept that I would not see Mary again unless she outlived him. It is unfortunate that this was necessary in order for me to heal and rejuvenate, but I have learned to accept it. Like so many of life's more ordinary decisions, options had to be weighed in light of how they would either help or hinder my own growth and healing. When viewed with that in mind, the decision was clear. Informing the family of the writing project cemented my resolve to complete the memoir and to find the appropriate means of publication.

*Mother and Daddy 50th Anniversary*
*May 9, 1976*

## CHAPTER 22

# CRIES IN THE NIGHT—ONSET

*But what am I?*
*An infant crying in the night:*
*An infant crying for the light:*
*And with no language but a cry*
Alfred, Lord Tennyson
(1809-1892)

I thought the cries in the night were a thing of the past—no panthers in Houston—only non-threatening neighborhood cats hoping to satisfy their periodic mating urges. But a voice rose out of my chest with no hint of its approach such as flashing lights that announce the onset of a migraine or a bout of vertigo. But still my cries resurfaced, disguised in a scary voice, unrecognizable even to myself and those who witnessed it.

My cries in the night were just as stealthy, persistent, and invasive as Daniel's presence. Their intrusion sprawled onto others who shared my space, showing no respect for my privacy. With unharnessed power, they temporarily turned me into something I was not: an unaware, helpless victim—silent and alone in my darkness.

Perhaps the unrecognizable voice was an expression of my childhood belief that Mother could not hear me; maybe the simultaneous fear that she would not respond even if she did hear my true voice; or it could have been the hoarse attempt to be heard during a laryngospasm—an involuntary contraction of the vocal folds due to anxiety or stress. The only thing that is certain is that there was no sign of infection or allergies.

My first cries in childhood were silent, choked off initially by fears of my environment, my adherence to the "act mature" admonition, and, eventually, by the fear that Mother would not respond to actual cries, even if she heard them. Scaredy-cats were afraid of the dark, but it wasn't the dark that bothered me.

As a child, the fear of not being heard forced me to lie awake at night as I struggled between staying in bed or risking getting up without a flashlight to find the oil drum chamber pot without stepping on roaches or feeling them scamper across my feet as I sat on the rusty rim of the oil drum.

The chamber pot for that side of the house was in a small area between the sleeping porch and the storage area under the stairs that led up to the attic. It felt like I was calling out in a stage whisper, but I couldn't find the strength to make my voice louder. Bed-wetting was never an issue with me, so I must have found the courage to find the chamber pot in the dark when absolutely necessary. Dodging the cock-roaches in the house was the same as dodging the chicken shit in the back yard except the roaches roamed and the chicken droppings stayed in place until they were forced to ooze between toes. I believed that if Mother did hear me, she would remind me that big girls can get up dur-ing the night by themselves.

On those nights when the Florida panthers made their trip through the woods behind our house, I initially covered my ears and buried my head in my pillow to lessen the volume of the scary sound. I didn't dare call out to Mother and admit my fear when I heard the panther's cries in the night because if I admitted I was afraid, she would know that I was not as mature as I pretended to be. Big girls were smart and knew that the panthers could not get into the house. And big girls ignored silly fears. Big girls did not need a mommy to hug and comfort them.

Once we knew about the panthers' regular route through our prop-erty, or near it, we knew to ignore the automatic response their screams caused. The grown-ups squelched the immediate impulse to find out what was going on to account for such an awful sound. We who were young learned to ignore the hair standing up on the back of our necks and to remind ourselves that the panthers couldn't get to us as long as we were in the house. But the structure that provided safety from wild preda-tors proved impotent when the domesticated predator stalked his prey.

With hindsight, I view the panthers as more humane than human sexual predators. Panthers attack humans only when threatened. Sexual predators attack with premeditation, fully intent on their narcissistic satisfaction. A panther kills in the wild for food and protection. Human predators kill others' selfhood while playing their hidden game of hideous self-aggrandizement. In time, whatever conscience they once had becomes immune to society's norms and their own rationalization becomes justified in their skewed view of a twisted world in which the only thing that matters is the successful search for the opportunity to feel power over a weak target—power to sustain them until the next urge demands repetition—a habit just as potent as narcotics or alcohol.

The difference between people who are addicted to drugs or alcohol and sexual predators who are addicted to the search and exercise of power, though, is that people with substance addictions primarily harm themselves. Sexual predators primarily harm others and almost never gain enough self-awareness to even admit their wrong to themselves, much less apologize to their victim(s) or change their behavior. Many may give lip service to change, but few ever break the cycle of abusive behavior. Almost always, it is a lifetime sentence to the one who allows himself (or herself) to pursue the exercise of power directly over victims and indirectly to all others in relationship with them. Thus, it becomes the victim/survivor's responsibility to face the history, to learn to forgive themselves for the false guilt planted by the perpetrator, and to rise to the challenge of their lifetime to overcome the premeditated attack(s) that defined their history. Statistically, there is almost never only one victim for each perpetrator.

It took more than three decades for me to give voice to the nightmares caused by the sexual abuse I suffered. I believe that they would not have surfaced without the trust I felt with Chris. Even though I had been successful in my teaching and graduate work, the underlying dregs of dread still smoldered.

When it was time to mail out surveys as part of my doctoral dissertation, Chris helped me seal the envelopes. At each step of the academic way, he was right there with all types of support and encouragement. In earlier relationships, the level of intimacy was not deep enough to call the outcries to the surface. Still tucked away, they lurked at-the-ready, but were patient until the time was right for me to face them.

While Chris and I were still dating, we saw the movie, *Ghost*. There was a character in the movie who reminded me of Daniel—not in looks or mannerisms—but in personality. That night, Chris went back to his apartment, so I was alone. Toward morning, I woke myself up with a voice that I did not recognize as my own. It was pitched very low; the pace of speech was slow; and it was loud enough to wake me up. I have no way of knowing how many times I had cried out in the night without waking myself up, but I have to believe that they had been a frequent occurrence. The repeated outcries started after I married Chris. I feel certain that the silent cries of childhood persisted for decades.

The most obvious similarity between the character in *Ghost* and Daniel was the air of menace that encompassed their entire being. Willie Lopez, played by Rick Aviles, was of Puerto Rican descent with collar length bushy hair that framed a swarthy face in a perpetual five-o'clock shadow. Physically, his nose was the only feature similar to Daniel's, whose background included Cherokee heritage. But it was a less obvious attribute that connected these two characters. The sense of foreboding that surrounded each of them was the magnet that caused my subconscious to equate the two and to turn Willie into a symbol for the dread, fear, and loathing that Daniel's presence and behavior had created in me.

In my ground floor apartment, there were exterior French doors in my bedroom. When my disguised voice awakened me, I thought that someone who looked like the character in *Ghost* was standing at the foot of my bed. The impact was more than I even realized during and immediately after seeing the movie. In the nightmare, he had entered my bedroom through the French doors. With the loud, gravelly voice, I told the character, "Get out of here right now! Get out!"

He tried to give me some lame made-up excuse as to why he was in my room. While I listened to his talk, I had only one eye open while I slowly ran my hand under the extra pillow, thinking I had put a pair of scissors there. It was so real that I said, "You'd better walk through that door right now, or I'll make you wish you had. I have a weapon in my hand."

With that uncharacteristic bravura, I began to slowly ease toward the edge of the bed, trying not to make a sound. In my sleepy haze, I thought that I had scared him so badly that he began to back out toward the French doors. By the time my feet hit the floor, he was on the patio, heading for the street. Once my feet felt the texture of the carpet, I snapped out of it and realized I had been talking to a character in a nightmare and that it was Willie from *Ghost* who had triggered the nightmare so reminiscent of my experience with Daniel.

This terrifying nightmare scene was a re-living of the nights when Daniel was the intruder in my own bedroom, but I was powerless and without a voice on those nights, just as I was without someone to comfort me on the night of the first outcry. The dam of sequestered feelings had burst and I was freed from denial of the pain. It was a surreal verbal and emotional reenactment of the actual personal violation, but this time with the twist of fighting back and making myself heard—a first small step toward reclaiming internal permission to speak up and protect myself.

My own voice woke me up, and it took a long time for me to realize that I was not in danger and that there was no intruder in my bedroom. Despite the fact that the *intruder* existed only in my bad dream, my response to the merely-dreamed encounter encouraged me to speak up in real life. Even a voice unmatched to my usual timbre and pitch was a source of strength and served as a rehearsal if I would ever need to speak up with authority and authenticity.

It is no coincidence that the weapon of choice in the first (so far as I know) nightmare was a pair of scissors. To me, the scissors represent the way that the brother-in-law cut me to shreds. My threatened use of them in the dream represents my hidden, repressed desire to hurt him as badly as he had hurt me. Perhaps it was even a thinly veiled wish to emasculate him, to both punish him and protect others. But in the dream, I was not able to find the scissors. Exposing his pathological behavior toward me would have, in my view at the time, eviscerated my entire family, whether or not they believed me. It would take an additional twenty years for me to be honest with my family about what Daniel had done to me.

The glass doors leading from my bedroom onto the patio were real and to me reflected my belief that Daniel's behavior should have been visible to someone else in the family, particularly his wife, my sister. The transparence of glass panels should have been clear enough to reveal what he was doing. I asked myself so many times, *How could she not have known? How could she remain silent and allow such disgusting, hateful behavior to continue? How could she pretend to love me and not protect me?*

With mature reflection, it is hard for me to believe that I had never cried out in the night until 1990. After Chris and I were married (1993), the cries in the night occurred fairly often—perhaps every two or three months. Since Chris and I shared a deep, close friendship, I think his commitment to me and his unfailing attempt to make fun and joy a part of our everyday life account for me feeling free to let those feelings surface, if only in bad dreams.

Because of conflicting sleep habits, Chris and I often slept in separate rooms. The bedrooms we used were adjoining and we kept the doors closed so that his all-night TV habit would not disturb me and my night-owl schedule would not disturb him. The first time he heard my cries in the night he came into my room, lay down beside me, and gently shook my shoulder until I woke up. "Sue, wake up. You're having a bad dream. Your voice doesn't even sound like you."

Groggy, but curious, I said, "What'd I say"?

"You were yelling so loudly that I thought you might alarm the neighbors, saying, 'Stop! Don't do that! Get away from me. I hate you; I hate you!'"

I knew the nightmare had only one source. Later that evening, as we ate dinner, he said,

"Do you know who you were dreaming about? Are you angry with me about something? If so, please tell me so we can talk about it."

"No, I'm not angry at you. This is all old stuff surfacing from the personal history I told you about."

I reminded him about the nightmare I had experienced before we were married. Concerned that he feared I was angry with him, I went on to tell him that he should feel complimented because it was the first time I had felt free and secure enough to stop squelching those old feelings that were still too raw to deal with at a conscious level. Whenever the nightmares surfaced, he came in to wake me up and help me get back to sleep. There was one time when he cradled me and rocked me as he said over and over again, "You're with me now; I will never hurt you. And neither will anyone else hurt you as long as I'm alive."

I am grateful that my relationship with Chris freed me from the albatross that secrecy and the pain of self-recrimination had turned me into—a hardened mass of unhealed wounds marked with indelible scars.

Gradually, the night-time terrors haunted me less and less frequently. When we built our dream house the year before his death, our rooms were much farther apart than in the first house we bought. Even then, there were a couple of episodes when he heard me and came in to reassure me that I was safe.

After going through the grieving process following his death and the frenzy of closing his office, being re-hired at a different school (I thought I had retired), and finding my way out of the numbness that a sudden loss can cause, I turned to playing bridge with church and community friends. It was an enjoyable means to establish a thorough meness. Although I was always quite independent, being an independent single senior citizen was far different from being an independent part of a couple.

It was natural for me to go right back into the classroom. But my position had already been filled. There was only one position open in my district, and it required teaching violin in an enrichment program in addition to the usual elementary music education curriculum. I had never even held a violin. But I needed full-time income for at least a year, and I needed the collegiality of a teaching partner. As always, the relationships with children supported my need to nurture.

I reasoned that if we expected young violin students to learn a little each week, I should be able to stay far enough ahead of them to teach them. My main concern was that I not inadvertently allow them to develop bad practice habits. It was fortunate for me that the school had two music teachers. My colleague was a concert pianist whose brother was a violinist in a symphony orchestra in another city in Texas. She had picked up a lot of technical expertise from him and could always call him if either of us had a question or concern.

So far as I knew, the nightmare cries had ceased. After Chris' death, I never woke myself up in the midst of night-time terrors. Perhaps knowing that he was not there to comfort me accounts, at least in part, for the receding of the terrors. I prefer to think, though, that my beginning of therapy was the main reason for the retreat. In therapy, I faced every single aspect of the history and my feelings about it, developed the courage to face my family regarding the writing of my memoir, and accepted aspects of the effects that cannot be changed. Therapy also enabled me to forgive myself for maintaining over sixty years of silence.

Through therapy, I grew from attempting to deal emotionally with the jumble of feelings being fired in all different directions to focusing on the effects of the sexual abuse and its secrecy, the forced exposure brought about by Curtis Winfrey's book, and the fear of facing the family with honesty. I don't mean to say that everything is absolutely perfect now, but I live a very fulfilling life that is productive for myself and for my piano students; I travel fairly often; I enjoy many friendships; and I am in a healthy relationship with someone who also would comfort me if the nightmares made an unexpected re-entry into my world. Because of daily joy grounded in self-acceptance and artistic expression, I don't expect to experience a relapse of cries in the night.

# CHAPTER 23

# CRIES IN THE NIGHT— RELAPSE AND RELEASE

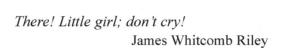

*There! Little girl; don't cry!*
James Whitcomb Riley
(1849-1916)

As recently as the spring of 2015, while on a bridge retreat at Camp Allen (a conference center owned by the Episcopal Diocese of Texas), I again was jolted by night-time terrors. A group of friends has gathered there annually for many years to play bridge in the sanctuary of rural quietude.

Camp Allen offers a beautiful, peaceful setting in the woods away from city noise and the pressures of fast-paced living. Rustic cottages built beside the lakes on the grounds feel like a second home after so many such retreats. On the drive to the camp grounds, heart rate and blood pressure drop. The four-lane highway shrinks to a two-lane road that lures bicyclists almost year-round. Fields lie ready for bluebonnets that will soon spread as far as the hills rise and fall. In the early spring, a few Indian paintbrush wildflowers grace the roadsides in time to welcome the arrival of the bluebonnets.

By the time Camp Allen's turnoff is in view, the knots in my shoulders and jaw gradually unsnarl themselves. A barely paved lane narrows to become a gravel-covered car path where one car must take to the shoulder to let the other pass. It reminds me of Spring Garden Ranch Road as it was when we first moved to Mockingbird Hill.

As long as four people are awake, a bridge game is in progress. And as soon as four people have their first cup of coffee in the mornings, a new game is started. There can be as few as one table or as many as five. We have played together long enough so that we can tell when one of the group is about to slip into an attitude that borders on becoming overly serious about the game's outcome. Tension is rare, and cross words are discouraged. The intent to have fun is much stronger than any tendency to let egos overcome the atmosphere of play. We act and organize just as pre-teen or teenage campers would. Everyone takes a turn at helping to prepare a meal, set the table, and clean up afterwards. If we have an odd number of people for a while, whoever is not playing has other options such as hiking, fishing, or paddle-boating to work out any kinks that the drive has not already removed.

Although I was aware that I had cried out in the night prior to Chris' death, I thought the ugly leftover symptom of post-traumatic stress had archived itself in a closed file in the back of my mind. I thought I was safe—that I could sleep without disturbing my own or someone else's rest. I hated that my history of sexual abuse had long forced me to explain to potential roommates, my lover, or even extended family members that I might cause a disturbance while I slept—and most likely would not even know it had happened unless a witness told me. On the bridge retreat, I found out that those archived emotional files had not yet sunk to their final resting place. They remained perfectly capable of bursting from the unconscious and causing me to lash out verbally in repose. A vague feeling of fatigue and malaise might hint that my rest had been interrupted by the transition from sequestered silence to involuntary volcanic eruption both of what I said and what I wish I had said to my abuser.

On the second day at Camp Allen, a woman I barely knew arrived to spend two of the three nights with the group. I had arrived on the first evening, so had claimed the queen-size bed, and she chose the lower of the bunk beds in the room we shared. Being a retired school counselor, she displayed the sweetness and sensitivity that would be expected from such a professional. We got along fine and enjoyed playing bridge together. On our last morning at the retreat, I awoke earlier than usual and was already out in the kitchen sipping coffee when she came out in her pajamas. I went into the bedroom to get a Kleenex and was still there when she came back in. She asked, "Did you hear me get up to go to the bathroom in the middle of the night?"

"I vaguely remember hearing you leave the room, but I don't remember hearing you return."

"I almost decided to wake you up, but I wasn't sure whether I should or not. You were not thrashing around in the bed, but you were using a weird, growly voice and were shouting, "No! No! Don't touch me. Get away from me. Go away! Now!'"

My mind was startled into hyper-wakefulness, swathed in deep sorrow. I thought, *Oh, no! I thought I was beyond having those terrifying flashbacks in bad dreams.*

Trusting her genuine concern, I told my new friend about the history that accounted for the night-time outburst. When she heard about how Chris was the first to hear the cries in the night, she commented on how fortunate I had been to have his love and support when I first began to process some of my pain within the safety net of sound sleep. If anyone else was going to witness the cries in the night, I was glad that it was someone who not only was a sensitive, caring person, but also one who happened to be a mental health caregiver. She said that she understood how my husband might have thought that the verbiage was a guised expression toward him rather than to the abuser. The words that had caused the most concern for my husband were, "I hate you! I hate you!" But as the occurrences decreased in both frequency and intensity, he came to trust and believe my explanation

My roommate at Camp Allen said she understood my story and that she had not meant to pry. Her assumption, though, was that I would want to know about the episode. "When I first heard you, I had expected to see you sitting up in bed and pointing to some door. You sounded very assertive and completely clear about your expectations. I was surprised to notice how completely still your body was while all this was going on. You didn't seem to be moving at all, just crying out. I thought maybe you had heard me and thought someone else was in the room since our conversation over dinner included the assumption that we didn't need to lock the doors."

"No, it has nothing to do with anyone here or anyone else other than the brother-in-law who abused me."

I went on to tell her about the writing project and stated that it probably had surfaced in the form of a nightmare because the history was on my mind almost constantly as I worked through the writing. I thanked her for letting me know about the cries in the night. "If someone had to be exposed to the outburst, I'm glad it turned out to be you. When I write this scene, would you be willing to read it and let me know if I have told the story accurately?"

"Sure. Just email it to me and I'll get right back to you after I've read it." When I sent her the file, she verified that I had told the story accurately. She also mentioned that she would be glad to read the entire manuscript when it was complete.

I wondered at the time if finding out about the cries in the night from a new acquaintance would affect their return or release any differently than when I first became aware of them or from the time my husband first let me know about them. If I have had any additional episodes of nighttime terrors after the bridge retreat at Camp Allen, they have not awakened me.

Finding out about the cries in the night so quickly did not trigger any recollection of the dream/flashback or of the outcries. As a child, there had been many times when I would awaken and remember a bad dream in which I cried out for help and there was nobody to hear or respond to my cries. And there were times when I called out to Mother, but she either didn't hear me or ignored the cries. I recall those times clearly. But after this relapse, I had absolutely no recollection of the experience.

Once I finished the two chapters on the two rapes, I have not cried out in the night. I believe that if I had, my general energy level would be less, and my mood would be far less joyful. My significant other verified that he has never heard any unusual sounds from me during the night.

When I alerted someone to the possibility of my crying out in the night, it was not a matter of shame; rather, it was a deep sense of regret and sadness that events from such a long time ago might find a way to burst into my life as though they were entitled to torment me. It was a fear that the memories might always have at least a subconscious hold on me, no matter how emotionally healthy I feel and how successful and fulfilling my life is. But the evidence of the last decade clearly indicates that the cries in the night have only surfaced once since Chris's death. I believe they are a thing of the past—not so much vaulted and buried as released.

In Florida in the 1950s, it was not uncommon for one or more panthers to be seen in a large portion of the state. Now, they are on the endangered species list. There still are occasional sightings in my home county, but such sightings are likely to be covered in the local or state news media because of their rarity.

I think back to how it seemed that the roving panthers invaded private property and caused fear in those who knew nothing about their habits. Now, the situation is reversed. In the name of growth and progress, humans claimed more and more of their habitat and forced them to cluster near the Everglades. When first studied, they lived from East Texas all the way through the Gulf states to all of Florida. Now, the last fifty are almost trapped. If they branch out in any direction, they run the risk of being hit by automobiles or being deliberately killed by homeowners ignorant of their plight.

The cries of the panther called to me. I learned not to fear the nocturnal animals that screamed in operatic volume and power. Mother had told all of the family as soon as her friend alerted her to the possibility that we might hear them when the panthers used the woods near our house as part of their seasonal circuit. I understood that they would not approach our house because they habitually sought the shelter of the woods.

The panthers were lucky, I thought, because there was no panther leader to make them sleep when they really wanted to travel and hunt. No panther leader squelched their cries. It was as if they were completely free to be as they were meant to be—powerful hunters with bodies evolved for long leaps and quick, quiet movements.

I can't help but be in awe of the irony of the reversal in situation and characteristics between the Florida panthers and me since the 1950s. They have become trapped; I have become free. Their geographic area has shrunk; mine has expanded beyond my expectations; their voice is heard less and less; mine is clearly audible and will continue to grow in strength and volume; and the external boundaries that defined them have tangled into a death trap with utter extinction likely to be documented in the near future. My future is wide open, inviting me to continue my journey, offering me all I need or want to maintain my expansion of self and to continue my pursuit of knowledge, understanding, and insight as I share my story with all who want to hear.

The only time I get really angry now is when I think of how unfair it is for people to get away with such brutally cruel behavior as sexual predators do and how inexcusable it is for others to enable the crimes. Enablers' behavior may be somewhat understandable, but at some point, they must take on the responsibility of stepping up, speaking out, and accepting the consequences of their own poor choices or decisions. I would never have been able to forgive myself if I had remained silent. Although I still resent Curtis Winfrey's publishing the false statement in which he claimed that I accused my father of the crime of child sexual assault and abuse, I am thankful that his blunder caused me to break my silence.

The final outburst of cries in the night enabled a global release of the perpetrator's power over me—not a one-time, all-purpose sigh of relief, but the culmination of multiple small steps that finally vaulted me over and beyond the highest obstacle there was—the hidden effects of sexual abuse and the gnarled feelings capable of causing flashbacks and aftershocks.

Now, I find the freedom of spirit that returned after the global release lets me imagine the feeling of grasping a pole vault forged from the message from friends and mentors: *Come soar with us.* Their invitation combined with my own stubborn ambition to create fuel for the propulsion, and the welcoming arms of all who had beckoned waited, outstretched and ready to buoy my footfall onto the ground.

It is easy to think of being on a carousel at age three without any feelings of detachment, but with connections that live beyond earth's bounds—a happy preschooler on her chosen steed, knowing that

Grandmother waited for me to dismount, wriggle in the warmth of her arms, and to hold her hand as her hobbled steps became smooth and swift, as though she were young again.

Floundering between success and setbacks carved a journey with an exaggerated trend line for me. But with the release, I am grounded—firmly a-foot with those who led the way—wings ready to fly to chosen destinations rather than from intolerable abuse; space to breathe; time to refresh; and optimism to fuel hope.

The powers and pain encased in the global release are gone—so far away that their effects are now impotent. In turn, my own strength is emboldened. My intent in writing this memoir has never been revenge; yet, there is a certain comeuppance in my successful shrug of Daniel's shoulder seconds after Mother's death that set the rest of my life in motion—a life of purpose; release of the demonic power he held over me; and joy beyond my imagination.

One of the most tender images I have of Mother was a ritual of maternal love that she most likely established even before my conscious memory set in. She always got up to use the bathroom at least once during the night. During the years when I was single and visited her and Daddy and, for twenty-five years, her alone, without fail, she would come into the bedroom I was using. It was as though she was reclaiming the closeness she had felt and the care she had given me when I was an infant and very young child—a bedtime tuck-in ritual. She would stand near the head of the bed and stroke my forehead and hair as she adjusted the covers with her other hand. With her gentle voice, she would whisper, "God, bless my precious Sue."

Still resisting closeness to her, I would pretend to be asleep. The odd thing is that I have no memory of her doing that when I had grown into later childhood and so badly needed just those strokes. In fact, every time I visited her, up until she entered the nursing home in her late 80s, she unfailingly maintained this loving maternal ritual during the night. The only exceptions were when my husband was with me. In my childhood, there was not much of a bedtime ritual other than saying a prayer, brushing the sand off my feet, and having whoever was putting me to bed place the covers over me. I recall no nighttime bedside visits during my later childhood.

I want to believe that she would have responded to my cries in the night if she had heard them and if things in the household had not been in such disarray. In fairness to her, I must say that she grieved over the lack of closeness between us just as much as I did. There was too much going on within each of us to be able to heal the breach that my arm's-length attitude toward her created. Part of my pulling away from her was my quest for independence and my determination to be my own person with my own beliefs, attitudes, and values. I was simply not willing to acquiesce to the dogma of the rural church and her undertone of what, to me, smacked of conditional love. In reality, it was not so much conditional love as conditional acceptance.

Once sexual abuse within the family was added to my emotional challenge, we didn't stand a chance to become close until I was out on my own and our visits could *accentuate the positive*. Once we finally talked about my history, we were able to reclaim a lot of our relationship and to love each other more fully.

Mother could not have met my needs without, in her mind, turning her back on Mary and Margaret, particularly Mary. I understand the agony she must have felt when I lashed out at her verbally for allowing Mary and Daniel to move in with us time and time again. But she had no idea of how betrayed I felt when she let me know that I had better tell her if I had done something I shouldn't do when I tried to tell her about the first rape. That was the final blow to seal the long-term distance between us. At the same time, she tried to accommodate my desire to live in town. She reinforced my own commitment to education by showing how she could manage to drive a school bus to pay for her classes at Stetson University. Yet, the irony is that her school bus duties kept her from catching Daniel in the second rape. Every family or church event that included him was tainted by his stalking and my attempts to avoid him.

When she was able to be honest with me about her feelings toward Daniel solely apart from anything I told her, I began to feel closer to her and enjoyed the limited time I spent with her during the last fifteen years or so of her life. I was deeply proud of her accomplishments, her talents, and identified with her in many ways. Her family heritage gave me a set of academic standards to claim and aspire to equal. The aspects of her personality that I did not accept gave me the friction to allow me to find my own footing. And the adult tuck-ins during visits to her home gave me a tender tendril to grasp when tempted to dwell on regrets.

The strength, power, and courage that I absorbed from the symbolism of the panther have become the foundation upon which my selfhood is built. Even though I never was able to bring a baby home from the hospital and live out the mothering instinct in my home, I was able to claim that maternal characteristic of the panther's embodiment and use it in the school and church settings where I worked. That need was fulfilled long before I learned about the symbolism of the panther. Now, I recognize the correlation and claim it as I take care of myself and my students—not in a physical way as a birth mother would, but as a teacher, mentor, and music coach.

Completing this writing project by realizing how I have become the panther and how the physical panther I feared as a child has become trapped and incapacitated has given me deep fulfillment. The understanding feels right. The most significant part of this realization is the certain knowledge that the beast of sexual molestation, abuse, and attack is now impotent. I am free of fear, shame, and false guilt—free to live out my life as I believe it was meant to be—in touch with my aspirations with confidence and courage for the remainder of my personal journey. I trust that there are many stories yet to discover and live. Perhaps some will find their way into the next manuscript. No more interruptive cries in the night; no more dodging; no more dreading the required pretense; no more being on high alert for acceptable ways to avoid additional abuse; no more squelching myself in order to collude with familial and cultural prescriptions for behavior; no more donning the cloak of secrecy that was woven for the sole sake of keeping women in their place and allowing the *status quo* to be the crippling appendage that could trip and trample the self of anyone seeking relief from a sexual predator. Our culture still has a long way to go to remedy this age-old problem, but progress is being made.

# CHAPTER 24

# WRITING:
# PROCESS AND EFFECTS

*Style is knowing who you are, what you want to say... .*
Gore Vidal
(1925-2012)

In the late 1960's, at the beginning of my career in Music Education, I heard that there was a visiting professor from Hungry at the local college—Limestone College in Gaffney, South Carolina. Word soon spread that she had a serious interest and extensive training in astrology. A friend told me that the professor was particularly interested in studying the charts of people born under the sign of Libra. That got my attention and piqued my interest. When I met the professor on campus, she said, "Oh, yes. I heard that your sign is Libra. Would you permit me to study your astrological chart? I am especially interested in people born under the sign of Libra because that is my sign." I told her she was welcome to do the study.

"I just need the date, time, and location of your birth. With that information, I will be able to do a complete workup of your chart and will not charge you anything because I need the practice."

After verifying the time of my birth with my mother, I gave the information to the visiting professor. With only the basic information at hand, she said, "Are you aware that you were born on the cusp of Libra and Scorpio? I consider you a strong Libra, though, because of considerations beyond your basic sun sign."

She went on to say that she was aware I taught elementary music. Later, when she turned over the chart to me, she said, "I need to let you know that you are not in the best career for your talents. You are an A+

teacher and a B+ performer; but you will never realize your highest and best calling until you become a writer."

She speculated that the career change would not happen until later in life when I would find my way into the field of creative writing. Not until then would I be completely fulfilled. She went on to say that I had an unusually deep understanding of others because (in her opinion) my soul was very old. Additionally (in her view), being born on the cusp meant that I would not be reincarnated again.

Being curious, if not a firm believer, her astrological report almost left me speechless. There are several writers on my mother's side of the family and at least an equal number on my father's side. I had dabbled in creative writing, but never with any depth or training. Yet, it tapped on my brain and heart. So, the professor from Hungary planted seeds of expectation and speculation that germinated for a long time. Now, I look back at her prediction and smile.

When I first became acquainted with Grace B. Freeman, Poet Laureate of South Carolina, in the early 1970's, I knew I would have to write about the two rapes, other molestations, and the effects of those experiences. At that point, and for another quarter of a century, my underlying assumption was that I would write for my own expression. I had no plans or desire to write for the public. Rather, I thought that any bent toward writing beyond self expression would be realized through writing choral music.

Once the acquiescence to silence had been seared into my mind, the only hope I had of ever divulging the secret I carried was perhaps to be able to share my pain with someone who would care about me enough to at least try to understand what I had been through. I speculated that the media for such sharing would be either poetry or prose.

The book of so-called genealogy published by Curtis Winfrey spun my assessment of where my writing would lead completely around. Keeping my work private was no longer permissible. My mission was clear, as stated earlier in this book. But it took about ten years from the publication date to the shift in practice from private expression to crafting a full-length memoir.

Although I was comfortable with academic writing, I felt the need to study creative writing as craft and as a form of expression. I also felt a need for camaraderie with other writers. I wanted and needed the underpinning of a supportive community of people who understood the role that writing plays in the process of healing.

When deciding on the title for this book, I thought that the image of the panther would represent Daniel, while at the same time, the cries would represent me. But as the narrative of the story unfolded, I realized that he is much more like a hyena or a jackal. He lacks the innate strength, beauty, and courage of the panther. His hunt was not for sex or food, but for power. A panther can kill a deer, but sexual predators prey only on smaller and weaker targets. Daniel's grin and giggle were like a hyena's—a proud announcement that he had found his target and that he smelled success just as other animals smell their prey's fear. Perhaps human predators also possess the ability to smell their victim's fear. They certainly have uncanny accuracy when identifying those who become their targets.

Like a jackal, he is small—small in stature, in mind, and in spirit. Like all predators, he is sneaky. Like a jackal in search of the spoils of others' hunts, he sought easy prey, never putting himself into situations where he would be held accountable—smart enough to beat the system and pursue his pathetic pleasure in plain sight, but not smart enough to compete academically, socially, or economically. He functioned like a trophy hunter who kills for sport on a game preserve, then brags about it in photos posted on social media platforms.

In time, Gramma's little wildcat evolved into the panther. The permission and fundamental understanding embedded in Grandmother's nickname for me guided my quest for self awareness and expression. It seemed that my need to be different from my sisters was acceptable since Grandmother celebrated my rebellion in song.

Wanting pretty clothes appeared to be permissible since Grandmother, aunts, and teachers shared my desire. Wishing for a reasonably nice house and furnishings seemed also to be acceptable when friends and relatives enjoyed their homes. But when I was introduced to the reality of the wandering panthers that roamed at night through the woods next to our property, I had feared that my immediate response to their shrill cries would either be unheard or ignored. Fear of their cries and fear of my unspeakable fears stalked me at night as I lay on the couch in the living room, trying to get back to sleep after giving up on making Mother hear my real and choked-off cries.

I learned of using writing as part of the process of healing through extensive reading after I retired from full-time teaching. I alternated reading actual memoirs with studying craft books. When I shared the original poem that ultimately led to this memoir, my therapist strongly encouraged me to continue to express my memories, thoughts, and feelings through writing. She does not write creative nonfiction herself, but listened to me read portions of my work as a means of focusing our attention on various aspects of my experience.

After taking two nine-week creative nonfiction courses in Houston, I attended a two-week intense retreat and workshop for writers at the Port Townsend Writers Conference in Washington. Wendy Call taught the memoir class. It was an outstanding immersion in the writing process. Although there was no announced statement, or even suggestion, that learning to write would lead to healing, there was a certain presumption that the process of writing could and would customize itself for each practitioner's needs and focus.

The following year, I attended a similar retreat and workshop held at Wildacres in North Carolina. Jessica Handler taught the memoir section of the workshop. Although her story in her own memoir bears a much different profile than mine, her knowledge and experience in writing and publication and her outstanding ability as a teacher broadened the more general aspects of writing I had learned at the Port Townsend location.

The more I wrote and shared my writing with others, the stronger I grew, both as a writer, and as a survivor. The more I wrote, the more I wanted to write. It was simply right for me. Every class within every course I took taught me more about the mechanics and artistry necessary to create a book of meaning and value beyond my own desk.

Much of the strength I gained through writing and therapy involved forgiving myself for staying silent for so long. I had always feared that my silence could have served as an enabling factor for the perpetrator. Maintaining the familial and cultural code of silence stifled my sense of self and reinforced the burden of shame. Staying silent made me feel weak and cowardly. The false shame and guilt I had assumed darkened ambition with dreadful uncertainty.

I had to forgive myself for not forcing someone to listen to me. I had to shake off the misplaced responsibilities I had accepted toward my family. It was shocking to realize that any hurt to the family by breaking the code of silence was the fault of the perpetrator's behavior, not mine. And I had to accept the real responsibility to clear my father's name. Writing a letter to my late father was one of the first assignments I gave myself. (See end pages.)

In 2018, I attended the Murphy Get Away to Write course held in Wales and sponsored by Stockton University of New Jersey. Classes taught by Peter Murphy and his team were almost magical. Classmates and the surrounding environment were inspiring. Reading some of my work for peers built both support and self confidence.

Because the experience last summer in Wales was so meaningful, I attended another Murphy Writing workshop held at the Atlantic Center for the Arts in New Smyrna Beach, Florida, just last month (February, 2019). Barbara Hurd taught the class for memoirists. Her warm personality combined with precise expertise and inspirational presence gave my classmates and me a week of close support while learning new techniques to use in our respective projects. Now, I continue to put into my writing practice what I learned and absorbed in that class. The environment made me feel proud of being free enough to read for peers from both the memoir and poetry sections and faculty members without hesitation.

Panthers, particularly black ones, symbolize the feminine: powerful motherly protection. Their presence in my life and memory functioned as instruction regarding my need to mother myself, to claim my own voice, and to exert my own strength. The little wildcat at the core of my being could morph into the sleek coat of warmth with strength to escape danger, to charge toward necessary nourishment; to cry when and how my urge to cry requires: tears of joy, tears of anger, of grief, surprise, tears of release, and tears of relief.

Black panthers in the southwestern wild of Florida are rare. So am I—the crying little wildcat who hated to take naps; the older child who couldn't cry out in fear; the silent victim of long-term familial sexual abuse; and the survivor who claimed the power of the panther and found her own strength of voice. I whisper; I speak; I sing; and I shout.

While writing this memoir, I researched wildcats and panthers and found similarities and differences between them. Characteristics of the wildcat, also called *bobcat*, that fit me were a sense of aloofness, wanderlust, and comfort in grooming. The tufts on their ears give them extraordinary hearing, a trait necessary to my career in music education and now, as a piano teacher.

One of Mother's sisters, Aunt Miriam, used to talk about babies being marked either before or soon after birth. The marking could be something as natural as a thunder storm or as environmental as a mother's fear of snakes. The belief or superstition was that any event or encounter could mark the baby in either positive or negative ways—a classic case of correlation being elevated to causation. For a brief moment when I first heard their cries, I wondered if it were possible for the cries and my fear of them to mark me in some way.

Healing comes in both predictable and serendipitous packages. Feeling what life can be like out from under the burden of abuse's power makes me interact differently with others, particularly new acquaintances. For me, the healing that has come from the process of writing in combination with on-gong therapy has brought back wonder, joy, confidence, and so much more. Mostly, it has returned me to more me-ness with still more potential for development. It has given me a life of calm freedom, like sheep shorn of the burden of wool they assumed they were doomed to carry forever. No, I don't expect my *wool* to grow back, but I know that certain associations may trigger some reflection, perhaps even some pain; yet, I feel certain that I can recognize any symptoms that such occurrences might produce and cope with negative memories in a positive way. I can't say that life is perfect, but it is good, worthwhile, productive, and self enhancing.

Thank you, Grandmother Orrell, for marking me. Thank you, Mockingbird Hill, for hosting the black panther that became family lore and whose symbolism provided concretized imagery for my long journey. Thank you, all who served as positive enablers along the way. Gramma's little wildcat has taken on the attributes of the panther—strength, courage, powerful voice, and contentment within my own environment.

In time, I came to see the panther not as sleep-shattering threat, but as the embodiment of my aspirations, the animation of innate dormant traits in search of a birth canal—a being perfectly fit for its environment, content unless threatened by impending danger. Today, with the very existence of the panthers of my childhood threatened, it seems possible that the Florida panther will become a mystical creature whose existence in the future will be limited to archival memories. Without a doubt, their cries I heard as a child and their characteristics I learned to admire are embodied as a permanent part of me.

Now, I feel like an eagle soaring on high in John Denver's music, watching a frisky wildcat and a graceful black panther play together in joyful abandon. I glide down and plant all four toes of each foot on firm ground, wings spread to cover the wildcat and the panther with my seven-foot wing span. All three relax in peace, content in their essence, tolerant and encouraging of each other.

The energetic wildcat is like a mascot—a charm for good luck. The panther soothes with her motherly protection and promise of nurturance—a provider to fulfill needs. And the eagle is the regal sovereign, fit and worthy to be monarch. Now together, the three form one being whose name looks the same for each, but has a different accent for each aspect of the new being: MARsutonell for the frisky young wildcat; marSUtonell for the matriarchal panther; and marsutonELL for the potentate eagle. All three are different, yet complimentary; the same in so many ways; each part enhanced and fulfilled by melding into an essence of completeness; one self, woven and knit—mascot, matriarch, and monarch, all in one—healed, whole, embellished by permanence and renewed by flexibility's tempered stretch.

In the distance, an ugly, cackling hyena slinks away, already sniffing leftovers or even infant hyenas unaware that they rest in harm's way. The sound of the hysterical laugh is drowned out by the powerful cries of the panther, no longer making the rounds at Mockingbird Hill, but confined to the natural environment where it chooses to cavort. Rather than riling fear, the cries soothe with familiarity, blending with the wildcat's meows and the eagle's calls.

They are cries of jubilation with loud reverberations echoing on Mockingbird Hill; harmonized by my own voice; accompanied by a choir made up of every person whose influence created just the right wind currents to launch my flight above the reach of the abuser's snare and beyond the limits he attempted to graft onto my soul and into my spirit. I stand apart, baton in hand, my face reflecting joy of fulfillment and triumph over the childhood cries that nearly drowned my hope.

I plan to continue attending writing retreats and workshops in attractive environments as the process of healing and the process of writing maintain a mutually dependent relationship. In the summer of 2019, I was a part of the Get Away to Write course held in Dundee, Scotland. I look forward to additional study with Peter Murphy and Roberta Clipper. Writing has become the essence through which pain is released and joy is set free. Writing and writers are connected collaborators that push and pull me toward an ever-present target of wholeness. Writing is a cherished companion, always available, ready to guide or to be guided. I have no expectation to jump up and down and declare, "I'm cured!" But I do attest that I am free—free from the power of the perpetrator and all the chains he attempted to bind around me with permanent dead bolts. My spirit is renewed; my creativity is bursting; and the lure of the rest of my life beckons with no bars holding me back.

*It is well with my soul.*
(Hymn title—Horatio G. Spafford, 1828-1888)

# CHAPTER 25

# MUSIC, WATER, AND TREES

*The setting sun, and music at the close,*
*As the last taste of sweets, is sweetest last,*
*Writ in remembrance more than things long past.*
William Shakespeare (1554-1616)

*When the well's dry, we know the worth of water.*
Benjamin Franklin (1706-1790)

*Flowers are lovely; love is flower-like;*
*Friendship is a sheltering tree.*
Samuel Taylor Coleridge (1772-1834)

Dear Music, Water, and Trees,

Please accept these thoughts in the same way you have always accepted me. Each of you individually and all of you collectively stand as the undergirding that saw me through emotional dissonance, whitewater rapids, and storm-severed branches. Without you in my life, I would have withered rather than thrived.

Without you in my life, I would have had no respite from destructive forces that threatened my selfhood. Without you in my life, there would have been no joy to balance and temper the pain and scars. Without the safety net of your sound, your touch, your constancy—in sum, without your very being what you are and giving what you had to offer, I could not have overcome the hideous reality of my late childhood and adolescence. Without Music, Water, and Trees, I would never have sung, swum, or climbed away from the trap and into harmony, calm buoyancy, and ever-renewing growth.

Music that I created is published; tsunamis have been tamed into clear streams with ripples of silver, colorful stones washed smooth as beach glass; and the withered broken branches went away with the wind—the fresh breeze of clarity, assurance, and pride.

So now ends the story of my earliest beginnings, my adolescent strivings, and the beginnings of older age. Current beginnings are the most exciting, the most joyful I have ever known: beginnings filled with promise of fulfillment; optimism more abundant than pessimism; and re-start charged by success. Past is reconciled within me. Present is lived moment by moment. And Future brightly calls.

With eternal gratitude,

Sue Skilton Orrell

*And now abide these three: Music, Water, and*
*Trees; but the greatest of these is Music.*
                    (Parody, I Corinthians 13:13)

# LETTER TO MY FATHER

*Your story may be the key that unlocks someone
else's prison. Don't be afraid to share it.*
Battlefield Assembly of God web site

My Dearest Father, (Daddy),

I have written this memoir to honor you by revealing the truth concerning my personal history. In his book, *Ancestors and Relatives of Arthur C.S.S. Winfrey (Gateway Press, 1999),* your nephew, Curtis Winfrey, claimed that I had accused you of child sexual abuse. That accusation is absolutely false. His mistake was to make such a claim; my mistake was to trust him enough to share a poem I had written concerning my history of sexual abuse. After reading the poem, Curtis jumped to an unjustified conclusion and used the poem as the basis for his false claim. He never attempted to verify his interpretation of the poem. By relying on his misperception without verification, he blatantly betrayed my trust in him and came to his categorically incorrect conclusion.

I will not attempt to make sense of Curtin Winfrey's motivations, to interpret his own personal writings that he shared with me, or to find a logical rationale for his actions. Rather, I will focus on the main two goals of this memoir. The first, and primary, goal is to clear your name. I believe there are few, if any, people who would believe the false claim, but it is still important to me to set the record straight for the sake of your reputation and for the sake of others who will read my memoir. At long last, the truth will be available to anyone who is interested and willing to learn it.

The second goal of this memoir has been to come to an understanding of what happened to me and how I coped with the ongoing abuse throughout my adolescence and the after effects throughout the decades since the assaults and molestations occurred. The process of writing my story played a large part in the healing process.

Forgive the mistake in judgment I made when I trusted Curtis Winfrey, and know that every effort has been made to honor you by telling the truth.

With so much more love than I was ever able to give you,

Sue
Suzie-Q
Sioux City Sue *
Daddy's Little Girl

Daddy's parody of *Sioux City Sue* *

Sioux City Sue,
Sioux City Sue,
Your hair is red; Your eyes are brown,
And, oh, that frown turned upside-down,
Sioux City Sue,
Sioux City Sue,
There's just none to compare with my
Sweet Sioux City Sue

*Sioux City Sue* was a popular song that made its way almost to the top of the charts in 1945. Ray Freedman wrote the lyrics; Dick Thomas wrote the music.

# LISTEN TO THE SILENCE

Sue Skilton Orrell


Listen ---- ---- to the silence ---- ---- ----.
Listen to the silence as it speaks in whispers and shouts,
Praying to be heard. ---- Soundless cries, sighs, give-ins.
Listen ---- ---- to the silence ---- ---- ---.
Screams from fathomless depths,
Sequestered under green marine snow.
Sympathetic undulations, seabed's harmony,
Static white noise, pressure cooker's call.

Can't you hear the anguish of the silent din's roar?
See the facial signs of silence's betrayal;
Ruts in rusted armor wrought by salty river tears,
Pores clogged shut by detritus in the wake
Of rage clambering cell by cell,
Bent posture bears the weight,
Gnarled into a knot, compressed, muffled and stuffed.
Niggling nudge, tsunami wave,
Colon motion clamped and constricted.
Taste the vile bile of scalding caustic reflux;
Erosive, corrosive, scourge of vocal health.
Smell the slow rot of soured self-worth.
Can't you feel the brutal bludgeoned beating of a young, tender soul?


• Long dashes represent silent beats.

Silence speaks in wasted dreams, nighttime terrors,
Imagined hope, ugly reality, a waterfall crawling uphill,
Liquid footprints fading—drop by drop.
Silence speaks through fingernails bit—bit to the bloody quick----.
Silence speaks in waves of nausea, dizzy spells----malaise----
Energy gone, victim of a vacuum, squandered on depression's *tells*.

The *see's* about to *saw*; tipping point has come;
No more stasis of society's fulcrum point.
We have found our voice; shattered crushing silence;
Finally, we have said, *Enough is enough.*
No more ignoring *lesser* offenses.
No more settling for culture's acquiescence;
No more isolation after *greater* offenses.
Enough is enough!
No more silence;
NO MORE!
NOW, LISTEN TO THE ROAR!

# ACKNOWLEDGMENTS

Writing Teachers (listed chronologically)

Grace C. Nash (1909-2010) (primary mentor in Music Education, particularly the Orff- Schulwerk approach to teaching and learning; led me into creativity, 1969-2010)

Samuel D. Miller, Ph. D. (1932-2009) (Chair of Dissertation Committee, University of Houston; supervised my academic writing)

Nancy Geyer (teacher of Creative Writing, Rice University, 2013)

Nancy Patterson (teacher of Memoir Writing at Inprint Houston, 2014)

Ellie Mathews (teacher of Creative Nonfiction at Port Townsend Writer's Retreat, Washington, 2015)

Wendy Call (teacher of Memoir Writing at Port Townsend Writer's Conference, Washington, 2015)

Jessica Handler (teacher of Creative Nonfiction at Wildacres Writers Workshop, North Carolina, 2016)

Peter Murphy (Murphy Writing of Stockton University, Wales, 2018; Scotland, 2019)

Barbara Hurd (teacher of Memoir at Murphy Writing of Stockton University, New Smyrna Beach, FL, 2019)

Technical Assistance

Rick Orrell (photo restoration; nephew)

Veronica Resendez (document preparation)

Editorial Assistance

Penelope Schwartz (initial overview)

Roberta Clipper (detailed edit)

First Readers
> Grace B. Freeman (1916-2002) (Poet Laureate of South Carolina, 1985, the first to read the poem that led to the writing of this memoir and who encouraged me to keep writing)
> ClaireBeth Langston Link (first reader of nearly complete first draft)
> Stan Pieringer (1948-2016) (the voice of formal expertise with abiding support)

Writer's Group
> Wendy Levine (the voice of critique tempered with encouragement)
> Merideth Melville (the voice of humor with imaginative suggestions)
> Claire Poole (the voice of technical expertise wrapped in compassion)
> Don Sanders (1943-2017) (the voice of wisdom, perspective, and understanding)

Other Readers
> Christina (Tina) Finney (friend)
> Genie Nash (gentle inquirer when baffled by my cries in the night)
> Sonia Simon, Psy. D. (outstanding therapist whose support never wavered)

Family
> Richard B. Orrell (verifier of facts where possible; brother)
> Robert S. Orrell (cousin on Daddy's side; respected author of family history)
> Suzanne Orrell Guest (cousin on Daddy's side)
> Kimberly Reading (third cousin on Mother's side)
> Patti Gould Saathoff (second cousin on Mother's side)

Others Who Made a Difference
   Christopher A. Colvert (friend and husband who first witnessed
      my cries in the night)
   Numerous friends, mentors, and even strangers who cared

Each of the readers served a unique purpose. All made meaningful contributions that led to improvements and added to the ultimate success of this book. Everyone listed offered friendship, encouragement, and various strengths that powered and sustained my perseverance. Without the combined effects of their individual contributions, I could not have told my story with the same clarity or impact. Without their belief in me and in the project I undertook, I might not have found the strength or courage to complete the daunting task of getting the truth of my story into print. I am truly grateful to all who pulled and pushed me as needed throughout this long journey.

Every attempt has been made to be accurate and to let the reader know when I was offering an opinion apart from objective verification. Most of the family history came from the stories that Mother and Daddy often repeated when we were together as a family. What I witnessed, experienced, and endured, is my true story. No names or places have been changed because such an alteration would not conceal the identities of people and place. A deliberate attempt to cover up the identity of my abuser would only contribute to the cultural climate that caused my decades of silence. That is a syndrome of which I want no part. Rather, I hope this book will encourage abuse survivors to speak up with strength, step out with courage, and to seek help when necessary in their own journeys toward renewed wholeness. Writing served me well, as it has others. May each person who has survived abuse of any sort find his or her own way to self-forgiveness. The abusive acts of others are not your fault.

Any remaining flaws in the manuscript are solely my responsibility.